MEGA BUILDER

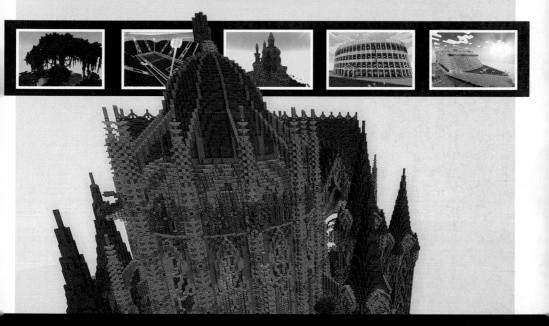

THE MOST COMPLETE GUIDE TO
MINECRAFT®™ SECRETS,
CREATIONS, HACKS, AND STRATEGIES

TRIUMPH
B O O K S

Triumph Books LLC
814 North Franklin Street
Chicago, Illinois 60610
Phone: (312) 337-0747
www.triumphbooks.com
Printed in U.S.A.

ISBN: 978-1-62937-348-5

Contents

Chapter 1

Basic Minecraft

Getting Started

So here you are, you've taken the plunge and bought Minecraft. You're staring at that menu screen, and you're ready to dive into this crazy world you've heard so much about.

Now, you could start up a new world and try and wing it, but trust us, that path leads to darkness (literally), frustration and, yes, death. Minecraft is a game that's at once very simple on the surface and incredibly complex underneath, and what you do when you first start out can make a huge difference in your success at crafting the world you want. That, plus it's really not much fun to die in the dark from your fourth Creeper attack in a row and lose all of your gear over and over.

To get the most out of Minecraft, you'll have a much better and less death-filled time if you know a few things about the game before jumping right in.

This is a great starting location between two Biomes

A simple spawn point beacon

Looking Around

When starting a new game, the first thing to do is put a marker down where you started. To do this, dig out some dirt from the ground with your hand and stack it in a column. This will help a lot later. Now, simply look around a bit and see where you've started. Minecraft is split up into different environments called "Biomes," and each Biome contains specific plants, animals, resources and terrain-types. You can build and mine in any Biome, but some are much more convenient and safe when it comes to creating a shelter to live in. The number one priority is trees, because without trees, you aren't going to be able to craft important tools and items. After that, look for areas with water, animals and easily defendable terrain such as mountaintops. One good trick is to find a spot where two Biomes meet and build there. Remember though: nighttime comes fast, so don't spend too much time traveling on your first day.

Gathering Resources

On your first day out, you want to make every second count, so while you're looking for a nice place to set up a shelter, you'll need to be gathering resources. At the beginning of the game, certain resources are more important than others. The smartest order for gathering goes Wood>Cobblestone>Food>Wool, but if something is very close to you (say a Pig wanders by), take the opportunity to pick it up.

To gather Wood, you need to punch some trees. The noble art of tree-punching is what starts just about every game of Minecraft, and to do this, point the crosshairs at the wood of the trunk and punch the blocks until they break. This is the slowest way of collecting wood, however, and you'll want an Axe as soon as possible.

Two types of trees

When you've collected at least 3 Wood, open your crafting menu and create a set of four Wood Planks, then create a Crafting Table. The recipe for the Crafting Table is one block of Wood Planks in each of the four squares of the menu. You can then place your crafting table anywhere in the environment. Now, to make an Axe. Point at your Crafting Table after you place it and open the Crafting Table menu. You should then turn all of your remaining Wood into Wood Planks and turn at least 2 of your new Wood Planks into Sticks. Once you have at least 3 Wood Planks and 2 Sticks, you can create your first tool, an Axe!

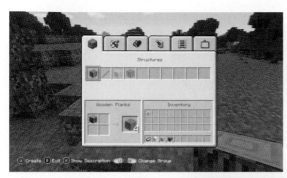

Wooden Planks

*Your first
crafting table!*

Building A Shelter

With your Axe, you can now chop down trees much quicker. Continue doing this until you have about 30-40 Wood (you may need to create another Axe if yours breaks), then break up your Crafting Table by chopping it, pick it up and move to where you want to build a house.

Place your Crafting Table and turn about 2/3 of your Wood into Wood Planks (you need about 60-100). Put the Wood Planks in your inventory tray, and start building a house! The quickest way to do this is to create a rectangular shelter at least 4 blocks long, 2 blocks wide and 4 blocks tall. Build the bottom layer first, then jump on top and run around it putting up the second layer. Repeat for the third and fourth layers, and then jump in.

*Your first shelter should
be simple and effective*

Screenshot: Minecraft®™ & © 2009–2015 Mojang/Notch.

A good first shelter

Before you fill in the hole with a ceiling, you need light, and light means Torches. Torches are created with one Stick and one Coal or Charcoal. To get Coal, you have to find a Coal deposit and mine it with a Pickaxe, and to get Charcoal, you need to burn Wood in a Furnace, which means you need to gather Cobblestone.

Gathering More Resources

At this point, you need to build your first Pickaxe, the most famous and useful tool in the game! To do this, open your Crafting Table menu up again and create the Wooden Pickaxe. (you may need to make more Wood Planks and Sticks to do this)

With your trusty new Wooden Pickaxe, you are now able to mine your first Stone (a big moment!). Leave your house by chopping a hole 2 blocks high and 1 block wide in the wall, and look around where you are. Try to find a hill or mountainside with exposed Stone. If you can't see any, you can just pick a spot and dig down until you hit some. Remember to leave a few blocks that you can jump on to get out.

Wooden Pickaxe

A typical first mine. This one was a natural cave that was widened.

At this point, you need at least 8 Cobblestone, but gathering around 20-30 won't hurt if you have time. Once you have some Cobblestone, head back to your shelter.

Before you build a furnace, let's put a door on that home. Open your Crafting Table, and create the Wooden Door (this takes some Planks). Step outside your home again, select the door in your Inventory Tray and point your crosshairs at the hole in the side of your shelter. Use the Left Trigger to place the door, then open it and walk in.

A shelter that's ready for night

Doors are a necessity.
You don't want those Creepers sneakin' in!

Go to your Crafting Table again and move to the Chest icon. Push down on the D-Pad, and then create the Furnace when it shows up. Place the Furnace anywhere in your shelter, and then open it up with Left Trigger. Furnaces take fuel, which is something burnable like Wood or Coal. Put some of your remaining Wood in the top item slot, and then use Wood, Wood Planks or something else made of wood in the bottom one. You'll see the Furnace come on as it starts to turn your wood into Charcoal.

While this is happening, finish the roof to your home. Make sure it's fully enclosed, or else a Spider could fall on your head during the night!

Now, check your Furnace. Take the Charcoal from the Furnace, and open your Crafting Table back up. In the Tools section, you'll see Torches. Use all of your Charcoal up making Torches, and then start placing your Torches on the walls and ground around your home.

Once you've got a completed shelter, you can continue gathering resources until Nighttime. Soon enough, you'll start seeing the sun go down, which means Nighttime is about to arrive with all of its terrors. But no worries, because you've got a handy little shelter to protect you! Congrats on your first day in Minecraft.

It won't take long before your simple home starts to look like a mighty dwelling

Nighttime

Here's the deal: when night falls on the world of Minecraft, things are going to try and kill you. A lot. All night long. This is because the monsters in Minecraft, known as "hostile mobs," can only survive when the level of light is low (except for Slimes, Spiders and the dreaded Creeper, which can survive in the day). Add that to the fact that hostile mobs spawn randomly at nighttime and then attack you on sight, and you've got yourself a bit of a dangerous situation for your character.

To put it simply, when that sun goes down, you had better be prepared to deal with the perils of night until that blissful moment when you see the light start to peek back over the horizon. If you're not prepared, you can be sure that your character is not going to survive.

So, what can you do to protect yourself in the dark, dangerous Minecraft nighttime? Luckily, you've got quite a few options, and you should have no problem keeping safe and snug with even the most basic preparation during the day.

The Necessaries

You need two things for certain if you're going to live to see another day in Minecraft: Shelter and Lighting.

Shelter

The Primary Number One Super Important Thing to have that will keep you safe from all of the Zombies, Skeletons, Endermen, Spiders and (shudder) Creepers at night is a nice shelter. You can read all the details on how to build a good basic shelter in the "Getting Started/Your First Day" section of this guide, but the basic idea is that you need an enclosed area with no open spaces to hide in. That's actually all you need to stay safe at night, but it'll be a dark, boring nighttime without at least a little light.

This situation is very easy to fall into at night...

...As is this one

Lighting

Torches are your best friend in Minecraft, and you definitely need some in your shelter. Again, check out the "Getting Started/Your First Day" section to see exactly how to make a few torches. Another way torches are super useful at night besides letting you see (which is pretty darn useful, we'd say) is to keep monsters from spawning. Light in Minecraft is measured on a scale of 1-15, and monsters cannot spawn in any light level above 7. By placing torches in an area, you can keep monsters from spawning there, though they can still travel through it. To do this, you need to put torches so that there are no more than 11 blocks between them in a straight line and no more than 5 between them diagonally.

The Secondary Ideas

While you don't absolutely need these things, your nighttime experience will be a heck of a lot safer and more fun if you have them.

A Bed

This is the most useful tool to have at night, and it's one of the first things you should try and build in Minecraft. A Bed is a 2 block long item that can be placed in your world and slept in during the night, which instantly makes it day again. Not only that, but sleeping in a Bed sets your spawn point to

A nicely lit room

Everyone needs a bed!

that bed, meaning that when you die, you won't have to run back to your shelter!

To build a bed takes 3 Wood Planks and 3 Wool of any color. Wool is relatively easy to come by, as it drops when you kill Sheep. Use your Crafting Table to combine the Wood Planks and Wool, and set your Bed someplace where the sides are unobstructed. Then, just sleep in it when it's nighttime, and you'll skip right through the danger to daytime.

Weapons & Armor

When you start a game in Minecraft, you're basically an unprotected weakling. Sad to say, but it's true. That doesn't have to remain the case though, as you can beef up your character's power through crafting weapons and armor to use in combat.

Basic weapons are easy to get early on, as you only need 1 Stick and 2 Wood Planks or Cobblestone to make a Sword. Do this as soon as you can, as it makes a huge difference in your attack and will often save your life during combat. In fact, even a Wooden Sword does four times the damage that punching does, and that damage rating goes up with better materials (except Gold).

Other weapons in Minecraft include Bows, Tools and Potions, each of which does differing amounts of damage, with Tools being the least effective. You can also use other items in the game, such as Cobwebs, Cactus, Snowballs, Fishing Rods and Buckets of Water or Lava to hinder or damage mobs in various ways, so get creative!

A Crafter fully decked out in armor and weapons

Armor, unlike weapons, can take a while to create because it requires a large amount of rare materials. Basic armor is made of Leather (dropped from a killed Cow), while better armor is crafted of Iron or Diamond (you can also use Gold, but this is not effective or recommended). Armor is worth making once you have enough Leather or a few extra Iron, as it makes an enormous difference in the amount of damage you can take.

On the attack!

With weapons and armor handy, you can actually brave the nighttime a little, though your chances at dying are still pretty high.

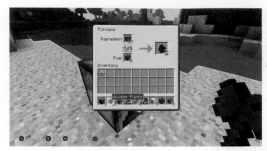

You need Torches, so you need Coal or Charcoal

Some mobs burn at night!

Something To Do

Once you've got a Bed, you don't need to deal with the night, but having to return to your Bed to sleep can get annoying after a while, especially if you're playing multiplayer (players must sleep at the same time). Because of that, it can be useful and fun to take the nighttime as a chance to do a few things.

The most obvious thing to do at night is to work on the inside of your shelter! Whether you decorate it, reorganize your materials, build more Crafting Tables, Furnaces or other useful items or even create another room or story, this is a great time to do this.

Nighttime is also a good time to refine your materials, such as making Iron Ingots out of Iron Ore or creating some extra Tools. Use your extra few minutes and get some stuff made!

Another great idea is to create a mineshaft that's accessible through your own home. You'll want to make sure this has a door on it to keep out mobs, but this can be an easy and efficient way to mine for resources while staying relatively safe.

Finally, once you're pretty confident in your weapons, armor and combat skills, you can go monster hunting at night...if you dare. Most mobs drop useful items when killed, and a small excursion out to hunt monsters can be very rewarding.

When you're ready, go mob hunting   *A few walls and some Torches are all you need*

Nighttime Facts

Here are a few facts about nighttime that can help you out:

Nighttime lasts 7 minutes of real time

Sunset/dusk is a short period of 1½ minutes real time during which players can go to sleep

Light decreases by 1 every 10 seconds during dusk

The natural light level at nighttime is 4

Crops can still grow at night

Sleeping through night, however, essentially stops time, so no crops grow and Furnaces pick up where they left off when you went to sleep

The day/night cycle continues even when you're in The Nether or The End

Spiders, Creepers and Slime are the only hostile mobs that do not die in the daylight

A random song will start to play at the beginning of each cycle of time

Materials

Materials are everything in Minecraft, and we mean that quite literally. Except for player characters, NPCs (Non Player Characters, such as animals and mobs) and a few rare objects, everything you see in Minecraft is either a material or can be made with materials. This is what makes Minecraft so awesome: since everything breaks down into materials, you can destroy and build just about anything you want in the world.

This section of the guide will give you a quick look at the most important materials in the game, as well as a look at what you can make with them. Play enough Minecraft, and you'll come to know each and every one of these materials by heart. You'll know 'em, you'll learn to love 'em (or hate 'em—we're looking at you, Gravel) and soon enough you'll be squealing with glee every time you stumble on some precious, precious Diamond just like the rest of us.

Building Blocks

These are what the world of Minecraft is made up of, and they're what you'll mine and harvest to use in your own creations.

Dirt

Found: Overworld almost everywhere
Used In: Early shelters, farming
Best Tool to Use: Shovel

Look around you in the Overworld, and there's probably some dirt. Dirt is one of the most common blocks, but it's only real uses are for aesthetics and farming. You can make a shelter of it in a pinch, but it's always recommended to use something more stable (and better looking!) when you can. However,

Dirt can have things grow on it, including "natural" materials like Snow, Mycelium and Grass as well as farmable materials like Trees and Wheat.

Stone

Types: Cobblestone, Stone
Found: Overworld, especially underground
Used In: Stone, Stone Bricks, other Stone building materials, Furnace, Stone tools, mechanisms
Best Tool to Use: Pickaxe

If you play Minecraft at all, you're going to end up with a whole lot of stone in the form of Cobblestone. Much of the Minecraft world, especially underground, is made of Stone or Cobblestone, both of which drop Cobblestone when mined. This stuff is required to craft a huge number of items, and you'll definitely want to keep a large stock of Stone tools on hand, as they're the easiest advanced tool to craft.

Wood

Types: Oak, Spruce, Birch
Found: Overworld in most Biomes except Desert, Plains and Mushroom
Used In: Wood Planks, which are needed for many items including tools and building materials
Best Tool to Use: Axe

Wood is without a doubt the most important resource in the game for one major reason: you need it to build tools. You also need it for many other items, but without tools, you're not going to be able to do much in Minecraft. You can find Wood just by looking around most worlds.

Gravel

Found: Overworld everywhere, usually between Stone and Dirt

Used In: Traps and nothing else. It is evil.

Best Tool to Use: Shovel

Drops: Flint

Gravel is evil. We say this because it's basically just there for variety and to make digging a bit more challenging. It's one of the only two blocks that drops when there's not a block below it (the other is Sand), and it can cause damage when falling far enough and can suffocate creatures it falls on that can't get out. Because of this, it's used in traps. It's only other useful feature is that it drops Flint, used in Flint and Steel.

Sand

Types: Sand, Sandstone

Found: Overworld near water and in Deserts

Used In: Glass, Sandstone, Sandstone Brick

Best Tool to Use: Pickaxe

Sand is the other block that, like Gravel, falls when there's nothing supporting it. Sand is the base block, from which Sandstone can be crafted, but you can also find naturally occurring Sandstone. Unlike Stone, Sandstone actually drops a Sandstone block when broken with a Pickaxe. Sand is mostly useful for making Sandstone to build with and Glass, which is also needed for Glass Panes.

Clay

Found: Overworld in water, usually in groups. Rare.

Used In: Clay Block, Bricks

Best Tool to Use: Shovel

Perhaps the rarest construction material block out there, Clay is found in water mixed up with Sand and Sandstone blocks, but is much less common than either of those. Clay is only used in two things: Clay Blocks and Bricks. Bricks can make a Bricks block, which is one of the more rarely seen building materials, as it takes a lot of Clay to get enough to make much.

Obsidian

Found: Overworld where running water has met standing lava, The End

Used In: Nether Portal, building shelter, Enchantment Table

Best Tool to Use: Diamond Pickaxe (nothing else works)

Obsidian is one tough material. In fact, you can only mine it with a Diamond Pickaxe, and its resistance level is 6000 (compare to Cobblestone's 30). That makes Obsidian hard to get, but it's necessary if trying to build a portal to the Nether or an Enchantment Table. You can find Obsidian only where running water has hit still lava, or you can create it by pouring water over lava. Because of its high resistance to damage, Obsidian makes for good safe rooms and walls.

Netherrack

Found: The Nether, all over

Used In: Nether Brick, can be lit on fire indefinitely

Best Tool to Use: hand, Pickaxe or Golden Pickaxe

This is what the Nether is made of, literally. It's incredibly quick to mine and is plentiful, which is nice if you like the way Nether Brick materials look. It has a very, very low damage resistance and can only be turned into Nether Brick, however, so it's not exactly the ideal for most players. Netherrack's ability to be lit on fire indefinitely makes it a common choice for traps and fireplaces.

Glowstone

Found: The Nether

Used In: Lighting

Drops: Glowstone Dust

Best Tool to Use: Any

A special block from the Nether, Glowstone is the best source of light in the game (level 15, Torches are 14). To get it, you'll have to break some Glowstone blocks and collect the Glowstone Dust that drops. This can then be converted back into Glowstone at a Crafting Table.

Soul Sand

Found: the Nether, often near large lava lakes
Used In: Traps and slowing mechanisms
Best Tool to Use: Shovel

Soul Sand is another unique Nether block that isn't used for much as of yet. Soul Sand's primary feature is that it slows down any creature that moves across it (items as well), making it useful in traps and mechanisms where slowing is desired. Its slowness effect is compounded when used in conjunction with water or ice.

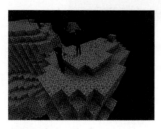

End Stone

Found: The End
Used In: protection from the **Ender Dragon**
Best Tool to Use: Pickaxe

Another rarely seen block, End Stone is only found in The End, and its main use is as a building material

when fighting the Ender Dragon. The Ender Dragon's attack can't destroy End Stone like it can other blocks, but End Stone is a lot easier to mine than Obsidian, making it the best choice for protective shelter in The End.

Ores/Minerals

When we're talking about the "mining" part of Minecraft, these are the things you'll be looking to find, for the most part. All ores and minerals form in "veins," or pockets that are usually surrounded by Stone, Dirt and Gravel (though sometimes water and lava too). They are much harder to find than most blocks, and they are used in most of the complex or advanced creations.

Note: You can craft solid blocks of each of the ores and minerals for use in decoration or certain recipes.

Coal

Types: Charcoal, Coal
Found: Charcoal—Burn Wood in a Furnace, Coal—the Overworld in formations at any level (1% of Stone blocks are Coal)
Used In: Torches, smelting, Fire Charge, running Powered Minecarts
Drops: 2/3 chance of experience dropping
Best Tool to Use: Pickaxe

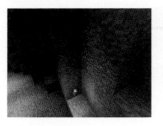

Iron

Found: Overworld from layer 1-63
Used In: Iron tools and armor, Buckets, Minecarts, Cauldron, Rails, Flint and Steel, Compass, Piston, Iron Door, and Iron Bars
Best Tool to Use: Stone Pickaxe or better required

If Diamond is the most coveted ore, Iron is the second, because Iron is necessary for so many important items. Whether building a railway with Minecarts, moving water or lava, setting a Nether Portal alight, trying to make a Map or even just mine Diamond and other rare materials, you'll need Iron. Iron is pretty common, luckily, though not nearly so as Coal. Look for it underground below sea level.

The most plentiful ore is Coal, and that's good because you're going to need a whole lot of it. Coal is what makes Torches, which are the primary light source in your game. Without Coal, you won't have any torches, and you probably won't be able to see. Luckily, you can either burn Wood in Furnaces to make Charcoal or find Coal deposits easily in formations. Both work the same, despite their different names. Coal is also one of the best fuels for smelting in Furnaces (behind Lava Buckets and Blaze Rods). Covet your Coal, kids.

Gold

Found: Overworld from layer 1-32
Used In: Gold Ingot, which makes Gold tools and Armor, Golden Apples, Clocks and Powered Rails
Best Tool to Use: Iron Pickaxe or better required

Gold is a very rare ore, with only 0.1473% of the underground of the world having Gold Ore in it. It can be

crafted into Gold Ingots, whose main use is to craft Clocks, Golden Apples and Powered Rails. Gold items like tools and armor are weak, but can be enchanted, though the benefits rarely outweigh the cost. Gold tools are however the fastest mining tools in the game, but they also break the easiest (even easier than Wood tools).

harvesting, it can mine any other block, it makes the best weapons and armor and it's necessary for some recipes. Unfortunately, Diamond is also by far the hardest material to find. Diamond is only in small deposits in the bottom 16 layers of the game, and it's only mineable with an Iron or Diamond Pickaxe. To find Diamond, you'll need to look in those low levels and try to find lava, which it's often nearby. A note: you need Diamond tools to mine Obsidian, which you need to get to the Nether, which you probably need to do to get to The End.

Diamond

Found: Overworld from layer 1-16
Used In: Diamond tools and armor, Jukebox, Enchantment Table
Best Tool to Use: Iron Pickaxe or better required
Diamond is king. No seriously, in Minecraft, you want Diamond, more Diamond and all the Diamond. This is because Diamond makes the second fastest and longest lasting tools in the game for mining and

Redstone

Found: Overworld from layer 1-16
Used In: Redstone mechanisms and circuits, Compass, Clock, Note Block
Best Tool to Use: Iron Pickaxe or better required
Another mineral found deep, deep down, Redstone is much more common than Diamond, and in fact will drop multiple pieces of Redstone for each block. It's one of the most interesting materials in the game due to it being the

thing you need to create powered circuits and mechanisms. Redstone placed by itself acts like a wire connecting mechanisms to each other and power (which comes from Redstone Torches, Buttons, Levers or Pressure Plates), and when used with those mechanisms and other Redstone items, you can create complex machinery and devices. Look for Redstone by lava.

Lapis Lazuli

Found: Overworld from layer 1-32
Used In: dying things blue
Best Tool to Use: Stone Pickaxe or better required
Lapis Lazuli is fairly rare in the game, but it also drops multiple pieces when it breaks, and it's not used for anything except to dye Wool blue. It's fun to come across, especially if you love blue, but it isn't as valuable as some of the other ores.

"Natural" Materials

These are materials you'll come across in the world that aren't used in building except indirectly. In fact, you can only even pick up water or lava, but all of these natural materials have particular features that are worth noting.

Water

Found: the Overworld in any area
Uses: farming, creating Obsidian, putting out fire, decoration, shelter defenses, damaging Endermen
Water is important in Minecraft. You need it to farm, first of all, but you also want to have some with you most of the time when exploring so that you can put yourself out if you light on fire. Water is also used in decorating, in building barriers or traps for hostile mobs and in creating Obsidian, which occurs when running water touches still

lava. Endermen are also damaged by water easily, and it has a high blast resistance, making it a good tool for attacking and defending. Water can be carried in Buckets.

Lava

Found: Overworld, the Nether
Uses: Defenses, decorations, building trash cans, creating Obsidian

Lava is found in pools on the surface of the Overworld, in underground caves and, most commonly, all over the Nether. It damages almost all creatures that touch it, and it also lights them on fire. This makes it dangerous, but also useful as a defensive decoration. You need lava to make Obsidian, which happens when running water hits still lava. Its biggest use, however, is perhaps its ability to destroy unwanted blocks. You can then set up a pit of lava in your shelter to throw unwanted items into, where they will be destroyed.

Note: Bookshelves, Leaves, Wool, Fences (but not gates), Vines, TNT, tall grass, Wood Planks, and Wooden Stairs are flammable and will be lit on fire by lava.

Snow

Found: Cold Biomes in the Overworld
Drops: Snowballs

Snow is mostly a decoration that sits on top of blocks, but if broken, it drops Snowballs. These can be used to create Snow Blocks, which can then be used as decoration or to make Snow Golems.

Grass

Found: the Overworld
Drops: Grass Seeds

Similar to snow, grass doesn't do much, but it does break into Seeds. Seeds are used to grow Wheat, and are thus worth keeping in your stockpile.

Mycelium

Found: in the Mushroom Biome in the Overworld
Uses: Growing Mushrooms
Mycelium is another growing material that sits on top of blocks in the Mushroom Biome. It doesn't drop anything and can't be picked up, but it can be used to grow Mushrooms, which grow faster on mycelium.

Craftable Materials

Other than for building, materials are gathered in Minecraft in order to turn them into other items with your Crafting Table. Of these there are many, and since half of the fun is discovering what materials create

what kind of items, we're just going to give a basic breakdown of the types of things you can craft in the game.

Tools

Of course, the most important thing to craft is tools. Without tools, you're going to have a very slow and incomplete experience, so they're very important to know about.

Tools in the game come in five varieties: Wooden, Stone, Iron, Gold and Diamond. Leaving out Gold tools, which break easily (though they mine quickest), the other tools are tough, mine quickly and can mine the most types of materials in this order Wooden<Stone<Iron<Diamond. In fact, you need a tool of the material before each in that order to even mine the next one.

Tools come in many varieties: Shovel, Hoe, Axe, Pickaxe, Shears and Fishing Pole. Some people consider Maps, Compasses,

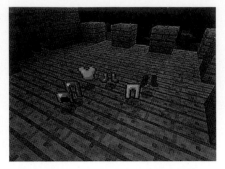

Buckets etc. to be tools, but we think it's simplest to stick with the definition that tools are items that are used to mine or harvest materials.

Weapons and Armor

Like tools, armor as well as one weapon (the sword) are made of different materials, each of which is better than the last.

The order of strength goes Leather<Gold<Iron<Diamond. There is also Chain armor in the game, which is between Gold and Iron in strength, but there is no natural way to get this in Survival at the moment. The other weapon in the game is the Bow, which is a ranged weapon made from a Stick and String.

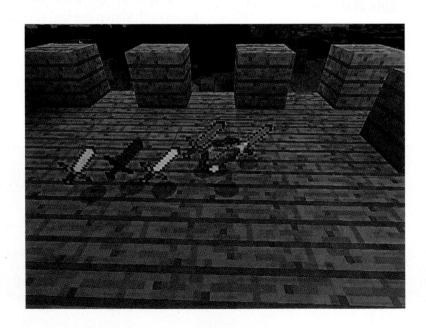

Material Refining

These are items that can be crafted to help craft other items. This includes:

Crafting Table: Your basic item-creation station

Furnace: Refines ores, makes Charcoal and cooks food

Enchantment Table: Enchants items with power-ups

Brewing Stand: Creates potions with buffs and debuffs as well as attacks

Cauldrons: Hold water, used to be for brewing before Brewing Stand was added

Mechanisms

Everything you use for Redstone devices! This includes Buttons, Levers, Pistons and more, and they're some of the more complex and difficult-to-master items in the game. Play around with a few and a bit of Redstone, and you can create anything from a food dispenser to a trapdoor to even a working computer.

Transportation

Rails, Minecarts and Boats fall in this category. This is everything you can create that helps you move without using your feet.

Decorations

Some folks are all about the building, some love adventure, and some love to design cool houses. Minecraft obliges this last group of Minecrafters by providing ample items to spruce up that shelter, including colored Wool blocks, Paintings and much more.

Food

Though not all food is crafted, some is, and others are cooked in the Furnace to make them better. Food is necessary in survival mode, and it comes in a wide variety of types. Food items are either used as ingredients in food that can be eaten, or they can be cooked or eaten themselves.

All Other Items

You'd think with a list this big that we'd be done, but nope! There are dozens of other items out there in the world of Minecraft, many of which are rare and difficult to acquire. We've covered everything we think is essential above, so we'll leave it to you to discover the other unique items in the game for yourself! Good luck, and here's a hint: keep on exploring. You never know what you'll find in the next chest.

A pair of towers sits atop an Extreme Hills Biome.

Biomes

What exactly do we mean by "Biomes"?
This might seem like an easy question to answer, and in a basic sense, the definition of "Biome" in Minecraft is pretty straightforward: Biomes are the different types of land you can find in Minecraft. However, there are actually two distinct types of Biomes that can be found in the game. For this book, we'll call them "Area Biomes" and "Feature Biomes," respectively, and you'll notice when you play that you'll often find them existing together, with the Feature Biome set within the larger Area Biome.

Area Biomes: We use this term to refer to the large sections of land that contain certain plants, mobs and aesthetics (for instance, Desert Biomes are mostly yellow and tan with little life, while the Jungle Biome is lush with life and is full of deep greens and browns). When running around the world of

Minecraft, Area Biomes are what you'll most often be in when above ground, and the border between one Area Biome and the next is usually pretty easy to see, as the ground will change color from one Biome to the next. Think of Area Biomes as different types of nature, or environments.

Feature Biomes: Where Area Biomes refer to areas where certain plants and mobs live, Feature Biomes are more recognizable by their shape. Think of them as natural structures, including Beaches, Rivers, Ravines and Hills. Caves aren't technically considered a Biome, but we've included them with Feature Biomes as they have many similarities.

Why You Should Know Your Biomes

Other than the obvious reason that you want to be an ultra-level, super-guru, Minecrafter genius-person, there is an important practical reason that knowing your various Biomes is a great idea: some items, mobs, structures and even Feature Biomes exist mostly or even exclusively in specific Biomes.

For instance, say you're looking for a lot of Wood and you need it really quickly. Well, if you know your Biomes, you know to stay away from the Desert Biome, and hopefully there's a Jungle Biome nearby. Ready to go cave-diving? The Extreme Hills Biome is your best bet, and you're unlikely to find what you're looking for in the Jungle.

The fact that not all Biomes are created equal, and that some contain resources you'll need more often (like Wood) and others don't, also makes it important to know Biomes at the beginning of your game when choosing a spot for a home. There's nothing worse than building a super-sweet house and then realizing that you'll have to hoof it about five minutes to the north to get more Wood because you built your home in a Biome without many trees.

The Biome Breakdown

So now that you know why you'll be an even better Crafter when you get your Biome game on lock-down, let's get into it! While we're not going to get into the crazy math that goes behind each Biome (it's out there online, if you're interested), we are going to give you a basic idea of what each Biome is like, what you can find there, why you might want to visit it and whether or

not it's a good spot to build a base. We've simplified the info for the Feature Biomes, as they are more about looks and things don't spawn exclusively in them.

Plains Biome:

What It's Like: One of the more common Biomes, the Plains (or Grasslands) is full of Grass, Flowers and some smaller trees. It usually features plenty of mobs (both hostile and friendly) roaming about, and you can sometimes find caves, lakes, Villages and Lava pools scattered around it.

Unique Items, Resources and Mobs: None

Reasons to Visit: It's peaceful and has plentiful Grass (for Seeds) and peaceful mobs to hunt. It's also good for later in the game when you have a lot of resources and want a big space to build something in.

Good for a Base? Only on the edges. Building too far into the Plains will lead to lots of time spent running to Forest Biomes and others with more resources, but building on the edges of the Plains can be fun.

Screenshot: Minecraft®™ & © 2009–2015 Mojang/Notch.

Forest Biome

What It's Like: Trees, trees and more Trees! Another very common Biome, the Forest Biome is one of the most useful early in the game, as they provide large amounts of Wood.

Unique Items, Resources and Mobs:
- Wolves are often found wandering outside of Forest Biomes, but they tend to spawn here.
- Though you can find plenty of trees elsewhere, the Jungle Biome is the only Biome with a greater concentration of trees (and those are almost exclusively Jungle Trees).

Reasons to Visit: You need Wood! Also, they are excellent for mob hunting, even in the day, as the shadows created by trees are ideal for keeping hostile mobs spawned.

Good for a Base? Absolutely! The easy access to Wood makes Forests great for your first base, though you might want to find an edge of the Forest so that you don't have to clear out so many leaves.

Desert Biome

What It's Like: Sparse of life and resources, the Desert is pretty cool-looking, but is not a great place to spend large amounts of time unless it is near another, more resource-heavy Biome.

Unique Items, Resources and Mobs:
- Cactus grows in the Desert and can be used for traps and decoration.
- Sand and Sandstone, while not exclusive to the Desert, will be found in the largest amounts here.
- Dry Bushes also grow here and are mostly used for decoration.

Reasons to Visit: The three primary reasons people head to the Desert are Sand, Cactus and Desert Villages. For whatever reason, Villagers love the Desert, and you'll often find a Village or two within. Primarily, however, Deserts are best for grabbing Sand for making Glass and Sandstone.

Good for a Base? Only at the edge of the Desert and another Biome. It's good to have a Desert near your base (as you'll probably want Glass at some point), but its utter lack of trees is a huge drawback for building a base there.

Swamp Biome

What It's Like: Lots of little bits of land surrounded by Water. Features short Oak Trees covered in Vines, and often has Mushrooms and Lily Pads around.

Unique Items, Resources and Mobs:
- Lily Pads are most commonly found here. These are fun decorations, but you can also build bridges across Water with them.

Reasons to Visit: Swamps are okay for Wood, but you're always better off finding a Forest Biome when you need large amounts. Most of the reason players go to Swamps is to find the resources that are common there, such as Lily Pads, Vines and Mushrooms.

Good for a Base? Can be a cool-looking spot for your home, but you'll need to have a Forest nearby in the long-run.

Extreme Hills Biome

What It's Like: You'll know this one when you see it: huge hills with massive cliffs, overhangs and even waterfalls. One of the most interesting-looking Biomes there is, and a fan-favorite.

Unique Items, Resources and Mobs: None as of now (Emerald Ore is exclusive here but not yet included on the console versions of Minecraft).

Reasons to Visit: When looking for Caves and resources, this is by far your best bet. Extreme Hills Biomes are absolutely riddled with Cave openings, and because there's so much exposed rock, you'll often be able to simply look around outside for Coal and Iron Ore.

Good for a Base? Again, yes, but only if there's a Forest nearby. One trick is to start at a Forest, collecting a lot of Wood and Saplings, and then move to a nearby Extreme Hills Biome to build your home. As they're great for caves, it helps you later in the game, and you can always plant your Saplings on the Extreme Hills (which looks awesome too).

Mushroom Island Biome

What It's Like: Maybe the most unique Biome, this features purple-ish Mycelium as its primary building block and has Huge Mushrooms that look like trees. Always found out in the Ocean Biome.

Unique Items, Resources and Mobs:
- Mycelium, a unique Dirt-like building block that is purple/grey and which Mushrooms like to grow on.
- Mooshrooms hang out on the Mushroom Island. These are Cows that have Mushrooms growing on them. These are great food sources, as you can get Milk, Beef, Mushrooms and Mushroom Stew from them, as well as Leather.
    - Giant Mushrooms are another great food source, as chopping them down gives you large amounts of Mushrooms.

Reasons to Visit: For one, there are no hostile mobs on these islands, so they're nice as sanctuaries. They're also very good for food, and if you can manage to get a Mooshroom back to your base, you'll have a constant plentiful food source.

Good for a Base? Nope. You could always build a secondary base on one, or a bridge or tunnel connecting your base to one, but because they are so isolated out in the Water, you're going to constantly have to go back to the main landmass to get other resources.

Taiga Biome

What It's Like: Can often be snowy and is a sort-of "Russian"-style forest with Spruce Trees and Wolves.

Unique Items, Resources and Mobs:
- Another great place to find Wolves (though again, they aren't unique to here).
- The best bet for Spruce Trees.

Reasons to Visit: Mostly just to chop down Spruce Trees or find Wolves to tame.

Good for a Base? Can be, though you'll be stuck with just one Wood type for the most part. Mostly good for raiding for Spruce Wood.

Jungle Biome

What It's Like: BIIIIIG trees. Like, really, really big trees. And lots of them. Tons of foliage in general, and usually some hilly areas and lakes.

Unique Items, Resources and Mobs:
- Jungle Trees. These are absolutely the best Wood resource out there, and you'll love finding a Jungle just to get at these giant trees. They can be as big as four times wider than a normal Tree and many, many times taller. You'll often find them covered in Vines as well.
- Cocoa Pods are sometimes found on Jungle trees and are used in food crafting.
- Ocelots! One of the cutest and most useful mobs, the Ocelot is very hard to catch but when tamed they can be used as pets or as guards against Creepers (that's right, Creepers hate Cats and won't go near 'em!)

Reasons to Visit: Get on top of Jungle Tree and chop down all the Wood you'll ever need (well, for about a project or so at least). You'll also want Cats at some point to protect your stuff, so Ocelot taming is a good reason as well.

Good for a Base? Sure! With all that Wood around, why not try a tree-house? You'll probably need to visit others for certain resources, but the Jungle is a great Biome for building, if you can clear out a spot.

Ocean Biome

What It's Like: Lots and lots of Water, going off into the distance. There are also underwater Caves and Squids!

Unique Items, Resources and Mobs:
- Squids can sometimes find their ways into Rivers, but you're mostly gonna find these neat little guys (that drop Ink Sacs) in the Ocean.

Reasons to Visit: If you're feeling adventurous and want to try an underwater cave, or if you need a Squid. They can also be pretty good for taking a Boat around, as you can explore the coast.

Good for a Base? Not at all. The Ocean has zero Wood and is hard to build in, not to mention breathe. Of course, everyone wants to have an underwater base at some point, so if you've got the resources, it's a fun place for a secondary home later in the game.

Nether Biome

What It's Like: Fire, Lava, things trying to kill you constantly, little in the way of food. Basically super, super hostile.

Unique Items, Resources and Mobs:
TONS. The Nether is like a whole new world, and most of what you'll find there is exclusive.

- Nether Rack is a red building block that when set on fire stays on fire.
- Nether Brick is made from Nether Rack and has a similar relationship to Stone's relationship to Cobblestone.
- Soul Sand is a building block that makes things move slow, great for docks for your Boat.
- Glowstone is a building block that produces light.
- Nether Wart is a plant resource that is used in recipes and only found in the Nether.
- Magma Cubes are like Slimes, but made of fire and Lava and are pretty darn dangerous.

- Ghasts are huge, flying creatures that shoot fireballs and will seriously mess you up.
- Zombie Pigmen are passive, unless you attack them, and they wield weapons.
- Blazes are some of the more dangerous mobs, floating around and shooting Fire Charges at you.

You'll need to kill some at some point if you want to make it to The End.

Reasons to Visit: Besides all of the unique resources, the mobs and the unique things they drop, you'll need to get to the Nether to get items you need to get to The End.

Good for a Base? You can try, but Beds explode on placement in the Nether, so don't expect to get too comfy. Take Stone and Cobblestone with you, as you're going to need something to protect you from Ghast blasts.

Feature Biomes

River Biome

What It's Like: Neat little rivers, cutting through the land and giving it definition.

Reasons to Visit: They look very cool, and it's always fun to build near one.

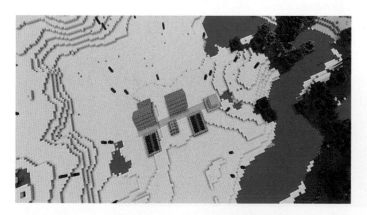

Ravine Biome

What It's Like: Giant gashes cut into the land that go down very, very far. These can be on the surface or underground, and can often contain waterfalls and Lava falls.

Reasons to Visit: They can be neat to build across or on either side of, but mostly they are just spectacular for getting ore and finding caves, as you can just look at the wall and see where the deposits are.

Hills Biome

What It's Like: Just plain ole hills, these can occur on many Biomes including Desert, Plains and Forests.

Reasons to Visit: Good for building on top of, as they offer a view of the surrounding mobs at night.

Beach Biome

What It's Like: Little bits of Sand on the edge of Water.

Reasons to Visit: Mostly just for Sand, and sometimes they have Clay as well!

Cave Biome

What It's Like: Winding, often-complex tunnels through the ground, full of hostile mobs.

Reasons to Visit: These are your best-bet for running into the best resources and structures in the game (like Diamond, Redstone, Fortresses and Abandoned Mineshafts). You'll be spending a lot of time in caves, and it's a good idea to find one very big one and build a little base in it to explore from.

Deep Ocean Biome

What It's Like: The Ocean Biome, except with massive underwater mountains and Ravines.

Reasons to Visit: Same as the Ocean Biome, but good for giant underwater structures.

"Snowy" Biomes

What It's Like: Many Biomes have "cold" or "Snowy" versions where you can find Ice and Snow, as well as get actual snow-falling animations. Plains, Taiga, Rivers and Beaches can all have "Snowy" versions.

Reasons to Visit: You can get Snowballs here, which can be turned into Snow Blocks. Ice is also fun to use, as you slip across it, and the "Snowy" Biomes just look plain awesome

A Jungle Biome sits just above a Cave Biome, giving this area a quite cool look.

"Infinite power just isn't very interesting, no matter what game you're playing. It's much more fun when you have a limited tool set to use against the odds. Usually, a new player to Minecraft doesn't make it through the first night. They're just not prepared for the danger. It's a harsh lesson but it establishes the rules."

— Notch on why Minecraft is the way it is

Screenshot: Minecraft®™ & © 2009-2015 Mojang/Notch.

Mesa Biome

What It's Like: Dry and covered in beautiful bands of Clay and Sand of different types. These are pretty hard to find, but there's no better source of Clay in the game. There are two types of Mesas: the regular Mesa and the Bryce Mesa, which features tall spires of Clay as well as the regular hills and mesas.

Unique Items, Resources and Mobs:
The Mesa Biome has

- Hardened Clay
- 6 varieties of Stained Clay
- Red Sand and Red Sandstone

Reasons to Visit: The Clay, and because they look great!

Good for a Base? Only if it's near a Forest. There's no wood on the Mesa Biome.

Savanna Biome

What It's Like: Somewhat like a Plain Biome with a few more short rises and falls, but with dry Grass and Acacia Trees. Like Plains, the Savanna can spawn Horses, and like a Desert, there's no rain on the Savanna.

Unique Items, Resources and Mobs:

* Acacia Trees
* Horses

Reasons to Visit: That cool, colorful Acacia Wood, and Horses.

Good for a Base? If there's a Forest nearby, then yeah, they can make for very picturesque base locations.

Ice Plain Spikes

Biome Variations

Many Biomes have variations on the basic Biome, including the Mega Taiga and a variety of "M-type" Biomes. Here are the different variations and what makes them different:

Ice Plains Spikes: Plains with snow and a large number of spike structures made of Ice blocks sticking into the air. Some are very tall, going up over 50 blocks

Cold Taiga M: Mountainous variation on the Taiga

Extreme Hills M: Higher peaks, mostly made of Gravel, not many trees

Taiga M: Mountains on the non-snowy version of the Taiga

Mega Taiga: Has giant Spruce Trees, has Podzol blocks and Moss Stone boulders

Extreme Hills+/+ M: Adds Spruce and Oak Trees, the M version has fewer of these but massive Gravel mountains

Stone Beach: Where the Water runs into Stone and not Sand

Plains M: Plains with Water patches and a little bit of mountains

Sunflower Plains: Large patches of lovely Sunflowers on the Plains

Flower Forest: Just like it sounds: beautiful flowers of all kinds on the floor of a regular Forest

Swampland M: More hills than on the Swamps, no Witch Huts

Jungle M: More mountains and heavy plant-life

Jungle Edge/M: A more sparse version of the Jungle without the big trees that happens at the edge of Jungle Biomes, M version is more mountain-y

Birch Forest M: Tall Birch Trees

Birch Forest Hills/M: Adds hills to the Birch Forest, M version adds mountains and tall Birch Trees

Roofed Forest/M: A very cool Biome where Dark Oak Trees grow so close together that it's actually dark beneath their leaves. Contains Huge Mushrooms and other mushrooms, and hostile mobs can survive the day there. M version has cliffs on the edges

Desert M: Patches of water can be found here, unlike the regular Desert

Savanna M: Crazy, weird mountains mixed into the Savanna. Can create the largest natural mountains outside of using the AMPLIFIED setting

Plateau/Plateau M: Hills Biome with flattened tops, often found in Savanna and Mesas. M version for Savanna is much taller and steeper, while for Mesa it's flatter

Friends & Foes

It only takes a few seconds in Survival Mode to realize that your character in Minecraft is not alone. Nope, the world of Minecraft is a full one, teeming with everything from tiny Chickens to Wolves to Zombie Pigmen to the giant Ghast, and if you're going to thrive in this crowded land, you're gonna need to know a bit about these creatures, known as "mobs."

Notes:
1. This section focuses on location, behavior, drops and combat. For breeding, see the Mining & Farming section.
2. The Attack stats are approximate. Attack can change somewhat depending on circumstances and exact numbers have yet to be confirmed for the Xbox 360 console version of the game.
3. Health, Armor and Attack are measured in half-icons, so 1 "heart" icon = 2 Health, one "sword"

icon = 2 Attack, and one "chestplate" icon = 2 Armor.

Peaceful Mobs

There are quite a few mobs out there that won't ever attack you, no matter how many times you punch them in the face or otherwise pester them. These mobs are considered "peaceful."

Sheep

Sheep are everywhere, they are not smart and you will need them for Beds. Sheep tend to spawn in flocks and then roam about, and since they can both jump 1 block high and swim, they end up all over the place.

Sheep are usually white (81.836% chance) but can also spawn as dark grey, light grey, or black (5%), brown (3%) or pink (0.164%), and whatever color they are is the color of Wool you will get from them. Wool can be gathered either by killing the Sheep or by using Shears on it (1 block for killing, 1-3 for shearing). You can also dye sheep to change the color of their Wool.

Iron Golem

The mighty Iron Golem! These tough dudes spawn naturally in Villages with 10 Villagers and 21 houses or more, and they serve to protect the Village from Zombie sieges. Additionally, players can craft them with 4 Blocks of Iron in a T formation with a Pumpkin stuck on top as the head. They are very powerful, but they will only protect Villagers, not the player, and they will wander away from the player if there is nothing keeping them from doing so (a barrier).

Mooshroom

A rarer version of the Cow, the Mooshroom is a Cow that's been infected by Mushrooms. You can only find these guys in the uncommon Mushroom Biome, but they're even better than Cows for food and materials.

This is because, in addition to what a Cow drops, you can also get infinite Mushroom Stew (3 food units, 7.2 hunger saturation). On top of that, if you ever really need Mushrooms, you can use Shears on the Mooshroom and get 5.

Chicken

Chickens may be small and easy to kill, but they also drop a ton of useful items and are easy to farm. You usually find Chickens spread out across the ground and Water, and they can fall without taking damage, so they can end up in deep pits and ravines.

Chickens drop three potential food items: Eggs (used in cooking), Raw Chicken (2 units of the food bar, 1.2 hunger saturation [see Farming & Mining for more info], 30% chance of food poisoning) or Cooked Chicken (3 food units, 7.2 hunger saturation) if it was killed by fire. Chickens also drop Feathers, which are used in crafting Arrows.

Cow

Another pack wanderer, Cows often spawn in groups of 4-10 then wander off, sometimes even falling down cliffs and killing themselves.

Cows are one of the best sources of food, as Raw Beef gives 3 food units and 1.8 hunger saturation (no risk of poison), Steak gives 4 food units and 12.8 hunger saturation and Milk is used to cure status effects like poison and in cooking Cakes. Steak is the most balanced food item in the game, and Milk is infinite, making Cows very good to farm. Their other drop, Leather, is used in crafting the lowest level of armor.

Ocelot/Cat

Released when the Jungle Biome was added to the various versions of the game, the Ocelot/Cat is the cat lover's answer to the Wolf/Dog, and it's both super cute and super useful. Though they do not attack or cause damage at all, when tamed with an uncooked Fish, the Ocelot turns into a Cat. The Cat can either follow the character or be told to sit, and it will scare Creepers away from whatever area it's in! This makes Cats insanely useful at a base or important parts of your map. To tame, simply hold out an un-cooked Fish and wait 'til an Ocelot approaches. Feed the Fish to the Ocelot, and there's a 1/3 chance it'll turn into a Cat. Both Cats and Ocelots can breed by putting them into love mode with Fish.

Pig

Pigs spawn just about everywhere that's not underground, and their initial group is 3-4 Pigs, so you can often find quite a few together. Pig meat comes as Raw or Cooked Porkchops, and it gives identical health benefits to Raw Beef and Steak, respectively (3 food units, 1.8 hunger saturation / 4 food units, 12.8 hunger saturation), making Pigs a good source of food. It is possible to find a Saddle in a Chest, put it on the Pig and ride it around. To control the movement of the Pig, you need a Carrot on a Stick equipped.

Wolf

Though they start out neutral and will become hostile if attacked (and will attack in groups), Wolves can be "tamed" by feeding them Bones. You'll know a Wolf is successfully tamed when it gets a collar around its neck and starts following you.

Tamed wolves follow the player and attack any mobs that attack the player or are attacked by the player except Creepers. They are most effective versus Zombies and Skeletons, less against Spiders, Cave Spiders and Endermen and almost not at all against Creepers, Magma Cubes and Slimes. You can tell the health of a Wolf by the angle that its tail is pointing. A tail that is all the way up means full health, and all the way down means very low health, with corresponding positions in-between. To raise the health of your Wolf, feed it any meat, including Rotten Flesh (which won't hurt it). Wolves also have special behavioral traits when it comes to mobility. A Wolf told to follow you that gets outside of a 20x20x10 block from the player will automatically teleport to the player, unless there's no room for it to do so. Additionally, you can tell a wolf to "sit" with Left Trigger, which makes it stay where it is until otherwise ordered.

Bats

Bats are another mob that doesn't hurt the player at any point and will spawn anywhere where there is a light level of 3 or less below layer 63 in the world. They don't drop anything at all (not even experience), but they are pretty cool because they'll hang upside down to sleep on solid blocks, and then flap away when players approach like real bats. They're more for atmosphere than anything, and between October 20 and November 4 (so around Halloween), they'll spawn in a light level or 7 or less anywhere. Fun, spooky times in Minecraft!

Squid

The only Water mob out there, the Squid will not attack and just drops Ink Sacs. They do make cool pets if you can trap them, though.

Snow Golem

Snow Golems are creatures that are crafted by stacking two Snow Blocks on top of each other (4 Snowballs = 1 Snow Block) and topping it off with a Pumpkin.

Snow Golems are very weak and do no damage to any creature except Blazes and the Ender Dragon, and they are damaged by the Nether, Deserts, Jungles and Water of any kind. However, they do throw Snowballs at most hostile mobs (not Creepers, however), which pushes the mob back slightly and keeps them away when used in groups.

Villager

Villagers hang out in, not surprisingly, Villages, and they can breed with each other and trade with the player. Each Villager has a profession (Farmer, Librarian, Priest, Blacksmith, Butcher), and you can trade with them for profession-related items. Typically, Villagers request Emeralds for the items they offer for trade.

Zombie Pigman

All over the Nether, you'll find Zombie Pigmen, usually in groups. They spawn in fours, but can gather together in larger groups, and they hang out in most parts of the Nether.

Like Villagers, this mob is humanoid and initially neutral to the player, but unlike Villagers, Zombie Pigmen most definitely will attack you if you hurt one. In fact, attacking a Pigman alerts any other Pigmen within a 32 block radius, who will all go hostile and come at the player with Swords.

Rabbits

The hippity-hoppity, ear floppity Rabbit is a newer peaceful mob that spawns in Forest Biomes of all types (including Jungle), Taiga, Savanna, Plains, Swamp and Extreme Hills Biomes. They will not attack you, and you can get Raw Rabbit from them, as well as Rabbit's Foot, a brewing ingredient that is a rare drop. Rabbits are usually in small packs of three, will eat wild Carrots and can be led and bred with Carrots (also bred with Dandelions), and Wolves will hunt them down and kill them. There are six different fur types for Rabbits, and you can also get a special-colored Rabbit by using a Name Tag to name the Rabbit "Toast," which is a memorial to a player's missing rabbit in real life. There is a hostile version of the Rabbit called the Killer Bunny that is white with red eyes and will attack players and Wolves, but it does not spawn naturally and must be put in the world with commands.

Hostile Mobs

Now, these are the guys in Minecraft who want nothing more than to bite you, poison you, shoot you full of arrows, light you on fire, punch you in the face, blow you up and otherwise attempt to make you no more. Even with the best gear, a few of these guys ganging up on you can mean a quick death, often far from home, especially if you don't know their tendencies and weaknesses. Get familiar with these guys as much as possible, and it most definitely will save your life.

Creeper

Ah, the Creeper. He's the unofficial mascot of the game, the sneakiest mob and the one you'll find yourself most dreading.

When Creepers get within two blocks of you (so one separating), their "countdown" starts, and you have 1.5 seconds before it blows up all of the

blocks in about a 6x6x6 area around it. Yep, it's a pain. The only warning you get for this is a slight "hiss" sound when it gets close, and since they will attack any players they see within 16 blocks and are good at finding paths to you, it's pretty likely that you'll have at least one Creeper death in your Minecraft experience. This is made even more likely by the fact that they can survive in daylight, unlike most hostile mobs.

The good news is that Creepers can't blow up when they see you through Glass or a Door, and if you kill them from a distance or before they can do their countdown, they will die without exploding and will even drop Gunpowder, which you can use to make TNT. A harder drop to get from a Creeper is a Music Disc, which requires the Creeper be killed by a Skeleton's Arrow. Because of their ability to blow up your hard work, it's best to protect yourself from Creepers by paying attention to your surroundings and building safely where they can't get to you. Because, as they say, that'ssssss a very nice house you've got there...It'd be a sssssshame if anything were to happen to it.

Spider

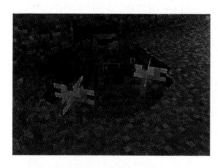

You're gonna see a lot of Spiders. Spiders are neutral until they've been exposed to darkness or attacked. This means that a Spider found in daylight will be neutral, but if he happens to wander into a dark area, he's gonna go hostile and stay that way. Spiders that start off in dark areas and move to light will remain hostile, however.

Despite their small attack, Spiders are dangerous because they can climb walls as if all blocks had Ladders on them and they can jump up to 3 blocks high. They also can see players through walls, meaning that if there's a hostile Spider within 16 blocks of you, it knows you're there and is trying to get to you, and they can even fit through one block high spaces.

To be safe around Spiders, wear armor, carry weapons and make sure your shelter is enclosed and well-lit. If you do kill a Spider, it may drop the very useful String or Spider Eyes.

Spider Jockey

A very rare mob, these have a 1% chance of spawning anytime a Spider does. They include a Skeleton archer riding on top of a Spider, both of which otherwise behave normally and take damage individually. Because of this, Spider Jockeys spawn, move and see like Spiders, though the Skeleton will simply attack anytime it sees you, whether the Spider is hostile or not. On top of that, the Skeleton can suffocate or burn in daylight, leaving the Spider on its own.

Skeleton

Skeletons are major pests in Minecraft because they spawn just about everywhere there's darkness and they attack with arrows from a distance. If you're being attacked in a dark cave and you can't see where it's coming from, then you've probably found a Skeleton.

Skeleton attacks don't do huge damage, however, and can even be entirely prevented by armor. You will want to make sure your shelter is completely sealed, however, because they can shoot through gaps. Skeletons also burn up in daylight.

Skeletons have two very useful drops when killed: Bones and Arrows. Bones can be turned into Bonemeal for use in farming, and picking up Arrows from Skeletons is a lot easier than crafting them.

Zombie

Another of the most common mobs, Zombies wander around the Overworld at night looking for you and your fleshy friends so they can feed on you. Zombies also attack Villages in swarms called Zombie Sieges and can eventually break down doors, both in Villages and otherwise.

Zombies attack by touching you, and they can quickly take your health down if they trap you in a small area. The main reason for killing Zombies, other than survival, is that they drop Rotten Flesh. This stuff can be eaten by your character in an emergency (4 food units, 80% chance of poisoning), but its main use is to feed tame Wolves. Like many mobs, Zombies burn during daylight.

Enderman

From the deep, dark lands of The End, the Endermen come to the Overworld to shift blocks around, look awesome and punch you for looking at them. No joke. Endermen are special mobs that aren't hostile to start, but if you're within 64 blocks and your crosshair points at an Enderman above their legs, they will come at you.

Endermen have a pretty tough attack, which is made worse by their ability to teleport around. This also means they can show up almost anywhere, though they tend to avoid sunlight, rain and Water. Sunlight, rain, Water and fire make them neutral, and any contact with Water damages an Enderman— useful tips for combat. It's suggested to attack the legs as well, as the Enderman can't teleport when taking leg damage.

Fighting an Enderman can be necessary when attempting to go to The End, because finding the necessary Ender Pearls otherwise can be very difficult.

Cave Spider

You won't run into Cave Spiders very often, as they only spawn in Abandoned Mineshafts from Monster Spawners, but they're much tougher than regular Spiders. To deal with Cave Spiders, you'll have to fight your way to their spawner and either break it or disable it.

Doing that is more than likely going to mean a bite or two from a Cave Spider, and since they're poisonous, you'll want to bring some Milk to counteract the effects.

Silverfish

Silverfish hang out in fake blocks called Monster Eggs in Strongholds and in caves in the Extreme Hills Biome. The Silverfish can make a Monster Egg out of a Cobblestone, Stone or Stone Brick block, and you can tell it's a Monster Egg by it taking longer than normal to break with a tool or quicker without one.

Breaking a Monster Egg releases a hostile Silverfish, and if it is attacked and not killed, it will wake every Silverfish in a 21x11x21 block radius and make them attack as well. Silverfish do damage every time you make a change on the Y axis (vertical) in relation to the Silverfish. You also hop every time you're damaged, which is a change on the Y axis, so Silverfish can do damage quickly.

Slime

Only spawning below level 40, Slimes have three sizes. When the Slime is killed, it splits into 2-4 more Slimes of the next smallest size until it is made tiny and killed again.

Slimes are great for experience and are further useful for their drop, Slimeballs, which are used to make Sticky Pistons and Magma Cream. They are also one of the few hostile mobs that can survive sunlight.

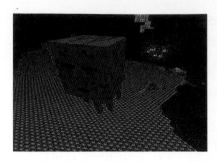

Ghast

The scourges of the Nether, Ghasts are huge and shoot at you with explosive fireballs from up to 100 blocks away. These fireballs do 17 damage at close range (8.5 hearts), but they also light the area around on fire, which deals more damage.

To defeat Ghasts, you'll need to build shelters that protect you from their line of site, and hit the Ghast fireballs away with your hand or item. Ghasts drop Gunpowder like Creepers as well as Ghast Tears, a potion ingredient.

Magma Cube

Similar to Slimes, Magma Cubes are hopping creatures found in the Nether that also split into smaller Magma Cubes. The main differences, besides their appearance, is that they can survive falls, Lava and Water, jump 4 blocks high and do more damage than a Slime.

As with Slime, Magma Cubes are great for experience, and they also drop Magma Cream, another potion ingredient.

Blaze

If you're looking for Blaze Powder, you'll need to find a Blaze, and these tough mobs only show up in Nether Forts. There, Blazes will start popping out once you're within 16 blocks of a Blaze Spawner and can spawn 1-4 at a time, meaning they will build in numbers quickly.

The best method for defeating Blazes is to kill those spawned by using weapons and Snowballs (which do 3 damage to the Blaze). While doing so, destroy or disable the Monster Spawner to avoid more. Snow Golems are also good against Blazes, but will melt in the Nether.

Blazes carry two rare items: Blaze Rods (used in creating Brewing Stands and Blaze Powder) and Glowstone Dust (used in brewing and making Glowstone). Since Blaze Powder is necessary to make an Eye of Ender (among other things), which you need to get to The End, many players find themselves needing to hunt Blazes at some point.

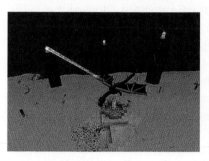

Ender Dragon

There's no greater foe in Minecraft than the Ender Dragon, and there are few greater challenges. Located in The End, the Ender Dragon has 200 health points and does huge damage in the Xbox 360 console version (the PC version has different attacks).

The Ender Dragon also gains health by having it beamed from a circle of Obsidian pillars that have Ender Crystals on the top. These will need to be destroyed before you can kill the Ender Dragon, either by shooting them with Arrows or (in the case of the caged Crystals) building to them and breaking them.

It's recommended to take enchanted Diamond weapons and armor and a lot of Obsidian to build with (it won't blow up like most blocks) to defeat the mighty Ender Dragon. Once you do, you'll be rewarded with 12,000 experience (enough to get you to level 78) and the infamous End Poem.

Endermites

There are no hostile mobs smaller than the Endermite, and these little guys will comes at any player within 16 blocks of them. They will get hurt on Soul Sand and Endermen don't like them and will try to kill them if a player isn't close. They spawn very rarely: only when an Enderman teleports (a 15% chance) or when the player throws an Ender Pearl (5% chance). They only do two hearts of damage, but that can add up!

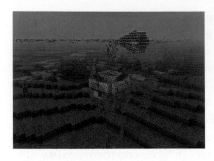

Guardian/Elder Guardian

The Guardian and its big sibling the Elder Guardian are two dangerous Water-based mobs that only spawn in and around Ocean Monuments. They will attack automatically when they see a player, but will stop attacking if you go out of their line of sight. They have two attacks: firing a laser that does high damage, and shooting out spikes when a player gets close as a defense, which does less. The Elder Guardian only spawns three times in each Monument and also causes the player to move slower and break blocks slower by putting a "mining fatigue" status on any player within 50 blocks (once a minute), while the regular Guardians can spawn in much larger numbers and don't have the status effect ability.

Wither Skeleton

A much badder, meaner version of the Skeleton that only spawns in Nether Fortresses in spots where the light level is 7 or lower. They move very fast as soon as they see a player, and they'll smack you not only with their Stone Sword, but also hit you with the Wither I effect, which will take your health bar down gradually. Weirdly, they can actually pick up Swords and armor dropped on the ground and use them. Very tough to kill, these guys!

Wither

Besides the Ender Dragon, the only other boss mob in the game is the Wither, and boy is this three-headed meany a hard thing to fight. To find one, you actually have to make it similar to a Golem. Take Soul Sand and make an upright T shape two blocks tall and three wide, and put a Wither Skeleton Skull (drops sometimes when killing Wither Skeletons) on each Soul Sand block on the top of the T. The Wither will spawn and start moving around while its health bar grows (it's invulnerable at this stage), and then it will cause a very large explosion that will damage players and blocks, but not the Wither. When this happens, you can attack. The Wither is immune to fire, Lava, drowning and suffocation, and it will attack anything except other undead mobs. Its attack features shooting a "Wither skull" shot at anything in its area from each of its three heads, all of which can attack a different thing at once. It can fly, but at half health it will only go as high as its target, but it also gains invulnerability to Arrows with "Wither armor." Healing potions will hurt it, but other effects don't work, and it also will heal itself a half heart every 1-second. Its skulls will put the Wither II effect on anything hit, which drains health over time, and it will heal the Wither 5 health.

Wiitch

The Witch is a solitary mob that you don't see too often, but when you do, it's gonna be a scary time. Witches use splash Potions to do damage to players and to buff themselves against attack, making them potentially one of the most dangerous mobs in Minecraft. Witches can spawn anywhere in the Overworld with a light level of 7 of less, but they also automatically spawn in Witch huts, which are small houses in Swamp Biomes. If lightning hits close to a Villager, this will also turn the Villager into a Witch. Witches have a lot of items they can drop, as well as quite a few attacks (see chart).

Peaceful Mobs

Friend/Foe	Found	Health	Exp.	Drop	Follows (when in hand)
SHEEP	Overworld	8 (4 Hearts)	1-3	Wool (1, 1-3 if dropped) Raw Mutton (1-2)	Wheat
CHICKEN	Overworld	4 (2 Hearts)	1-3	Feathers (0-2) Raw Chicken (1) Cooked Chicken (1 if killed by fire) Egg (1 every 5-10 minutes if alive)	Any seed
COW	Overworld	10 (5 Hearts)	1-3	Leather (0-2) Raw Beef (1-3) Steak (1-3 if killed by fire) Milk (when Bucket is used on it)	Wheat
MOOSHROOM	Overworld (Mushroom Biome)	10 (5 Hearts)	1-3	Leather (0-2) Raw Beef (1-3) Steak (1-3 if killed by fire) Milk (when Bucket is used on it) Mushroom Stew (when Bowl is used on it) Red Mushroom (5 when sheared)	Wheat
PIG	Overworld	10 (5 Hearts)	1-3	Raw Porkchop (1-3) Cooked Porkchop (1-3 if killed by fire)	Wheat

Friend/Foe	Found	Health	Attack	Exp.	Drop	Follows (when in hand)
WOLF	Overworld (spawns on grass)	Wild: 8 (4 Hearts) Tamed: 20 (10)	Wild: 2 (1 Heart) Tamed: 4	1-3	None	Bone

Friend/Foe	Found	Health	Exp.	Drop
SQUID	Overworld (Water, spawns between levels 46-62)	10 (5 Hearts)	1-3	Ink Sac (1-3)
VILLAGER	Overworld (Villages)	20 (10 Hearts)	0	Nothing

Friend/Foe	Found	Health	Armor	Attack	Exp.	Drop
ZOMBIE PIGMAN	The Nether, rarely in the Overworld	20 (10 Hearts)	2	Easy: 5 Normal: 9 Hard: 13	5	Rotten Flesh (0-1)

Friend/Foe	Found	Health	Attack	Exp.	Drop
SNOW GOLEM	Created	4 (2 Hearts)	0 (only pushes most mobs) 3 (Blazes only) 1 (Ender Dragon)	0	Snowball (0-15)
OCELOT	Jungle	10 (5 hearts)	None (scares Creepers, however)	1-3	None
IRON GOLEM	Villages or Crafted by Player	100 (50 hearts)	7-21 (3.5-10.5 hearts)	0	Iron Ingot (3-5) Poppy (0-2)

Friend/Foe	Found	Health	Exp.	Drop	Follows (when in hand)
RABBIT	Overworld (many biomes)	10 (5 hearts)	1-3	Rabbit Hide (0-1)	Wheat
BAT	Overworld (in light level 3 or below, below level 63)	6 (3 hearts)	0	None	None

Hostile Mobs

Friend/Foe	Found	Spawns	Health	Attack	Exp.	Drop
CREEPER	Overworld or Nether	Light Level: 7 or less	20 (10 Hearts)	Depends on how close, Maximum: 49 (24.5 hearts)	5	Gunpowder (0-2 when killed but not exploded) Music Disc (when killed by an arrow from a Skeleton)
SPIDER	Overworld	Light Level: 7 or Less, But Can Survive in Light (goes Peaceful)	16 (8 Hearts)	Easy: 2 Normal: 2 Hard: 3	5	String (0-2) Spider Eye (0-1
SPIDER JOCKEY	Overworld	Light Level: 7 or Less, But Can Survive in Light (goes Peaceful)	Spider: 16 (8 Hearts) Skeleton: 20 (10)	Spider- Easy: 2 Normal: 2 Hard: 3 Skeleton- Easy: 2	5 for each	Spider: String (0-2) Spider Eye (0-1) Skeleton: Bone (0-2) Arrow (0-2)
SKELETON	Overworld or Nether	Light Level: 7 or less	20 (10 Hearts)	Easy: 2 Normal:3-4 Hard: 4-6	5	Arrow (0-2) Bone (0-2)

Friend/Foe	Found	Spawns	Armor	Health	Attack	Exp.	Drop
ZOMBIE	Overworld or Nether	Light Level: 7 or Less	2	20 (10 Hearts)	3-6 depending on health	5	Rotten Flesh Rare: Carrot, Iron Ingot, Potato

Friend/Foe	Found	Spawns	Health	Attack	Exp.	Drop
ENDERMAN	Overworld or The End	Light Level: 7 or Less	40 (20 Hearts)	Easy: 4 Normal: 7 Hard: 10	5	Ender Pearl (0-1)
CAVE SPIDER	Overworld (Abandoned Mineshafts)	From Monster Spawner in Mineshaft Only	12 (6 Hearts)	Easy: 2 Normal: 2 (Poisoned) Hard: 3 (Poisoned) Poison Damage: 1 Every 1.5 seconds Normal: 7 Seconds Hard: 15 Seconds	5	String (0-2) Spider Eye (0-1)

Friend/Foe	Found	Spawns	Health	Attack	Exp.	Drop
SILVERFISH	Overworld (Strongholds and Rarely Underground in Extreme Hills Biomes)	From Monster Spawner (Strongholds) or Monster Egg (Fake Blocks, Strongholds and Extreme Hills Biomes)	8 (4 Hearts)	1	5	None
SLIME	Overworld	Below Level 40	Big: 16 (8 Hearts) Small: 4 (2) Tiny: 1 (0)	Big: 4 Small: 2 Tiny: 0	Big: 4 Small: 2 Tiny: 1	Slimeball (0-2, only from Tiny Slime)
GHAST	The Nether	Anywhere with space except in Nether Fortresses	10 (5 Hearts)	More the closer it gets, Max of 17	5	Gunpowder (0-2) Ghast Tear (0-1)

Hostile Mobs

Friend/Foe	Found	Spawns	Armor	Health	Attack	Exp.	Drop
MAGMA CUBE	The Nether	Anywhere, often near Nether Fortresses	Big: 12 Small: 6 Tiny: 3	Big: 16 (8 Hearts) Small: 4 (2) Tiny: 1 (1/2)	Big: 6 Small: 4 Tiny: 3	5	Magma Cream (0-1, only Big and Small)

Friend/Foe	Found	Spawns	Health	Attack	Exp.	Drop
BLAZE	The Nether (Nether Fortresses)	Light Level 11 or Less or Monster Spawners, both in Nether Fortresses	20 (10 Hearts)	Fireball- Easy: 3 Normal: 5 Hard: 7 Contact- Easy: 4 Normal: 6 Hard: 9	10	Blaze Rod (0-1) Glowstone (0-2)
ENDER DRAGON	The End	In The End	200 (100 Hearts)	Fireball- Easy: 6 Normal: 10 Hard: 15	12,000	Nothing

Friend/Foe	Found	Health	Attack	Exp.	Drop
ENDERMITE	Overworld (where Ender Pearls are thrown or where Endermen have teleported)	8 (4 hearts)	2	3	None
GUARDIAN	Overworld (Ocean Monuments)	30 (15 hearts)	Easy: 4 Normal: 6 Hard: 9 Defensive attack: 2	3	Prismarine Crystals Prismarine Shards Raw Fish Rare: Raw Fish Raw Salmon Blowfish Pufferfish
ELDER GUARDIAN	Overworld (Ocean Monuments)	80 (40 hearts)	Easy: 5 Normal: 8 Hard: 12 Defensive attack: 2	0	Prismarine Crystals Prismarine Shards Raw Fish Wet Sponge Rare: Raw Fish Raw Salmon Blowfish Pufferfish

Hostile Mobs

Friend/Foe	Found	Health	Attack	Exp.	Drop
WITHER SKELETON	Nether (Nether Fortresses)	20 (10 hearts)	Easy: 4 (Wither I effect) Normal: 7 (Wither I effect) Hard: 10 (Wither I effect)	5	Wither Skeleton Skull Stone sword Jack o'Lantern or Pumpkin (if during Halloween)
WITHER	Wherever the player builds it	300 (150 hearts)	Easy 5 Normal: 8 (Wither II effect) Hard: 12 (Wither II effect)	50	Nether Star
WITCH	Overworld (light levels of 7 or less, Witch Hut)	26 (13 hearts)	Potion of Slowness Potion of Poison (if player has 8 health left or more) Potion of Weakness Potion of Harming Defense: Potion of Water Breathing Potion of Fire Resistance Potion of Healing Potion of Swiftness 85% resistant to damage from magic	5	Glass Bottle Glowstone Dust Gunpowder Redstone Spider Eye Sugar Stick 1-3 drops or 0-2 items each

Quick! What do you do in this situation?

Top Tips

You might have noticed, but there is a ton of stuff to learn about Minecraft. In fact, if you ever find someone who tells you they know every single thing about the game, you've probably got a bit of an exaggerator on your hands. Even the pro-est of the pros always have something new to learn!

In order to get you a head start on some of that pro-knowledge so you can get around to the real crazy stuff in Minecraft, we've put together this little list of pro tips. The rest of this guide has been all about specific sections of the game, but here you'll find more general info that can help you out. Don't let that fool you though: some of these tips are among the most useful in the game. In fact, if we were to suggest just one part of the guide to players looking to take their game to the next level, it'd be this one.

So strap in kiddos, and get familiar with these pro tips and tricks!

DON'T DIG DOWN

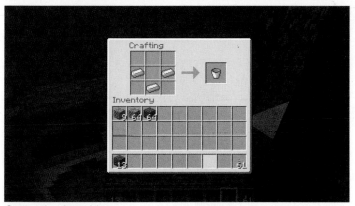

Carry a bucket with you

Exploring Tips

You've heard us say it, other people have said it and the game itself will even say it sometimes: never dig straight down or straight up. Straight down can lead to epic falls, possibly into dark areas, and straight up can drop lava or mountains of gravel or sand on your head. Even in Minecraft, lava on the head is usually pretty darn fatal.

Carry water with you in a Bucket whenever possible. Lava can show up out of the blue (sometimes literally, if you find a lava/water meet up),

Screenshot: Minecraft®™ & © 2009-2015 Mojang/Notch.

The ladder-in-water trick will save you from drowning

Build straight up if you need to find your way home

and it's pretty lame to get caught on fire far from home with a bunch of valuable materials on you. Plus, you can always pour the water out and turn lava to Obsidian and walk right over it.

Stuck underwater? Build a small air pocket to breathe! Doors, Trapdoors, Fences and Signs all create air pockets when placed underwater. You can also build a horizontal five block cross shape, then put one block on the block in the center of the cross. Swim under the middle of the cross and break the bottom center block. Voila, a pocket of air!

Torches to the right!

If you're stuck in a cave or other place underground, and you're tired of trying to get out, dig a diagonal staircase right into the wall. You can also risk digging straight up and placing blocks below you as you go, but there's a good chance you'll have lava, Sand or Gravel fall on your head and kill you if you do.

Buckets of Water can be used to climb up or down sheer faces a few steps without falling. You just need to aim it right above (for down) or below (for up) where you'd like to go, then drop the water. Swim up or down the waterfall, then when you get to your destination, turn around and pick the water back

Screenshot: Minecraft®™ & © 2009–2015 Mojang/Notch.

Beds just take up one inventory space, and they can save you a lot of trouble

up with the Bucket. When going down, make sure you don't pick a place too far away, or you won't be able to pick the water back up. This might not matter in some cases, if you just want off a cliff.

If lost with no Map, build a single-block tower underneath you by jumping and placing blocks below you as you're in the air (Dirt is best). Even better, have another player do it at the same time so you both end up high off the ground where you can see each other. Place torches on the side of the tower if it's night.

Keep a Bed on you so you can sleep if needed wherever you are, but make sure you put it in a safe place.

Carrying a stack of Coal and a stack of Wood is a great way to make sure you always have enough torches. Here's the formula: 1 Wood = 4 Wood Planks = 8 Sticks. 8 Sticks + 8 Coal = 32 Torches. So carrying just 1 Wood and 8 Coal means you can make 32 Torches at any time, or use the materials for other things if needed.

If you find yourself stuck someplace at night, turn it into a mini-shelter. Make it protected from mobs, light it up with Torches, build a Chest, Crafting Table and Bed if possible and leave a few useful items in the Chest, such as tools, materials and a few Torches. You never know when you'll be back this way.

Exploring areas with walls (caves, Strongholds, the Nether) is much easier when you leave Torches only on one side of the walls as you go in. When you need to find your way out, put the Torches on the other side and follow them to freedom.

There's a trick to finding north without a Compass: put down a block of Cobblestone and look on top for the "L" shape in the pattern. The short side of the "L" always points north, no matter what world you're in or how you place the Cobble down.

Use the right tool for the job—don't use a
Diamond Pickaxe on Sand

Lava = ore

Harvesting and Mining Tips

Another common tip: use the right tool for the job. This isn't just because your task will go faster; using the wrong tool for the job also makes that tool lose durability twice as fast. So, not only are you doing the job slower, you're losing your tools faster.

To get the most Wood from tall trees, leave the bottom block of Wood and take out as many as you can reach above it. Then, stand on the bottom block to reach one more before you break it too. If you still can't reach the top by leaving one block of Wood, stack Dirt on top of the Wood while jumping until you get to the right height, then break the Dirt back up.

Replace trees as you chop them down to keep enough Wood around. All you need to do is find a clear area and throw down a Sapling.

Ores often spawn near lava, so go looking for lava to find them. You can use a single bucket of water to turn an entire lava deposit into Obsidian piece by piece as you mine, and you can then mine all around the lava.

You can reach four blocks ahead of you and three blocks down without moving. The most efficient mining method is to point at a single direction and hold down the mining or harvesting button and mine blocks in a row. Because of this, it's good to think in groups of multiple blocks in horizontal or vertical lines, and not single blocks randomly.

Save Coal and a trip to the Furnace by killing food animals with a Flint and Steel. You can light them on fire, and they'll drop fully cooked food.

Cactus can make a good moat

Keep them Creepers away from your home!

Shelter Tips

Moats are awesome, but water is difficult to move through and lava will burn up the items of anything that falls in it. Try a Cactus filled moat that has a walkway over it. Or, if you're feeling fancy, build a system that causes water to flow over the cactus moat and down a hole when you push a lever. Make a little gathering room under the hole, and many of the items from killed mobs will flow down through the hole and into your room. Then, just turn the water off!

Don't put off making a bed and sleeping in it. Beginners are pretty good about this, but advanced players often put it off thinking that they'll be fine. And then a Creeper shows up.

Set up shelters in areas you're working extensively. You'll save a lot of time by making a small shelter with the essentials, and then you'll have a second base too!

Make your home as Creeper proof as possible. This means using Cobblestone or better for walls, as it has a much higher chance of resisting Creeper blasts. Also, build at least part of your house so it's inaccessible from the outside, or at least hard to get to.

Soul Sand can save your Boat from wrecking   *Creepers and other mobs can and will ride in Minecarts*

Transportation/Movement Tips

Boats damage easily, and will break quickly if they keep hitting blocks (it only takes one ice block), but Soul Sand doesn't damage them. Build harbors with Soul Sand to keep your boats around longer.

If you want to ride a Pig, you'll need to find a Saddle, and as of right now those are only in Strongholds in the Xbox version. However, there is no way to control a Pig when you're on one right now, as this requires a Carrot, which is not yet implemented on the Xbox.

Minecarts react differently to Powered Rails if they're occupied by a player or mob. Unoccupied carts will be able to travel a much shorter distance than occupied carts after a Powered Rail. This is due to occupied Minecarts supposedly having greater momentum. Carts with Chests still count as unoccupied carts.

Most mobs can ride in Minecarts, so don't be surprised to see this happen, and be prepared to kill a few now and then.

Jumping while sprinting can make you move faster, but each action done by the player drains your food. If you do this, keep food on you at all times.

Some weapons are better against certain mobs, like Bows with Ghasts

Combat Tips

Each armor icon (the things that look like Chestplates) indicates an 8% damage reduction from attacks, explosions, lava and cactus. A full set of Diamond armor gets the full amount of armor icons and protects from 80% of attacks, while Iron armor gives 60% protection.

What you eat before battle matters. You want your hunger saturation as high as possible, otherwise you'll get hungry much quicker as you attack and your health won't regenerate. Good choices for pre-fight meals include Cooked Steak and Porkchop and Cake.

Mobs do not take damage if they still glow red from the last attack.

Armor and a cake: two important combat items

TNT can really mess a player up

Attacking while in air after jumping and sprinting gives you the best chance for a critical hit.

If you're stuck in a battle you can't win, use the "turtle" strategy. Look down and jump repeatedly while placing blocks under your feet. Soon you'll be high above the battle, but you'll probably get bored pretty quickly!

In PVP, try unique strategies such as "Finn Fu," which involves creating a wall of flame with a Flint and Steel and hiding a lit block of TNT behind it. Then, run so the player chases you past the wall as the TNT goes off. There are tons of strategies like this online, so go check a few out if you're going to be in heavy combat.

Chapter 2

Advanced Strategy

Kill More Mobs

Thing is, when you play Minecraft in Survival mode, some creature at some point in the game will attempt to kill you, and it will succeed. We all know this when we start a world (which typically involves dying once or five times), but after a while you get comfy in your safe house and well-lit mine, and you forget that outside your cozy walls lies death. And then it comes for you, in the form of a sizzling Creeper you didn't see until it was too late, or a nest of Cave Spiders that you suddenly crack into, and you're dead. All your gear is probably lost, you're far from where you were, and then you remember: combat happens in Minecraft. **Let's get you ready to fight.**

Crafter Robot Noise is decked out in enchanted armor and a Diamond Sword, ready for battle.

You'll notice the difference that Diamond gear makes right away. There really is no substitute.

1. Prepare for Battle, Young Miner

Nothing you do in Minecraft is more important to your success in combat than preparation. Every good strategy involves at least some of it, and it is the core of almost all successful offense and defense. Fail to prepare, or at least think ahead a bit, and you're gonna die. Do even the smallest bit of prep work, and you're gonna kill some mobs, kiddo.

So let's get you prepared. These are far from the only ways to prepare in this game, but they'll at least get you set on the path to tasty triumph over the dark forces that wait outside the walls of your home.

Light up the area around your base. Hostile mobs only spawn where the light level is low. When you leave your base unlit, you're letting the mobs choose when to fight you. Turn the tables by lighting the area around your base, that way you only fight on your terms.

It's okay to spend on gear. We know, we know— you want to save that Diamond for <insert difficult to acquire item here>. Well, we get that, but trust us on this one. The amount of lesser materials you will save by spending that Iron or Diamond on good Armor and weapons is going to make that enchanted Diamond Sword pay for itself. You won't just die less, you'll die a lot less, and your ability to kill mobs quickly will result in experience and drops galore.

Eat This, Not That

Best before battle:
- Golden Apple
- Cooked Porkchop
- Steak

Good before battle:
- Cooked Chicken
- Mushroom Stew
- Bread
- Cooked Fish

Bad before battle:
- Apple
- Melon
- Uncooked meat
- Cookie

A miner's gotta eat. Food is the most often forgotten and perhaps most important part of combat. Health regeneration and the ability to sprint (and thus knock the mob back, aka "knockback") depend on your continuing to have a full food bar (the bar with the meat-on-bones). Eat foods that have good hunger-to-saturation restoration levels before battle for best effects, and avoid those with low hunger-to-sat. You should also bring such foods with you when going out hunting and eat them whenever hungry. Keeping yourself well-fed with the right foods all throughout your combat period is essential.

This pit and staircase combo is an excellent build for mob hunting, as it allows you to shoot from on top of it, drawing mobs toward you and hopefully into the pit. Make it even better by building a fence and a gate at the back.

Prepare the land. Make the battlefield your own, not just with lights, but with traps, murder holes and more. The thrill of attacking blind is great at times, but if you're looking to become a true hunter, take the daylight hours to prepare your hunting grounds for maximum success. Create pits, holes and cliffs to lead or knock mobs into and know where they are. Build tunnels and places to attack from above (little towers and forts) that you can access but keep you safe from mobs. This is where you can start to have the most fun with hunting (and essentially farming) mobs, and where you can get the most creative. Turn the area around your base into a place that invites mobs in, murders them brutally and leaves the spoils for you to collect.

2. Offense Is the Best Offense

When combat comes, and it will, don't go swinging blindly. And in fact, don't just swing. The Minecraft community has come up with a few tried and true methods that will amplify your ability to come out of a mob encounter on the life-having end by enormous amounts, and you'll find they'll lead to a lot fewer frantic trips back to your dropped pile of loot.

Sprint and hit to get a knockback. Attacking a mob at sprint causes you to knock it back. This is good for two reasons: It puts distance between you and the mob, and it gives you the opportunity to knock them off of something and damage them. This is especially useful when you know or have prepared the battleground.

Circle around while attacking: the circle strafe. One of Minecraft's two most trusted attack styles, circle strafing involves putting an enemy in the center of your vision while you walk around them in a circle, attacking the whole time. Called the circle strafe, this method makes it hard for most enemies to attack while giving you the opportunity to do damage. NOTE: does not work on Creepers unless you're just crazy good at it.

{ **Flint & Steel** }

Is, in fact, so useful in combat that it should be considered second most essential to a Sword.

Attack, pull back and draw them in, attack again: kiting. Kiting is the second of the two sacred Minecraft combat strategies. "Kiting a mob" is when you hit a mob and then back away while keeping your vision focused on the mob. Mobs immediately attack after you hit them, so by pulling away, you can direct them toward you (as if you were pulling them on a kite string). As your target comes to attack, time a second attack perfectly so that they are hit and knocked back a bit, giving you the chance to back away again and repeat the process. Kiting is one of the safer and most effective strategies in

Minecraft combat, and it can be used in combination with archery as well as with traps for seriously damaging attacks.

- Swords aren't your only weapons. The best hunters use all of their tools. Swords are the primary weapon, but you can also light blocks on fire with Flint and Steel, drop Lava, suffocate with Gravel or Sand (you have to time those just right), drown with Water and even slow mobs down with Cobwebs or Soulsand. Try all of these in combat at least once and arm yourself with the weapons you are best at using.

3. Keeping Alive: Defense in Minecraft

While prepping and attacking correctly are great, sometimes you just need to stay alive to win the fight. And, let's be honest, sometimes you just need to stay alive period. Don't let your first thirty deaths get ya down, Crafters: staying alive can be done, and done well.

Putting a wall between the Crafter and the Creeper will save you over and over.

Putting Torches down while attacking ensures that mobs won't spawn in this exact area again (though they might be able to travel there).

This angry Spider can't get to his attacker when he's underwater!

Use the zigzag method. Most mobs do not do well with direction change when it comes to attacking (the Silverfish being a definite exception). Skeletons in particular just can't handle it, so whether you're attacking or running away, strafing from side to side will boost your chances of success.

Put blocks between you and them. Mobs will chase you, but if you make a move when they can't see you, they won't know you did it. This means that getting behind something and then changing direction or tactics can save your butt more often than not. This is great for attacking, but even better when you need to get yourself out of combat quickly.

Go underwater. No mob can swim to try and kill you underwater, so if you need to get away, dive down, kid.

Spam those torches. Remember, mobs will keep spawning anywhere there is darkness, and if mobs have put you in a bad situation in one spot on the map once, they probably will do so again unless you do something. Spamming torches on the environment when running is a great preventative measure for now and the future.

4. Generally Good Ideas

Any good general will tell you: always take the higher ground when possible.

Just plain smart things to think about when it comes to Minecraft huntin'.

Creepers start their countdown when you are within three blocks and end it when you leave the three block range. That might sound like pretty specific advice, but anyone who's played the game much at all knows that no other mob really compares to the Creeper when it comes to doin' damage. Know this fact and use it to your advantage.

With full health, this Zombie should be no problem. If this Miner was hurtin', however, it would be best to avoid combat in this dark tunnel.

Don't Fight Unless You Can and Want to. You don't have to prove your bravery in Minecraft. Fighting when you are close to death, don't have good gear, are far from home or are otherwise unprepared leads to death, which leads to losing precious items and time. Run away first, fight when the odds are in your favor, and your game will progress a whole lot faster than that of your "brave" friends.

5. Colonel Creeperkiller's Strategy Corner

Okay we made that name up, but this neat little strategy section needed a flashy title. Pulled from the deep depths of the Crafter community, these specific strategies should be learned and used when you find yourself in a tough spot. When you get good at them all and combine them with the above tips, you'll find yourself wrecking your way through wave after endless wave of mobs, reaping their delicious experience orbs and laughing as you stand tall as the apex predator of the Minecraft world. Or something like that. NOTE: These tricks can be used on mobs or, if you're feeling rascally, on other players.

By digging above this Zombie, he has no idea he's about to die.

Getting past mobs in tunnels is a great use of the Ender Pearl (if you can afford to use one).

The Duck and Swing. Best on mobs, make the mob lose sight of you, then move to attack mode. Basically, move to a place where the mob can't see you. They will continue to come at the last place they saw you, so you can move yourself to a place where you can attack them. Swing around behind or above, and you'll have the advantage on the unsuspecting mob. This strategy is super tricky in PVP, but it feels pretty great when you pull it off.

When a Creeper's coming head-on like this, the best option is to get around him and hit from behind.

The Reverse Sapper. Tunnel above enemies or mobs and unleash your fury. Don't feel confined to the way the environment is set up. If you know where they'll be, dig so that you pop up just above them and rock them with attacks. One of the most effective strategies there is.

Ender Bouncing. Pretty straightforward, but expensive: throw Enderpearls to teleport around the battlefield. Especially effective when you throw them through throw walls of fire or where enemies can't see/reach, gaining you a tactical advantage.

A Creeper's about to learn what the Pit Knock is.

The Pit Knock. Set up a pit that's either deep enough to damage anything that falls in it or that has something damaging in it like Cactus or fire. Lure enemies near it and knock 'em in with a sprint attack or a weapon with the Knockback enchantment. Mob falls in, collect loot at the bottom, profit. Can also be made more complicated by creating a drowning or suffocating trap (see the Inventions section).

The Mini Murder Fort from a distance.

The Murder Hole. Create a border around a part of your base where you leave one block open just above where the ground level is on the outside of the base. On the inside of the base, make this spot accessible so that it is at your head-height. This will make it so you can attack the feet of mobs, while most can't get to you. Spiders, however, still sometimes can. Stlnkin' Spiders.

Stack your Mini Murder Fort with some useful items.

The Mini Murder Fort. Get yourself all geared up and find a good spot out in the wild during the day where mobs are likely to spawn at night. Build yourself a little spot where you can reach mobs on all sides but they have a hard time getting to you. This can either be slightly up in the air or slightly underground (or both, for The Ultra Mini Murder Fort), putting you just out of reach of most mobs. Wait til dark, and then wreck all that dare come near. Even Spiders will usually just jump on top, and if you have a one-block hole punched in the ceiling, you'll have a fine window to kill them through.

Screenshot: Minecraft®™ & © 2009–2015 Mojang/Notch.

Finn Fu done correctly is devastating.

Finn Fu. Start a ranged attack on an enemy with a Bow, then create a large firewall on a line of blocks in front of you using Flint and Steel. The enemy can't see through the fire, so drop TNT blocks behind it. Pull away from the firewall, shooting through it at the enemy. If hit, the enemy will usually kite, following you through the firewall. This will light them on fire, running them into the TNT and blowing them up. Works even better if you can put it in a pit and then escape out of the top of it. NOTE: Most items and blocks are destroyed by TNT. You will probably still find some resources that were hit with the shock-wave, however.

The hilarious Sato Technique about to make a Creeper pay.

The Sato Technique. Set a TNT trap by digging down two blocks and placing one TNT block at the bottom of the pit. Put a block that can take a Pressure Plate above the TNT and put a Pressure Plate on it. Now kite a mob or enemy over the plate, and if you can keep them in the general vicinity, they'll go sky-high when the TNT detonates. Also works best in a pit. NOTE: Also destroys most items. But is really, really funny. Can also be used as a trap around your base, but not too close of course (unless you've got an Obsidian blast wall).

Mine Better

When it's time to slam a Pickaxe into some Stone, you need to be ready to go. There's gonna be a lot going on out there in your mine, from caves to explore, to mobs that'll attack you, to ore to snag and more, and it's easy to get distracted (and killed). Remember miner: when you put Pickaxe into hand and you set out for ore, you've got one goal, and that's to mine as well as you darn can.

To do that, you need to do three things: find resources, extract them, and return them to be stored in a safe area in as large amounts as is possible and as fast as is possible without dying.

To do that more often than you end up dead and far from your base, you need to keep a few things in mind.

The Camp

Perhaps the best habit you can adopt for yourself as a miner is to never mine far from a base. This doesn't mean you need to stay by your home, far from it. We just mean that if you're mining and there isn't a Chest or five, a Crafting Table, a Furnace, maybe a Bed and certainly some safe, safe walls to get to quickly, you're mining dangerously.

Mining free, with a base farther than a minute or so away, is a fine tactic when you're out exploring, just starting a world or otherwise unable to invest any large amount of time into the effort, but once you've established a home, you should rarely be mining without having a secure area nearby in which to resupply, deposit gathered resources and hide from the elements.

Camps can be built just about anywhere, as all you need to do is build a small room wherever you are. Don't hesitate to wall off a section of a cave or build a safehouse within a structure like a ravine, Fortress or any other. You have mastery over this land, if you'll take it, and you can never really have enough safehouses.

To produce the best results, plan your mines by first picking a good spot for a mining camp/safehouse, such as at the bottom of a deep staircase, or built up in a natural structure such as a ravine or cave. Bring the stuff you'll need to build a good camp along with you to the spot you want to mine before actually mining, and it will make your ore collection progress much quicker than it otherwise would.

Well-lit tunnels are a must for any good camp.

Camps can be as elaborate or simple as you'd like, but each should meet a few requirements: they should be secure from mobs (meaning they should be well-lit and only accessible through Doors or Trapdoors), they should be easily accessible from your mine (no more than a minute or two away from where you're mining), and they should contain a Chest with helpful items, a Crafting Table, a Furnace and possibly a Bed at the least.

Good items to bring to start a base include Wood of any kind (as well as Planks and Sticks), Cobblestone, tools and weapons, food, and Coal, Charcoal and Torches. Unless you expand your mining camps into more permanent bases, you should think of them as places to resupply and work temporarily, so transport rare or valuable items back to your main bases when you can.

Another shot of a good mining camp, complete with Chests, a Crafting Table and a furnace.

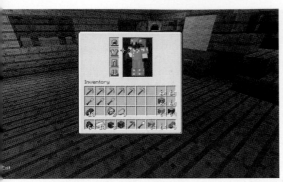

This Miner has all the gear he needs to set out in search of ore.

Don't forget the armor and the Sword when you go minin'!

For Mining

3 or 4 Stone Pickaxes

2 or 3 Stone Shovels

At least 2 Pickaxes of higher quality

At least 1 Shovel of higher quality

1 full stack of Torches or more
(4 stacks is a good number)

Enough food to get full from empty three times
(cooked meat and Bread are great options)

1 full stack of Cobblestone, 2 at most
(partially in order to make a Furnace)

Whatever Wood you can spare (a full stack of
Wood is ideal, but at least some Wood, Wood
Planks and/or Wood Sticks is a very good idea)

When First Setting Up Base Add

As many Torches as you can

As much Coal as you can

As much Wood as you can

3 more Shovels and Pickaxes of any type
except Wood or Gold

2 or more Chests

1 Crafting Table

Some Iron Ore or Iron Ingots

The Gear

A Pickaxe is all you need to mine, but it's not the only item you should take with you on your trips. When you need to mine, plan an extensive mining excursion that takes a bit of time and gear, and your trips will be much more rewarding.

Miners out on a serious resource acquiring jaunt should take as much of the following kit as possible for best results. You might not be able to acquire all of this gear at first, so just take as much as you can and improve your kit as you expand. Eventually, you'll be able to add to this kit and outdo it by adding better items as you progress in your world.

Each time you go out on a planned trip to mine, take the mining kit with you, and stay out mining until you use it all up or run out of inventory space. By doing this and combining it with the practices below, you'll end up with the maximum number of resources in the least amount of time.

The Exploratory Trips

As tempting as it might be, don't go just randomly mining when you find a cave or other structure (or at least don't do so for long). Plan your trips, get your gear ready, know where your base is, and head out with an area in mind.

- The best mines are centered around a mineshaft (a vertical shaft with a ladder) or a staircase that goes from ground level to the bedrock. Build tunnels or clear out levels around these, never going too far from the center staircase or mineshaft and always going straight out from the center. No twisting passages or changing levels, just straight halls, rooms and tunnels with flat floors.
- Keep your mine organized, but also collect all resources you see. When you find ore, follow it and mine it all out, but when it's done, repair your mine so that you keep it easy to understand. For instance, if you come across some ore that goes below the level that the rest of your mine is on, mine it out and then replace the floor so that it stays flat.
- Remember the two rules of ore finding: ore is most common below level 16 and near Lava. If you're really looking for ore, you want to have a base in the lower levels so you can explore them, and you want to look out for Lava. When you find Lava, dig around it, containing it as you go, and you'll more than likely come across some nice resource deposits.

Best Mining Practices

Some general tips for mining, these will refine your tactics into well-developed, highly efficient processes.

- Use tools to breaking. You're already out, and though you might have some other project you feel like rushing off to, you're best served by using up the tools you have when you're already in your mine. If you take our mining kit with you and use it all up, you'll collect more resources each time you're out, making the time you spent in your mine much more worthwhile.
- Your mine should have a straight shot to the surface. We've covered this a bit before, but it bears reiteration, as it's so key to good mining. It should never be hard to get back to the surface from your mine, and if it is, you should make an easy exit for yourself.
- You should have a quick shot back to base when mining as well. Again, we've covered this but we're going to say it again: it should never take more than a minute or two to get back to a base from where you're mining. Keep mining far away from base and we can tell you from experience that a Creeper's gonna find you and ruin your day sooner than later.
- Deposit resources often. It's a guaranteed win when you take your resources back to your secure base no matter how little or how much you've gathered. Do it as much as possible.

- Leave no dark spots in your mines. No matter how small the shadowy spots are in your mine, light them up. You should never, ever have mobs spawning in the areas you are mining, and you can make that  happen by using Torches and other light sources liberally.
- Use signs to direct yourself. Whether it's telling you what level you're on or that a cave or base is "This Way," use signs. There's never going to be a moment where you are sad that a sign told you where something is, and there will be many times you wish there was one to help out.
- Keep your tools close together in your tray. Switching between tools like Pickaxes and Shovels can take up a lot of time over many switches, so keep them right next to each other and you'll save a lot of minutes.
- Go in pairs, with one player mining and the other organizing. If playing multiplayer, split the responsibilities by having one player expand the mine and gather resources while the other cleans up behind them and keeps the mine organized. It really is worth the trouble.
- Leave a third of your Iron tools by switching to Stone for mining lesser materials. Use your Iron tools on all materials until there's about a third of them left. Then switch to Stone tools unless you find something that requires Iron to break. This allows you to stay out longer, as you can still collect the more valuable ores while continuing to expand your mine.

The Bedrock Tunnel

This mining strategy technically belongs in the structures section, but as its purpose is almost exclusively related to mining, we've included it here.

In our mining (and even exploring) of the Minecraft world, few structures have come in as handy as The Bedrock Tunnel, which is exactly what it sounds like. By digging down to the Bedrock and building a well-organized cavern or tunnel, you are able to expand over large areas of the map easily, giving you access to the layers above. The terrain right above teh Bedrock level is almost always solid Stone and ore, with maybe a little Lava and Gravel, so you can usually count on being able to dig out a simple rectangular room or tunnel with ease.

This tunnel or room can then be expanded on (we've even seem some Crafters who dug out the entire bottom layer of the map, incredibly), and you can build mineshafts with Ladders up out of the Bedrock Tunnel to access the entire map above. This means that you can use your Bedrock Tunnel to test out various areas of the map for caves, ravines, Fortresses and other structures while having an easy area to return to (the Bedrock Tunnel) that contains safe-houses and eventually leads back to your main base. Add rails and Minecarts for even quicker access to the entire map.

The Tutorial world has a great example of an animal farm

Sheep: they love Wheat

Farming

Farming also has two distinctive types, but the two types of farming are quite different from each other. One revolves around the capture of animals to breed and harvest meat and drops from, and the other revolves around planting and harvesting crops of plants.

Animal Farming

Don't worry, this isn't about to get all Orwellian. Animal farming is pretty simple in Minecraft, though some automated breeder inventions can take things to a whole 'nother level. What you need to do for an animal farm is fourfold: find the animals and get them to follow you, put them in an enclosure, breed them and then harvest them.

1. **Find and Follow:** Most peaceful animal mobs in Minecraft have a certain item that they really like, and when you hold it, they'll follow you. This is ultra-convenient for animal farming, as otherwise you have to shove animals one by one into your pens, or just hope they walk in on their own. Here's what animal follows what item:

- Wheat: Cows, Pigs, Sheep and Mooshrooms
- Wheat Seeds: Chickens
- Bone (use on to tame): Wolves

Screenshot: Minecraft®™ & © 2009–2015 Mojang/Notch.

A cool-lookin' farm on the side of a castle

Screenshot: Minecraft®™ & © 2009–2015 Mojang/Notch.

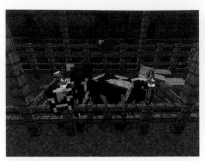

You can tell that animals are ready to breed when they display the floating hearts

A baby cow!

2. Put 'em in a Pen: Now that you've got some animals following, you need a place to put them. If you haven't built one already, just stick them in your home and close the door for now. Building pens is what Fences were made for, and this is where you should use 'em. Mobs need to be pretty close to each other to ensure breeding, so make a pen for each type of mob, and make them pretty small (maybe 8x8 at the largest, but more often smaller). Use Gates on each pen in order to get in and out, and remember that some mobs are hard to get in through a 1 block wide hole, so make double Gates if necessary. It's also a good idea to put all the pens near each other, and then fence around the entire section of pens. This makes it less likely that any mobs will get out, and it gives you a space to let some roam a bit if you need to do so.

3. Breed those Guys: Breeding is a necessity for any good farm because it allows you to turn your animals into renewable resources. There's not a lot of point in going out and collecting animals just to kill them, and then have to do it again, right? To breed animals, you simply need to find the right item to feed them, then feed two of them in the same area. They'll find each other, breed, and a new little baby animal will spawn!

Here's what each animal needs to breed:

- Wheat: Cows, Pigs, Sheep, Mooshrooms
- Any seed (not just Wheat Seeds): Chicken
- Any meat: Tamed Wolves

4. Time for the Harvest: Yes, they may be cute when they're bouncing around in your pens, but you need that food! To harvest meat and items from animals, simply kill them. You can light them on fire to kill them and have their meat drop already cooked (if they drop meat), but this method doesn't drop experience. Use a Sword, and take a few out. The key here is to make sure you leave at least two animals of each species alive so that they can keep breeding later. A note: there's no reason to kill Tamed Wolves. They don't drop any items, and besides, they're your friends!

Plant Farming

The primary plants for farming in Minecraft are Wheat, trees, and Pumpkins and Melons. You can also farm Sugar Cane, Mushrooms, Nether Wart and Cactus, but these are the plants that you're most likely to need and to farm in your game.

Wheat Farms: Wheat is probably the most commonly farmed plant (it's between Wheat and trees), and it's simple to farm. Wheat requires a light level of 9 or above and what's called farmland, which is what a block of Dirt turns into when you use a Hoe on it. For best Wheat growth, it should be no more than 4 blocks from a source of water as well. Wheat takes a variable amount of time to grow, but grows fastest under conditions where it's well-lit and on hydrated farmland. Harvested Wheat drops 0-3 Wheat Seeds when cut, making it a renewable resource. Use Torches or Glowstone near Wheat in order to make it grow even without sunlight.

Tree farming with friends

Set up your farm
in this pattern

Screenshot: Minecraft®™ & © 2009–2015 Mojang/Notch.

Wheat, Melons and Pumpkins need water and farmland

Tree Farms: Wood is a hugely important resource in Minecraft, so tree farms can make your virtual life a lot easier. Like Wheat, trees need light, but they don't need water to grow, so again use Torches to grow trees. The easiest tree to grow is the Oak, and the easiest way to grow it is to make a 5x5x2 space of Dirt. In each corner, dig a hole 1 block down and plant an Oak Sapling in each hole. Put 3 Torches to a side, and the trees will grow easily. Trees usually drop Saplings, making it easy to replace them.

Melon/Pumpkin Farming: Pumpkins and Melons are both farmed in the same way. Pumpkins and Melons work best on farmland with hydration, like Wheat, but they grow differently. When planted, their seeds make a stem, which when mature grows a Melon or Pumpkin in one of the 4 adjacent blocks. This means you need to leave at least one space and preferably more around a planted Pumpkin or Melon Seed. These also produce Seeds when harvested.

You can build an advanced farm by building it in tiers. By building the same shape of farm one on top of the next (leaving a little space between for movement and lighting it up with torches, of course). You only need one source of water if you let it flow down from one to the next!

Advanced Farming

Runnin' around and a'murderin' mobs in order to get food, or making maniacal runs on Villager Wheat farms, is all well and good, and will get you through the beginning of the game just fine. However, later in the game, having to leave your base for food trips can get exceedingly tedious and frustrating, and it usually leads to a cycle of taking quick hunting trips that never gather enough food, leading you have to go huntin' again not too far in the future.

In the end, having a ready food source built into your home such as a farm or ranch is almost a must for a Minecrafter, and they really aren't too hard to set up. We introduced you to a few neat and efficient ways to build some basic, high-yield farms and ranches that you can use to keep your food close and easy to get to, but despite making it a lot easier to acquire food than it would be by hunting, you still have to do a bit of work when it comes to harvesting the food.

This being Minecraft, however, there is almost always a way to turn most tasks into automated systems that require very little input, and this is certainly the case with farms. If you want to step up your food acquisition game to the next level, give these builds a go.

Screenshot: Minecraft®™ & © 2009–2015 Mojang/Notch.

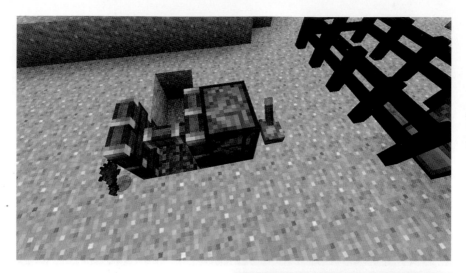

Two Styles of Automated Farms

The Piston Farmer

Piston Farms can easily be attached to most existing farms.

Pistons are one of the most dynamic and useful objects in the Minecraft universe, and when it comes to farming, they can help you out quite a lot. This build takes advantage of the fact that an activated Piston that shoves over a plot of grown Wheat will cause the Wheat to break and drop so you can grab it and use it.

This build can be added to most farms, but you'll need to leave at least one or two blocks next to each block where you will grow Wheat. All you need to do then is place a Piston on the empty block one block next to and one block above the block on which you're growing the Wheat. Make sure the Piston faces the Wheat, and do this for every block where there will be Wheat. Then, wire all of the Pistons together with Redstone so that they lead to one single Lever. (You may need some Repeaters.)

When you flip the Lever, all Pistons should extend across where the Wheat has grown, breaking the Wheat. Flip the Lever again so that the Pistons detract, and where there once was a Wheat farm, there is now a large

amount of Wheat icons floating on empty patches of Dirt, and you can just run down your farm and grab them, replanting as you go.

The Water Scythe

Piston farming's fun, but when it comes to efficiency, nothing beats the Water Scythe. Like Pistons, Water that flows over a block of growing Wheat will break it. Unlike Pistons, however, flowing Water will actually carry the dropped Wheat with it.

By using both of these features, we can harvest an entire farm with the flick of a Lever and direct the flow of the Water so that all of the harvested Wheat gathers in one spot for you to pick up.

For this, you'll want to build your farm in a terrace formation, with one level of the farm one block below the other. Before you plant, go to the far end of the top level of your farm, and build a little wall with alcoves (holes) in it that line up with where the Wheat will be planted. Now, place Buckets of Water in the alcoves so that it flows out over the whole farmland, making sure that it doesn't overflow the sides. Test this out a bit so that you get it right.

The Water Scythe caught in action as it harvests Wheat for you.

Screenshot: Minecraft®™ & © 2009–2015 Mojang/Notch.

Now move to the bottom level of your farm and see where the water is flowing out. Build around this so that all of the Water collects in one trench that goes downhill and ends in one single block (without overflowing).

Go back to the top of your farm and temporarily remove the Water. What you need to do now is control when the Water comes out. The best way to do this is by building a system of Sticky Pistons, blocks and a Lever, so that when you push the Lever, the Pistons remove the blocks from in front of the Water, allowing it to flow (and when you push it again, the Pistons put the blocks back and stop the Water). If you don't have or don't want to use Sticky Pistons, however, you can simply use a block of Dirt over the alcove that you punch out when you want to harvest your Wheat.

Once it's all set up, plant your Wheat and wait until harvest day, which will be the easiest one you've ever had.

Semi-Automated Breeding

Unfortunately, the console version of the game is not yet set up to where we can have fully automated breeding, as there's no way to automate feeding animals Wheat yet, but you can set up a fun if not always well-functioning automated breeder using a few Powered Rails, Detector Rails and some Water.

An above view of the somewhat-workable Automated Breeding machine.

Start your build with a pen for your selected animal. Make the pen lead to two Fence Gates that are separated by one block and that have a drop off immediately after them. You want your pen to funnel animals toward the Gates one at a time, and it's best if you can isolate two animals (one in front of each gate) if possible, so play around with Fences, Fence Gates, trenches and other methods to find the one that works best for you.

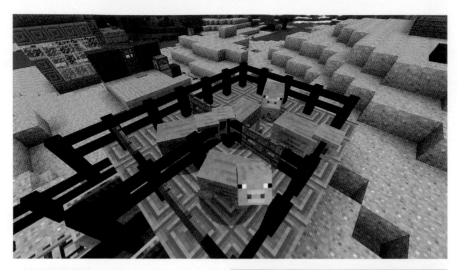

On the other side of each Gate (one block down from them), build a railway in this pattern: Powered Rail-Detector Rail-3 to 5 regular Rails-Detector Rail-Powered Rail. Make sure that there is a block at the end of the railway to stop the Minecart as well.

The machine in action!

In the space between the two rails, dig a trench that starts one block deep and then one block before the end of the rails goes two blocks deep, and then three deep one block beyond that. Build a little pool at the end, and then dump a Bucket of Water at the top of the trench by the Gates so that it flows away from the pen and past the railways into the pool. Build a Fence immediately around your rails, blocking off the end so that animals can go under the Fence and into the pool, but never outside of the build.

Finally, fill your pen with animals and set two Minecarts, one on each railway right in front of the fence. Use Wheat to put two animals into love mode (with the hearts above) and then open the Gates and lure them onto the carts.

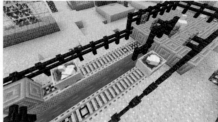

Note that these Pigs were brought down the canal and into the pen below, making them easy to harvest Pork from.

What should happen if all goes well is that the animals in love will fall into the Minecarts, which will bounce down the track and then back again forever. As they pass each other, you should start to see baby animals pop up between them, which will hopefully fall into the Water and be pushed out into the pool.

What can often happen, however, is that you will find it hard to get the mobs both in love mode and into the carts, and the baby mobs can often get in the way of the tracks meaning you need to give the carts a little push. You also tend to have to put animals back into love mode once they fall out, which can be hard to do while on carts.

Works for Chickens...and Cows too, as well as other breed-able mobs (though it still can get messed up just as easily).

It's not the best system, but it's pretty easy and fun to build, and as of right now, it's the best we've got for automated breeding. Tweak it here and there, such as maybe making there be a drop under the rails to where the water flows (so baby mobs simply have nowhere else to spawn), and you may be able to achieve better results. Hopefully in future they'll make this a little easier!

What To Do When

There's a moment in just about every long-haul Crafting session where you come up against something tough, and you're just not sure what to do about it. Minecraft is full of these kind of moments, whether it's deciding to stay down in your mine for another fifteen minutes before heading back to base, or whether you suddenly find yourself in peril and aren't sure if you should fight, fly or just throw in the towel and reload from your last save. While there are really no wrong answers in this game that's all about experimentation and playing how you like, there are some tips for certain situations that we can give you that can make your next mining trip go a bit smoother (by which we mean less full of death and woe).

Screenshot: Minecraft®™ & © 2009–2015 Mojang/Notch.

1. You're lost and can't find home (or anything else you recognize).

We all love the goofy, blocky graphics of Minecraft, but we also have to admit that they can make it hard to keep your sense of direction. Since there are only so many types of blocks and environments, you can quickly get turned around both above and below ground. If you're stuck out in the wild and are starting to think you'll never see home again, try these tips.

- Get up high. If you're above ground, create a dirt tower so you can look out over a bigger area, or climb a tree. If you're underground, stop trying to find your way out naturally and just dig up in a staircase pattern. Moving up is almost always beneficial in Minecraft when lost or stuck, and you can always go back down if you need to!

- Mark your path. Always, always mark your path, especially when you're already lost. Use towers, torches, just about anything you'll recognize, and you'll start to weed out all the wrong directions (and will stop going in circles, as can definitely happen).

- Use the Cobblestone/Nether Rack "north" trick. If you look at blocks of either of these, you'll see that they have an "L" shape on the texture (on the regular texture pack). If you situate your miner so that the L is facing the correct direction (meaning it looks like the letter should), you are facing north.

Spaun Spider

2. You're stuck outside/underground without resources and mobs are about.

Mobs don't care if you're ready for combat or not: they're coming for you. It's pretty likely that you're gonna find yourself in a bad spot at some point, with mobs a'comin' and no Sword, Bow or other weapons to speak of. What do you do?

- Get up high. Like with being lost, getting off the ground level is an excellent combat measure. Mobs have a hard time climbing even one block and most cant climb two (just Spiders), so put some air between you and your foes.

- Run straight through. Sometimes the best way to survive is to just put on a burst of speed and try and break through the line of mobs. If possible, eat something before you do this.

- Protect your resources. It's always easier to come back and find a Chest with items in it than it is to rush back to get the gear that dropped when you died. Bring Chests with you when you mine and store all of your important stuff when in a bad spot before trying to escape.

- If possible, build a mini-mini murder fort. Obviously you don't have time to do any major construction, but if you can surround yourself with blocks and leave just a little space to attack through, you should be able to time it so that you can hit mobs and they can't reach you. Very effective in a pinch.

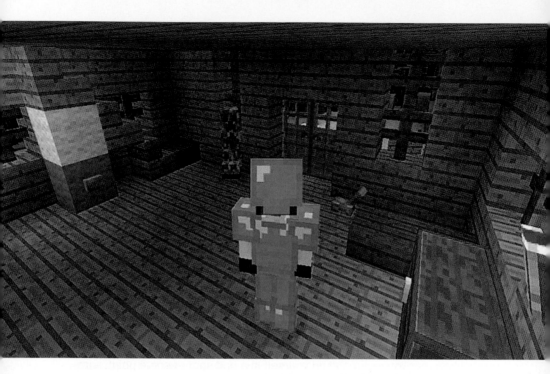

3. There's a Creeper in your home (or project, or mine, etc.).

It happens, sometimes a lot, and it's terrifying. There's one thing to do.

*   Get out. Immediately. It's the Creeper's home now. Okay, not really to that last bit, but seriously, just go. While you might be able to kill the thing, there's just too much at risk. Unless you don't care what happens to the place, it's always better to leave and let the creepy thing see itself

out or despawn than it is to risk having to put half your house back together.

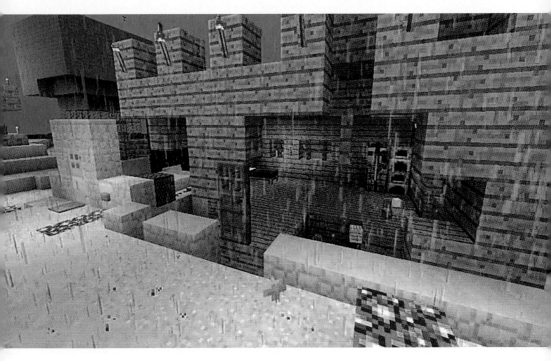

4. A Creeper done blew up your home.

But of course, sometimes you just can't get away in time. Creepers do be creepin'. But don't panic; you have options.

- Consider reloading. It may seem cheap, but so is showing up unannounced, sneaking right next to you and your beloved project and blowing it to smithereens. If you saved less than five minutes ago or if rebuilding would take more time than re-doing what you've been doing, you might want to reload.

- Take the opportunity to make it better. We all get distracted by new projects and tend to leave old ones sitting for a long time. It's super common to jump in someone's world and see that their bedroom is a lot shabbier than whatever the newest project they're workin' on is, as miners often get so caught up in other stuff that they don't take the time to update or upgrade their older work. If a Creeper knocks a hole in your house, well maybe it's time to add that moat you've always wanted! This is one of the greatest things about Minecraft: when things get destroyed, it gives you the chance to make it better!

5. You fell in a pit/cave/ravine without torches.

Falling into darkness is hard and a bit nerve-wracking; it usually starts with a bit of panic as you wonder how you can possibly get out without light. But...

- Just dig forward and up. Hopefully you have tools, but either way, just put a block in front of you (you can always kinda just a bit, even in the dark) and break it. Then point up and break the one above it, and then the one behind that. Jump up and repeat. You will eventually either A) find light, B) get out or C) crack into another drop and fall more, possibly to your death. Whatever happens, you'll at least get out.

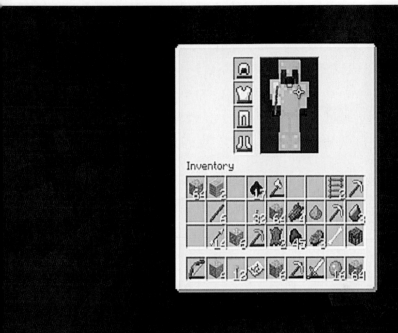

6. You have a bunch of resources and wonder if it's time to go back, but aren't sure if you want to yet.

Oh the many, many times we've thought to ourselves "I should find a Chest, but I'll just explore this one more cave." There's an answer:

- Don't stay out. If you're wondering if you should head to a Chest, the answer is almost always yes. Think of it like this: you just did a bunch of work, you have some good stuff, and you are currently safe, healthy and you know the way back. These are things you know for sure, right now. Give Minecraft the chance, and it will change one or all of those things within seconds. Err on the side of caution (and keeping your loot).

- Or, build a chest here and now and drop yer goods. You can always come back in a few minutes and grab it all, and at least you know it'll be safe.

- Or, save the game. Don't be afraid to use the save feature to your advantage. Hit pause and save real quick, that way you can load from right there and make a better decision if things go south.

7. You find somethin' awesome, but you aren't geared/prepared/ready to jump into it.

Cool things are around almost every corner, and you'll end up stumbling across a ton of them while you were on your way elsewhere.

- Don't overreach. Taking a peek is fine, but if you don't think you're prepped for a big cave encounter, **don't go down the big, dark, dangerous cave.**

- Mark it well. Light the place up with Torches, build a big tower of Dirt, make a Flower path back home or better yet bust out a Map and write down the coordinates. Just because you aren't ready to go now doesn't mean you should let neat places and valuable areas be forgotten. Make it so you'll definitely be able to find it again, and then do.

Abandoned Mineshafts are one of the more dangerous structures in the game. Don't go in unless you're ready.

8. A structure or area is giving you trouble because it is getting too complex and dangerous.

In most games, you're pretty much stuck with having to navigate complex areas as they are, but this is Minecraft. We have better ways of dealing with nests of enemies, such as...

• Take the area apart. Just start simplifying the area by removing blocks and making it into one big room. You don't have to play fair; mobs certainly don't. Turn that confusing cave system or dangerous mineshaft into *your* area. Eliminate the threat by controlling the land, and you'll find that Fortresses and the like are just oh so much less intimidating.

9. Something interesting pops up while you're in the middle of a project.

Say you're carving out a base, and you stumble across the entrance to a cave or a big deposit of ore. What do you do? Abandon your project and deal with this now, or save it for later?

- If it's ore, go for it. Get ore until there is no more, and then fill in the area so it is just Cobblestone. Your later projects will thank you, and you won't lose the organization of what you were working on.

- If it's a structure or system, secure the area, mark it, and come back later. There is nothing more dangerous than leaving an entrance to an open cave or structure in your base or project, because you never know what can come sneaking up out of the depths all the way through your home and even to your bedroom. Where there's dark, there's danger. Control the situation first, finish what you were working on, then come back and dominate that structure and whatever foolish mobs dare to dwell in it.

10. You can't find what you're looking for.

Sometimes you start a game and crack straight into a Diamond-filled ravine/Fortress, and sometimes you go weeks on a world without seeing either. While it's never guaranteed to find anything in the game, there is a system that can help.

* Use the Staircase Down, Ladder Up method. Seriously guys, this method works wonders. All you do is create a staircase down to the Bedrock and when you're at the bottom, build a Ladder that goes all the way to the surface from there. Create a few of these in different directions and on different parts of the map, and you end up covering an enormous area in very efficient manner. You'll find ore, you'll find structures, you'll find mobs; you'll find just about everything. Even more effective when combined with tunnels, branch mining and clearing out levels around the staircase.

Villages often have farms.

Navigation

If there's one thing that Minecraft is all about besides building, it's exploring, and this game does not slouch when it comes to giving you cool things to find. In fact, even a player that's plugged hundreds of hours into Minecraft can climb just one more mountain or break into just one more cavern and come across a gorgeous view that they've never seen in the game.

The world you see in Minecraft is essentially broken down into natural environments (Biomes) and environments spawned from building materials (Structures). In the Xbox 360 console version of Minecraft, there are currently four major Structures and two minor Structures, each of which has its own rules for where it can occur, what type of creatures populate it and what can be found or done within it. Knowing this info can make a big difference in your gameplay, especially when attempting to survive at the beginning of a game or when looking for certain items later on. There's nothing like coming across a Chest of Diamond right when you need it!

Note: when exploring just about any of these, except the Village, you'll want to bring plenty of Torches or other items to mark your path, or you most definitely will get lost.

Villages

If you're running around the Overworld (the part of the game that you spawn in), and you see a cluster of houses and think "Hey, I didn't build that!", you probably just found a Village. Villages are collections of buildings populated by neutral Villagers.

Where

Villages only spawn in Plains or Desert Biomes. They tend to spawn where it's flat, but they can also spawn on hills and across ravines, which can make for strange set-ups.

Structures

Depending on the available space, the game will place certain structures in a Village. The Hut, Butcher's Shop, Small House and Large House are simple structures made of Wood, Wood Planks and Cobble, and they usually contain a Villager or two. The Watch Tower and Church are taller structures with great views and a Villager, and you can also find Wells and Lamp Posts (made of one Black Wool block and some Torches). The most important Village structures, however, are the Farms, Library and Blacksmith, which contain useful items and in which Villagers live that can be traded with.

Village by night.

Villages are great places to find resources.

Mobs

The only mobs native to Villages are Villagers, baby Villagers and Iron Golems. Adult Villagers have professions and will breed with each other, and you can trade Emeralds with Villagers for various resources. You may also see Zombies attacking Villages in Zombie Sieges.

Materials

Villages are excellent places to raid for building materials in a pinch, as they're made of things like Wood Planks and Cobblestone. The best resources, however, are found at the Farms, the Library and the Blacksmith. Farms yield Wheat and Wheat Seeds, which means you can easily make Bread or start your own Wheat Farm. Libraries contain Books (helpful for Enchanting) and a Crafting Table you can snatch up. The Blacksmith, however, has a couple Furnaces and the true treasure: a Chest of items. Check out the graph to the left to see what goodies you can expect in a Blacksmith's Chest.

Strongholds

At some point in the game, you'll either accidentally pop into one of these (often massive) structures, or you'll need to find one to get to The End. Strongholds can sometimes be small, but usually they're huge, confusing and highly dangerous. There are only three Strongholds per world.

Where

Find a Stronghold by throwing an Eye of Ender. The direction it flies toward is the direction of a Stronghold. If you don't have an Eye of Ender, you're going to have to just dig around until you crack into one. Strongholds are always at

A Stronghold library.

Beware of mobs in Strongholds.

least 640 blocks from your start point and no farther than 1152, and they also often intersect sections like Ravines, Mineshafts and Caves.

Structures

Strongholds are mostly mazes of hallways, stairs and rooms, but they also include a few specific structures of note. These include Store Rooms, Libraries and the End Portal Room. Store Rooms are exactly what they sound like: an area that contains a Chest of useful stuff. Libraries are rooms full of Bookshelves and Cobwebs, and they come in one-story and two-story sizes. They also contain chests at the end of one or two bookshelves, depending on the size of the Library. The End Portal room is the only place in the world the player can get to The End, which is done by placing Eyes of Ender into the blocks of the End Portal, a structure that sits above a pool of Lava and is guarded by a Silverfish Monster Spawner.

Mobs

Fair warning: Strongholds are dangerous. They can contain just about every hostile mob in the Overworld, including Zombies, Skeletons, Spiders, Creepers and Silverfish. Silverfish are especially dangerous, as they can live in blocks called Monster Eggs that are disguised as normal blocks, and they attack in groups when one is damaged near others.

Materials

Large parts of Strongholds are built out of materials that are hard to come by elsewhere, such as Iron Bars, Iron Doors, Buttons, and special Stone blocks like Mossy or Cracked Stone. Even better, the Chests in Strongholds carry some great items, with possibilities including Ender Pearls, Apples, Bread, Coal, Redstone, Armor, Iron Ingots, Iron Swords, Iron Pickaxes and, rarely, Diamond, Golden Apples or Saddles.

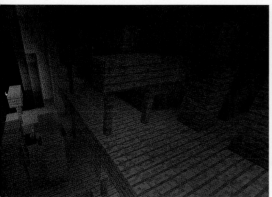

If you find an Abandoned Mineshaft, be ready for Cave Spiders.

Lucky players may find an Abandoned Mineshaft early and strip it of its Wood and other resources.

Abandoned Mineshaft

These are just what they sound like: mineshafts that spawn as if someone else had built them and then abandoned them.

Where

Randomly placed underground, especially intersecting with ravines and caves.

Structures

Mineshafts are simply hallways, stairways, crossings and rooms, often with Rail Tracks, supports and Minecarts in them.

Mobs

All mobs that can spawn in darkness have a chance of being in a Mineshaft, with the added danger of the smaller Cave Spider, which spawns from Monster Spawners and is unique to Abandoned Mineshafts. These little guys are poisonous, so watch out!

Materials

If you plan on making anything out of Rails, breaking them up in Mineshafts is the most efficient method. Other simple materials such as Wood Planks, Fences and Torches can be found, as well as Chests, usually in Minecarts. See the chart at the left for likely Chest items.

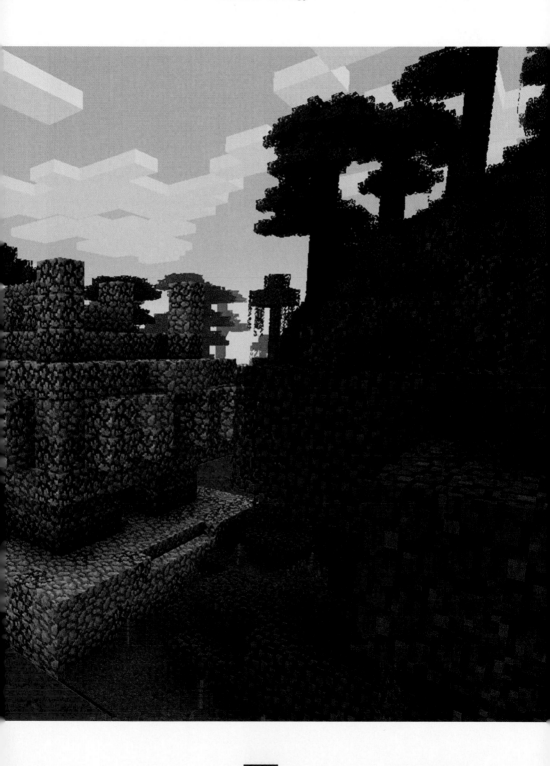

Screenshot: Minecraft®™ & © 2009–2015 Mojang/Notch.

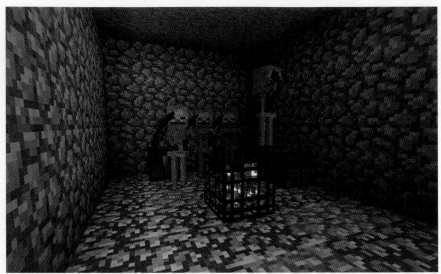

Get ready to fight if you find a Dungeon.

Dungeon

Small rooms randomly placed about the map, Dungeons contain a Monster Spawner and a Chest or two of items.

Where

Just about anywhere, but often in caves. Look for Mossy Stone and Cobblestone: those two together usually indicate a Dungeon.

Structures

Nothing more than one simple room!

Mobs

There will probably be tons of mobs of whatever type of Monster Spawner is in there (Zombie, Skeleton or Spider). Beware!

Materials

Just Cobble and Mossy Stone and the Monster Spawner, besides what's in the Chest.

Temples

Temples are awesome structures that look like big pyramids and which contain traps and Chests that contain useful items.

Where

Temples are only found in Jungles or in Deserts, and the two versions look slightly different from each other.

Structures

Both types of Temples are comprised of just one big building. Inside Jungle Temples, you'll find a puzzle that consists of three Levers and some Sticky Pistons. Desert Temples, on the other hand, have a secret room under a block of blue Wool. In the room is a trap consisting of a Stone Pressure Plate wired up to a large amount of TNT that will go off if the Plate is pressed. Also in the room will be 4 Chests with random loot from the same list as the Jungle Temple, making Desert Temples highly sought-after.

Nether Fortresses

The only Structure found in the Nether, these are enormous, hugely dangerous and are the only place to find Nether Wart and Blazes. They're not too hard to find, but getting out alive requires great gear, patience and skill.

Nether Fortresses are not to be lightly trifled with.

A Zombie Pigman stands guard over a crop of Nether Wart.

Where

The Nether, of course! Walk around long enough, and you're likely to find one, especially in big rooms, and when you do, the other Nether Forts will be laid out to the north and south in strips.

Structures

Nether Fortresses are comprised of tower-like structures connected by bridges. There are a few special rooms in the Forts: a stairwell with Nether Wart in it (the only place to find it), rooms with Blaze Spawners (also unique) and halls or rooms with Chests.

Mobs

You're most likely to come across Skeletons, Blazes and Magma Cubes in Nether Fortresses, while Ghasts may float above the bridges and Zombie Pigmen might be nearby. The rule for Nether Forts is to go in heavily armored and with the best weapons possible, as you will be attacked.

Materials

Besides the Nether Brick they're made of, which is immune to Ghast fireballs, and the items that spawn in chests (Iron Ingots, Gold Ingots,

Golden Chestplates and Swords, Saddles, Flint and Steel, Nether Wart and Diamonds are possible), Nether Forts are also the only place to get Blaze Rods (from killing Blazes) and Nether Wart, both of which are essential for crafting certain items (especially potions). You can also get Glowstone Dust from Blazes, occasionally.

Ocean Monuments

One of the newest additions to Minecraft in terms of things you can make a goal out of is the Ocean Monument, which is a very difficult to find and harder to conquer underwater temple of sorts. They're protected by dangerous Guardians and have many rooms, the top one of which is filled with Gold Blocks. A pretty nice reward!

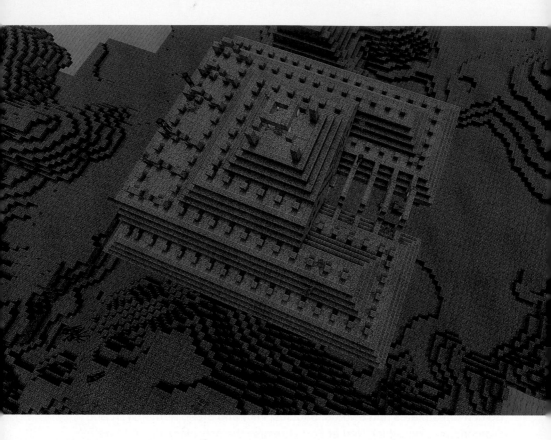

Where

Ocean Monuments are found only in the Deep Ocean Biome. They're pretty tough to find because of both that and the fact that the math for where they spawn makes them not spawn very often. Also, if you started your world before the update with Ocean Monuments (September 2014), then they will ONLY spawn in Deep Ocean where you have not spent more than 3 minutes of game time. That means you might have to go searching for other Deep Ocean spots to find an Ocean Monument if you tend to hang out near one.

Structures

The Ocean Monument is one single, big structure, and we do mean big. Like most other structures, the Monument randomly generates according to rules, so it can be different sizes. It will always have at least six rooms inside with a central shaft that goes up to the "penthouse" with the treasure chamber, and it will also have two wings on either side of it. The treasure chamber and both wings feature a tough Elder Guardian, and the whole of the place is lit by Sea Lamps. You can also find rooms with a bunch of Wet Sponges in many of the Monuments. To get to Ocean Monuments and stay alive, you're going to need to use Potions of Water Breathing, and probably a lot of other strong gear like heavy armor and weapons.

Mobs

The Guardian and the Elder Guardian are special mobs that only spawn in and around Ocean Monuments. Regular Guardians have a small chance of spawning outside of the Monument, but mostly will be inside, and Elder Guardians always spawn with one in each wing and one in the penthouse. They'll drop Raw Fish, Prismarine or Prismarine Shards sometimes, and have a very small chance of dropping another kind of fish.

These guys are tough and will go right at any player, attacking immediately with their laser that does three whole hearts of damage or their one heart-dealing spike defense. One good thing about the Guardians is that they will stop chasing the player if they lose sight of them, which you can use to your advantage.

Elder Guardians are much the same as Guardians but bigger, with a four heart attack, and they don't move as much. They also can inflict the "mining fatigue" status effect, which slows the player by 30% and makes breaking blocks slower. This is done without even touching the player once a minute if within 50 blocks of an Elder Guardian, and you'll see a ghostly form of the Guardian and a weird noise when it happens.

Materials

Besides the Gold Blocks in the treasure room, the Ocean Monument is made out of different types of the material Prismarine. Prismarine is only used as a construction material (you can make Prismarine Bricks or Dark Prismarine from it) except you can also make Sea Lamps from it.

Screenshot: Minecraft®™ & © 2009–2015 Mojang/Notch.

Beating the Game

Where You Should Be in Your Game

Most games of Minecraft that actually reach The End happen one of two ways: either the players collect the needed items as they otherwise play and get the opportunity naturally (which takes a very long time), or they specifically set out at some point to collect what they need to get to The End and make it a goal. It really isn't likely that you can play casually and even get to The End, and even if you do, you are even less likely to do well there, as it is arguably the toughest scenario in the entire game.

Because of this, your game should be fairly well along before you attempt The End. Check off as many items as possible from the following list before you make your trip, and your chances at success will multiply.

You Need
- Diamond gear (as much as possible)
- Lots of Obsidian (meaning more Diamonds needed in order to make Pickaxes)
- The ability to enchant (requires Diamonds, Obsidian and a Book to make an Enchantment Table)
- Potions (requires a Blaze Rod for a Brewing Stand)

As Diamonds are the hardest ore to find in the game, and two of the other three items on this list require Diamond (and the last a Blaze Rod, even harder to find), you'll need to either set out to find Diamonds early in the game, or be at a point where you've collected quite a bit already before you can think about going to The End.

Part 1: Getting to the Nether

One of the primary ingredients for getting to The End is the Blaze Rod, which drops when Blazes are killed in the Nether. Naturally then, getting to the Nether is your first goal, and of course, this means you need a Nether Portal.

There are two ways to create a Nether Portal: either mine Obsidian and create the Nether Portal shape (Obsidian surrounding an empty space that's

You'll need the best gear you can get to beat Minecraft.

two blocks wide and three tall), or use Water poured over Lava that is in the correct shape to create the Portal. The first method takes Diamond, but a lot less finagling with Lava, while the second lets you skip the Diamond. We suggest going the longer, Diamond-using route however, as the benefits of collecting a lot of Diamond will help you out later.

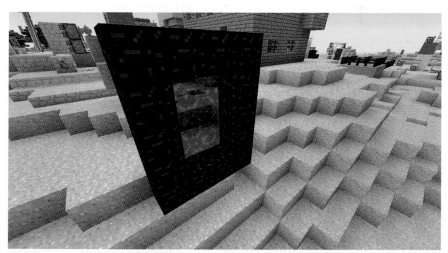

Ye Olde Nether Portal, ready to go.

Nether Forts can look like this when they spawn over Lava. Look for bridges and towers.

Part 2: The Nether

Once in the Nether, you need to create a safe area that you can base out of. Though you can't place Beds in the Nether (they will simply explode), you can bring building materials. Cobblestone is resistant to Ghast explosions, as is Obsidian, so using one or both of those materials to create a little base is an excellent idea. It's also prudent to take decent armor and weapons along, at the very least bringing some Iron gear if you can't go all the way for Diamond.

When you're set up with a safe place, you need to start looking around for Nether Forts. This can be a bit tricky, as your spawn point in the Nether can often be underground, requiring you to dig a while. However, if you find a pretty big room, especially one with a giant Lava pool at the bottom, you've probably found an area with a Nether Fort in it. The Nether is much smaller than the overworld, so if you don't see a Fort close around your base, you should try digging straight, skinny tunnels until you find one. Another option is to create a second Nether Portal in the overworld in a different spot, as this will spawn you elsewhere in the Nether.

The Blaze spawner in action, plus a random Magma Cube.

When you find a Nether Fort, look for Blaze spawners. These are usually on little Nether Brick platforms at the end of bridges in Nether Forts, and you can see them pretty easily due to all the yellow Blaze flying around.

Killing Blazes is tricky. You want good gear, preferably some Golden Apples to resist the Blaze's fire attack, some Snowballs and some blocks to build with. Blazes can fly and shoot at you from a distance, so use the blocks to contain the area around the spawner, making it so they can't get out of your range. Snowballs do 3 damage to Blazes and are cheap and easy to throw, so they can be your best weapon against these fiery foes. Use those, Bows and Arrows and the best Sword and Armor you can make, and you should be okay.

Screenshot: Minecraft®™ & © 2009–2015 Mojang/Notch.

When you find the End Portal room, you'll need to deal with this Silverfish spawner first.

Part 3: Opening the End Gate

To open the End Gate, you need to collect a certain amount of items and then find the gate. On the collection side, your first object is to get at least 9 Blaze Rods. One Blaze Rod makes two Blaze Powders, and one Blaze Powder plus one Ender Pearl makes one Eye of Ender. End Portals require 12 Eyes of Ender to open (at the maximum, some already have a few in them), and you'll need a few more in order to actually find the Portal. Additionally, you'll want an Enchantment Table, which takes another Blaze Rod. Add all of that together, and you need at least 9 Blaze Rods.

We've already shown you how to kill Blazes for Blaze Rods above, but you'll also need the Ender Pearls as well, which you get from killing Endermen. This is when the Kill More Mobs section of this guide will come in handy, and you'll probably have to kill quite a few as they don't always drop the Pearls. You should collect at least 16 Ender Pearls, and 20 is even safer.

Once you have your Rods and have made them into Powder (leaving one for your Enchantment Table) and have combined the Powder with the Pearls to make Eyes of Ender, you need to find a Stronghold. This is where your extra Eyes come into play: throw your Eyes of Ender, and they will shoot out toward a Stronghold. You may be able to pick up the Eye again, but they can also break so be careful about not throwing too many (make sure you keep at least 12).

Follow the Eyes, and eventually you'll get to a Stronghold. You'll have to explore the Stronghold, but somewhere in it you will find a room with Lava, a Nether Portal and some Silverfish blocks. Make sure to kill and contain the Silverfish, then build a containment area/mini-base around the Portal. Finally, activate it by placing the Eyes of Ender into the Portal blocks, and you'll see it kick on!

Give your Portal base everything you can, especially a Bed. You'll probably be dying a few times, so you'll be back here soon.

Part 4: Prep

Now hold yer horses young Crafter: you need to get ready before you dive through that Portal. Besides getting all the best gear you can, you also need to do a few more things before you make the plunge.

* Get the area around your Portal ready. If you die in The End, you just go back to your spawn point in the overworld. Make that mini-base around your Portal and include a Bed that you've slept in and Chests with tons of gear in them. This way when you die, you just gear up again and head right back to The End.
* Take the best gear, and enchant as much of it as is possible.
* In addition to a Diamond Sword or so, bring a Bow and as many Arrows as you can.
* Also bring Potions, a Pumpkin (to wear if the Endermen bother you too much), Water Buckets (to scare off the Endermen), Obsidian, Ladders, Chests and food. This is your kit to beat The End.

Once you've got your base prepared and have everything you need, you're ready to go wreck you an Ender Dragon. Whoo!

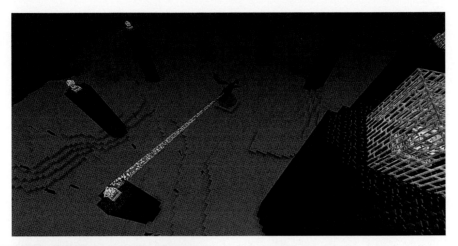

Part 5: Dealing with The End

You'll notice right off the bat that The End is different from the other areas. First thing's first: you need to get off the little area you're floating on and over to the main island. Use Obsidian to build a bridge over, and be careful! The main island is covered in Endermen, not to mention that big ole Ender Dragon flying around.

Build a little fort of Obsidian like this in order to survive your attack on the Dragon.

You can always go straight to the attack, but this isn't likely to get you anywhere but dead unless you are just insanely geared up and good at combat. The best bet for survival and success is to control the area.

Use your Obsidian to build yourself a small fort or safe area in The End. Make this so that Endermen can't get in and the Ender Dragon can't see you (so you'll need to make a few layers within it, or some entrance passageways that twist and are too small for the Endermen to get through). The Dragon can't break Obsidian, so you'll be relatively safe to put down resupply Chests in your Obsidian fort, as well as to use it to shoot at your enemies.

Endermen are mostly just pests in The End, so it's best just to kill them quickly or avoid them altogether. Use your Buckets of Water and Pumpkin for this (Endermen won't see you with a Pumpkin on your head, and they hate and are damaged by Water).

Part 6: Killing the Ender Dragon

Shoot these crystal, Dragon-charger things with arrows if possible, as they explode.

Building an Obsidian fort and messin' with Endermen is pretty fun, but you're here for one reason: to kill that big darn Dragon. You'll notice that beams are flying out of those giant Obsidian pillars and touching the Dragon as he flies around: these come out of crystals on the tops of the pillars, and they heal the Dragon. You can't kill him with these still going, as he'll just heal, so you need to take them out.

There are two common methods for this: shoot out the crystals from below with a Bow or Snowballs, or climb the pillars and break the crystals with a Sword. Either method works, though you'll have to be a good shot for the first, and you'll have to deal with the crystals exploding when broken for the second.

Once the crystals are out, attack the Dragon. Enchanted Bows are probably the best weapon here, as you can hit the Dragon when flying, but you can use just about any combat method you want. The keys here are these: have a big supply of the best gear you can get, avoid the fire blasts (they're pretty slow), hide when you need to (in fact, staying in your base and shooting out of it is a great method), and use items like food and potions to keep your health and strength up constantly.

It will be expensive, you will die a lot, and it will take a long time. But when you finally see that health bar drop to nil, and the Dragon starts exploding light everywhere and dropping the craziest amount of experience you've ever seen, you'll know it was all worth it. You've just "beat" Minecraft, brave young Crafter!

Note: Make sure to read the infamous "End Poem" after killing the Ender Dragon. It's a very cool piece of writing, and it'll make you see the game in a different light! It's also one of the only actual "story" parts in the game, so be sure not to miss it.

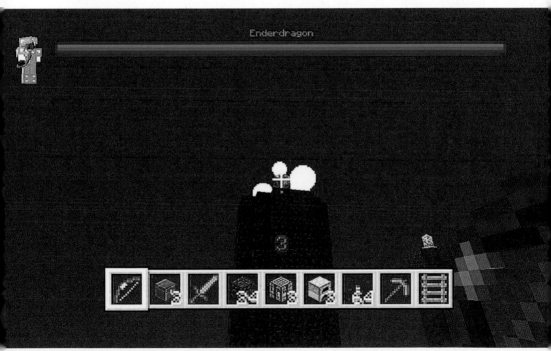

A crystal shatters from a bow shot.

Screenshot: Minecraft®™ & © 2009–2015 Mojang/Notch.

Chapter 3

Secrets of Redstone

The Basics

Ready to start your journey to becoming a master of all that is Redstone? Well then, let's dive right on in and get familiar with the basics of the Redstone world!

Before we do so, however, let's talk for a moment about how to best use this book to get the most out of it and to become the most knowledgable Redstone engineer you can:

How to Use This Chapter

Redstone is a massive topic, almost infinitely so because there are always players finding new ways to use it, and also because it often gets updated when Minecraft itself gets an update. This chapter is not meant to contain every single piece of information about Redstone, as that would be impossible, at the worst, or require a book that was a few thousand pages longer at best.

What this chapter is meant to do is to give you all of the basic information you need to begin learning how to use Redstone in the easiest and most pain-free way we can teach it to you. We want to make Redstone fun and inviting, and to dispel the air of intimidation and difficulty that often surrounds the subject.

We'll take you from the very most basic concepts of Redstone, starting here in this section, and as we go through the chapter, we'll add a little more with each section, stopping along the way to test out the ideas we present with some fun builds and cool applications.

We suggest that you approach this chapter from one end to the other, working through each section in turn and learning its lessons before moving on to the next. By the end of the chapter, we'll have you building some pretty highly advanced Redstone constructions and starting to think like a real Redstone engineer!

That being said, these concepts are also very complex, and there's a lot of information to internalize, so we'd also make one more suggestion for how to have the best and most successful Redstone learning experience:

Don't worry about getting it all perfect. Even the best Redstone engineers out there took a long time to understand and memorize this information, and there's no rush to do so. The best way to learn Redstone is to read through this book and test out the different builds, and then to just keep messing around with the stuff, referring back to the book when you need to know something. Over time, you'll start to naturally remember the nitty gritty details of Redstone items, rules and concepts without having to look them up, so there's no need to get discouraged if you keep having to look back at the book as you go.

In fact, we'd even suggest seeking out more resources on Redstone as well, such as watching videos online or finding other players to learn from. This chapter is meant to be your introduction to the world of Redstone and a handy reference guide, but we won't have our feelings hurt if you need to seek out a little extra help! The goal here is to help you learn Redstone, and we are simply trying give you as many resources in these pages as possible to help you do that.

One final note before we get going: Almost everything we talk about in this chapter assumes that you are playing in Creative Mode. This is because the builds take very, very many items of different types, and while you might have them in your Survival World, they will be pretty expensive. Additionally, Creative Mode allows you to fly and to turn off hostile mobs, allowing you to be able to learn in peace. We can't suggest doing this enough to learn Redstone's rules. Additionally, this chapter is primarily focused on the full version of Minecraft as it is on the PC and Mac. This is because the console versions do not contain all Redstone items quite yet, but they are being updated frequently. If you are playing on a console, you'll have to wait to try some of these concepts until the updates happen, but the basic rules and many of the builds are still the same and will work.

With that in mind, let's get into this!

The Concept

In a nutshell, Redstone is a system that uses power signals to cause something to happen in the game of Minecraft. This "something" could be as simple as opening a Door or turning on a light, or it could be something a bit more complex like causing a mechanism such as a Piston to activate and interact with the world, or it could be as complex as causing a mini-game to begin. A simple Redstone power signal can even cause something as intricate and massive as a player-built Redstone simulation of a computer to turn on and function!

Redstone power is somewhat like real-life electricity, and thinking of it like this is very useful, especially when first starting out with the stuff. Here are the ways in which Redstone and real-world electricity are similar:

- Redstone has an ON state and an OFF state.
- Redstone signals can have various levels of power, in the case of Redstone it goes from 0-15.
- Redstone signals can be carried through a Minecraft world through items called Redstone Dust (as well as others) that are very similar to real-life wires.
- A powered Redstone signal that is "wired" up so that it runs into certain items in the game called "mechanisms" will give those mechanisms power and cause them to activate.
- Redstone can be used to build "circuits" that function in much the same way as real-life circuits function in computers and other electronics.

There are, however, quite a few ways in which Redstone and normal electricity differ, and they are equally important:

The power that Redstone builds use is not always held in a storage unit like a battery, or piped through from the outside, but is instead almost always created by the items that toggle the power ON and OFF. To further explain the difference, a real-world light switch controls electric power, but it does not create the power. In Minecraft, Levers, which are very similar in look to light-switches, can control Redstone power, but they also create that power themselves. Redstone items that create power are called "power components," and there are many types of these, including two that do act somewhat like a battery and/or permanent power source (Redstone Torches and Blocks of Redstone).

Redstone power signals only go 15 blocks in one direction before their power signal fades away. To get it to go farther, it must be boosted. This is actually similar to real electricity, except that the rules that govern the distance of real electric signals are far more complex.

Redstone signals can and often are influenced by the passage of time. This is also actually similar to real electricity, but again there is a major difference. This time the difference is that the time delays on real electricity are often so fast that we do not even recognize them, while in Redstone this is essentially slowed way down so that players can manipulate and use these delays. Time in Redstone is measured in "ticks," where each a tick happens 10 times a second, or once every 0.1 seconds in real time. Redstone components and mechanisms update their status every tick, checking to see if their inputs have changed in any way, and when the input does change, they respond by activating, deactivating or performing a special action. Note: time in the rest of Minecraft also operates on "ticks," but a regular Minecraft ticks happen 20 times a second, making them twice as fast. This often confuses players who are aware of regular Minecraft ticks, so it's a good idea to note the difference here. Additionally, when we refer to "ticks" from here on out in this book, we are referring exclusively to Redstone ticks.

When you know how to use these and the many other rules of Redstone together, you will be able to build incredible contraptions and systems, and the range of things you can do in everyone's favorite builder game expands in a huge way. In fact, Redstone is considered by many players to be the pinnacle of Minecraft knowledge, and many of the things that people build in the game that will cause less-experienced players to scratch their head and wonder how it even happened are made with Redstone.

The Components

Redstone is possible because of certain items and blocks in the game and the way they work together. In the next chapter, we'll look at each and every one of these very closely and give you all the details of how they work and what they're used in, but for now let's break the various Redstone components down into their most simple forms and talk about how they relate.

All Redstone items fall into one of the following categories:

1. Power & control components (usually just referred to as power components)
2. Transmission components
3. Mechanisms
4. Basic blocks
5. Rails and Rail-related items
6. Other items that interact with Redstone

In its most simple form, a Redstone build will have a power component and a mechanism, but most Redstone builds use items from at least three of these categories, and some can even use many items from all of these categories.

Let's take a second to get the basics of how the first three of these components interact with each other set in our minds. A typical simple Redstone build starts with a power component, which sends a power signal out. This is often carried by transmission components to either other Redstone circuits or to mechanisms. When mechanisms receive an ON power signal, they activate.

Somewhere in this process of sending a power signal from power component>transmission component>mechanism, the signal may interact with basic blocks of the game. What we mean by this is blocks that are usually used for building purposes, such as Cobblestone, Dirt, Wool, Glass, etc. There are two important types of blocks when it comes to Redstone, and they interact with Redstone in different ways:

Opaque blocks: "Opaque" is a word that means an object through which light does not travel. In Minecraft, this definition usually applies as well. Opaque blocks are important to Redstone because they can be powered by a Redstone signal. When a block is "powered," this means that a Redstone signal is going into it, and that Redstone mechanisms, as well as Repeaters and Comparators (more on these in the Items chapter), will be activated by the block. This property of allowing Redstone signals to travel through themselves makes opaque blocks very important to Redstone.

This is the basic Redstone setup: power component, wire and mechanism.

Transparent blocks: As you might guess "transparent" blocks are typically those that can be "seen through" in the game, though this term also refers to a few such as Glowstone and Slabs that the game merely treats as transparent, though they themselves block vision. In terms of Redstone, transparent blocks are important because they do not take a Redstone power signal, even if one is going straight into them. This makes transparent blocks very useful to separate and block currents in Redstone building.

Our final two types of Redstone items (Rail items, and other interactable blocks) are not nearly as core to Redstone concepts and building as the first four, though they can be integral parts of specific Redstone builds. These are essentially specialty items that can be used to create very specific results, as opposed to items that you'll be using in every build. More on these in the next chapter; all you really need to do now is to be aware that Rails and rail-related items as well as a few unique items can also interact with Redstone builds.

Some transparent blocks (left) and some opaque blocks (right).

Putting it All Together for the First Time

Okay! So we know a bit about what Redstone is, we know a few of its rules, and we know the basic types of items that are used in Redstone builds, so it's time to actually test the stuff out!

We'll wrap this first chapter up by doing some small Redstone placement, and talk a bit about what's happening with each thing we do. Open up your Minecraft, get a new world started in Creative Mode, and let's play with a little Redstone.

1. Component + Redstone Dust

First thing's first: let's see some Redstone actually powered up. Put a Lever, a Button (either kind) and some Redstone into your inventory. Place the Lever on the ground, and then place Redstone Dust on the ground right next to it. Now scoot over a bit and place the Button on a block (any opaque block is fine) and place Redstone Dust on the ground right in front of this. Make sure this second Dust is not touching the first and is not adjacent to the Lever. Now, activate the Lever. See how the Redstone Dust lights up when you flick the Lever? This means it's powered, and that the power state is constant. If you want to turn it OFF, just flip the Lever to the other state. Now press the Button. See the difference? For the Button, the Redstone was only powered for a brief moment, and then it went off. This example is just to show you how Redstone Dust can be powered, and that different power components power it differently (in this case a constant signal vs. a temporary one).

2. Trying A Mechanism

Now flip your Lever OFF, and then put a Piston into your inventory. Place the Piston down adjacent to the Redstone Dust you placed next to your Lever, and then flip the Lever ON. As you can see, as soon as you flip the Lever, the Piston will activate, extending. This is the simplest form of a Redstone build (perhaps your first ever!). All that's happening here is that the Lever is providing a signal, the Dust is carrying the signal to the Piston, and the Piston is recognizing that it is powered and is firing. Though most Redstone builds get much more complicated than this, essentially this is what is happening at the basic level in almost all Redstone creations.

3. Powering An Opaque Block

Next, get a second Piston in your inventory, as well as a Redstone Torch and an opaque block. Move away from the Redstone items you have already placed, and put the opaque block down on the ground. Place a dot of Redstone Dust on the ground adjacent to the block (not on top of it though, for now), and then place the Redstone Torch on the opposite side of this Dust from the block. Now, go around to the opposite side of the block, and place the Piston down adjacent to this side of the block so that it is touching the block. For this example, make sure that the Piston is not adjacent to the Dust. You'll notice that the Piston also fires in this situation. This is because the block it is on is now "powered," which we talked about earlier in this chapter. The Redstone Torch, in this case, is providing the power signal to the Dust, which goes into the block and powers it, which then transfers the power to the mechanism. In this way we can see how powering blocks works and can be useful in Redstone.

4. Making Things More Complex With A Repeater

We're going to look at a very basic example of how we can make a Redstone build more complex for our final example. We'll need another Piston, another Lever and a Redstone Repeater for this one. Move away from your other Redstone builds, and place your Lever down on the ground. Put one dot of Redstone Dust adjacent to this Lever, and then stand on that Dust so that you are facing the opposite direction of the Lever. Aim down at the block on the opposite side of the Dust from the Lever while still standing on the Dust, and place your Repeater down. Now place the Piston on the block just after the Repeater, so you have a line of items that goes Lever>Dust>Repeater>Piston. Now flip the Lever. As you'll see, the Redstone current will go through the Dust, hit the Repeater, and then a slight amount of time later the Piston will fire. One of the features of Repeaters is that they output a signal at a slight delay, which in this case causes the Piston to fire, but which also has many other uses. We'll get to those later, but for now just notice how we can make the standard Redstone configuration more complex with other items.

Alrighty, we've done a little Redstone! That wasn't so bad, was it? Now you've got a bit of experience with the stuff, are starting to understand how it works, and hey! You can even tell your friends that you've started using Redstone. Good job miner!

Your First 5 Redstone Builds

All this talk about the components and concepts and rules of Redstone has probably got you a bit overwhelmed, but don't worry: actually doing a little Redstone will help you tremendously in figuring out just what all that information means, as well as how to use it to make MInecraft even more awesome than it already is.

So, young crafters, here's the part where we stop just telling you about Redstone and start actually makin' some cool stuff! These are your first five true Redstone builds, starting from the simplest Redstone doorbell and going through an awesome-lookin' Piston wave that's a great and easy way to impress those who don't have your Redstone skills.

These builds are designed to be super simple to build, in order to get you comfortable with using Redstone, yet they'll also teach you important lessons about Redstone and its properties. The builds also incorporate a few more complex properties and functions of Redstone, such as a NOT Gate and a clock, which you'll become much more familiar with later in the book as we get into more complex and difficult Redstone builds.

For now, however, we just want to focus on building the five contraptions here and understanding the simple basics of how they work. Later, we'll get into the more complex ideas behind some of the functions in these builds, but this chapter is all about dipping your toes into the world of Redstone in the simplest, most pain-free way possible. All you've got to do is follow the instructions and then recreate what you see in the images, and you'll already be on your way to earning your honorary Master's degree in Redstone Engineering.

Note: We recommend doing this in Creative Mode in order to learn these builds, but you can do them in Survival Mode as well if you have the materials.

The Doorbell

What it does: Lets ya know someone wants in your house by making a ding (or y'know, whatever weird noise you set it to).

How it works: A Note Block inside your home makes a noise when someone outside pushes a Button, powering the Note Block.

You'll Need: 1 Button, 1 Note Block, Redstone (optional)

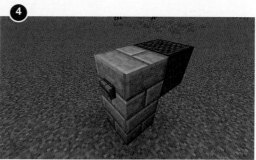

Makin' a working, useful doorbell is just about the easiest Redstone project you'll ever do. In fact, it can be done without any Redstone Wire at all if you don't mind the Note Block being right inside your door. This is a good project to just get an idea of how power-giving items such as Buttons work with items like the Note Block that take power, and it's a cute little way to spruce up your home. Plus, Note Blocks can be heard up to 48 blocks from its location, so it will inform you of visitors even at a good distance.

1. Find the spot where you'd like to put the button that will activate your doorbell. Typically these are placed by a Door, but you could do it anywhere you wanted. For the easiest Doorbell, pick a spot on a wall near a Door that is one block off the ground and where the wall is just one block thick behind where the Button will be. Place the Button on this block.

2. Place the Note Block on the other side of the block that now has a Button on it.

3. If the block under the Note Block is one you placed yourself, break it and leave the space empty. If you can't remember if you placed the block then go ahead and break it. This is done because the Note Block will change to a different sound than the beep we want if a human-placed block is underneath it.

4. Right-click the Note Block until it hits the note you'd like to use as your doorbell. This can be a little tricky, as sometimes the Note Block doesn't want to make noise, but just break the block and put it back down if you can't get it to work at first.

5. Press the Button back on the other side of the wall, and the Note Block will make its sound! The way this works is that the Button gives power to the block it is placed on, and this block gives power to the Note Block.

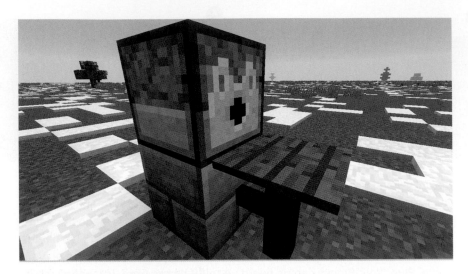

The Easy Potion Dispenser

What it does: Throws a Potion out at you when you run up and bump it (no need to click on this one).

How it works: A Dispenser is placed on a block, a Fence is placed in front of the block and Dispenser, and on top of the Fence is a Pressure Plate. When you run up to the Pressure Plate and push your crafter into it, it will press down, and whatever is in the Dispenser will launch out (Potions, in this case)

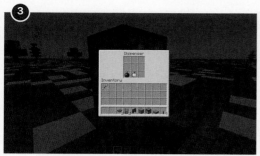

You'll Need: 1 Dispenser, 1 Fence, 1 Pressure Plate, 1 random block (optional, Dispenser could hang in the air), whatever Potions you want to dispense

Another quite simple little doohickey, the easy Potion dispenser makes taking Potions in Minecraft about as easy as it can be. Typically, you have to open your inventory or go to your hot bar and actually use a potion, or even run up to a Dispenser and push a Button or pull a Lever to get one to launch out at you. However, with the Easy Potion Dispenser, all you have to do is run up and bump the Pressure Plate, and you'll be smartly splashed with Potion.

1. **Place a block** of any kind down.

2. **Put a Dispenser** on top of this block.

3. **Fill the Dispenser** with a Potion of your choosing. This will actually work with anything a Dispenser can dispense at you, but Potions are one of the most useful options in this configuration.

4. **Stand so the Dispenser** is facing you (the side with the O-shaped hole) and look down at the block it is sitting on. Place one Fence on the block that is in front of this block that the Dispenser is on.

5. **Place a Pressure Plate** on top of the one Fence you have just placed.

6. **Run up to the Pressure Plate,** and it will press down and the Potion (or whatever else you've got in the Dispenser) will launch out. This is the Pressure Plate activating from interacting with your body and powering the Dispenser, which fires a random item inside of it at you.

The Trapdoor

What it does: Opens a hole in the ground wherever you'd like (in this case in front of a Door) at the flick of a Lever. Beneath this hole that opens is a big pit and/or Lava, which anything that was standing on the block above the hole will fall into.

How it works: A Sticky Piston is attached to a block and extended over a pit, covering the hole. The Sticky Piston is attached underground to a Redstone "gate" called a Not Gate (look to the Gates chapter for further explanation of this), which goes beneath the wall of a house using Redstone Wire. On the other side of the wall, a Lever on the ground surface turns the signal for the Redstone wire on and off, causing the Sticky Piston to expose and to cover the pit, alternatively. The whole contraption is hidden.

You'll Need: 1 Sticky Piston, 1 Lever, 1 Redstone Torch, 2 Redstone Wire, 2 Slabs of any kind, 1 random block

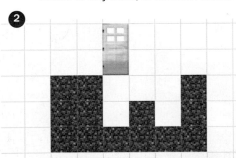

Diagram designed at mordritch.com

1. Find yourself a nice Door. This Door should be one which you would like to look out of, see a Creeper, and then kill that Creeper by making it drop to its doom. Also works with annoying players.

2. Dig out a pit in the pattern of Diagram 1. It should be only 1 block wide and 3 long, and it should alternate being 2 and 1 and then 2 blocks deep, as you also see in the Diagram.

3. Place a Redstone Torch on the wall as you see in the photo here.

4. Put a Sticky Piston in the space above the Redstone Torch facing toward the space in front of the Door (it will extend automatically), and then put a block of whatever type you'd like in front of the Sticky Piston. The 1 block deep hole in front of the Door should now be covered by the block stuck to the Sticky Piston.

5. Go to the other side of the wall which the Door is set in. Dig out a pit immediately on the other side of the wall from the block where the Sticky Piston and Redstone Torch are. Make this pit 1 block wide, 2 blocks long and 2 blocks deep.

6. Lay Redstone Wire down on the bottom of this pit. This is not essential to understand at this point, but what you have created in this section of the build is represented in the Diagram. By adding a power source to the end

Screenshot: Minecraft®™ & © 2009–2015 Mojang/Notch.

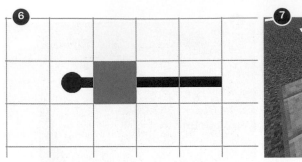

Diagram designed at mordritch.com

of the Redstone Wire in the Diagram (or on a block above it, as we will do in the next step), we create what is called a NOT Gate. A NOT Gate is a type of construction known as a logic gate, which manipulates a Redstone signal and is something we will learn in the future chapter on Gates.

7. Cover the last block of the pit (farthest from the wall) with the same type of block that makes up the rest of the floor. Put a Lever on top of this block. Now cover the second block of the pit with the same type of block, but with no Lever.

8. Flip the Lever and the Sticky Piston should pull back and uncover the hole in front of the Door.

9. Go back through the Door to the pit in front of it, and dig the pit deeper. Here you have a few options: place Lava or Cactus at the bottom of the pit to kill intruders with damage, make a long drop that will kill the intruder (at least 24 blocks down for a TKO), or build an area at the bottom for the intruders to fall into and just, y'know, hang out. Until you come to slice them up with your Sword, of course.

10. Go back up and cover up the Sticky Piston by placing 2 Slabs of any kind on top of the two blocks it takes up. Don't put one over the spot in front of the door, of course.

11. Wait for a Creeper to come stand outside your door, flip the Lever, profit.

The Simplest Clock

What it does: Creates a pulse of Redstone power that turns on and off at a regular interval, which allows many concepts to be created with Redstone, including but not limited to contraptions that keep time.

How it works: A Redstone Torch powers a Redstone Repeater, which slows down the signal slightly (in this case it is a '4 tick' delay). After 4 ticks the power goes through the Repeater and on to the Wire after it, which curves around to power the block that the original Redstone Torch was on. This turns off the Redstone Torch temporarily, in turn turning off the signal through the Redstone Repeater after 4 more ticks. This repeats indefinitely unless acted upon from an outside signal.

You'll Need: 1 Redstone Torch, 1 Redstone Repeater, 3 Redstone Wire, 1 Random Block

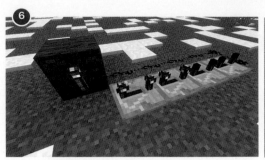

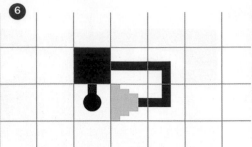

Diagram designed at mordritch.com

When referring to Redstone components, a "clock" is a Redstone construction that alternately causes an on signal and then an off signal to be transmitted from itself every so many seconds in a constant pulse.

Clocks are power loops, where a signal is transmitted from a power source, slowed down by Repeaters (or other ways, in more complex cases), and then is sent back to the original power source, temporarily turning it off. This causes the power to pulse with a consistent amount of time between each pulse, and the amount of time between each pulse can be customized by the builder through using multiple Repeaters in a row as well as other tactics.

This pulsing signal can be used to give something else power for a few ticks, and then take it away. So for instance, a Piston hooked up to a clock would continuously extend and pull back as long as it was hooked up to the clock.

This is the simplest version of a clock, and it's quite useful for everything from practical, mechanical Redstone builds to the most complex logic circuits.

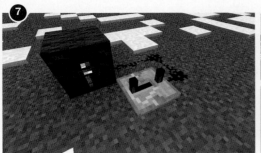 

1. Turn so that the direction you would like your power to go in is to your right. Make sure there are about five blocks of usable ground space to your right (if there is not, scooch over a bit so there is).

2. Place your random block down. This has to be one that can transfer power, so something like Stone, Wool or Wood of any type is good.

3. Keeping the direction you would like the signal to move in to your right, place a Redstone Torch on the side of the block facing you, as in the image.

4. As in the image, place a Redstone Repeater on the block to the right of the block that your Redstone Torch hangs over (so, caddy-corner to the block the Redstone Torch is on).

5. Set this repeater on the last setting (4 ticks). This is important- Redstone Torches cannot take a signal that is too fast coming back into them, and Redstone Torches will burn out after a while if you have too quick of a signal piping into them (turn your Repeater to a faster signal when your clock is fully built and test it out sometime, just to see this happen). The reason for this is somewhat complex, but all you need to know at this point is that you need to slow this signal down a bit with your Repeater.

6. Copy the Redstone pattern from the Diagram, taking it one block on the ground past the repeater, then both blocks on the ground to the right of the block you have a Torch on.

7. If you have set the Repeater to the right delay in step #5, your clock will start working immediately, doing a pulsing signal.

8. To use your clock, just put 1 Redstone Wire branching off the existing Redstone Wire in the clock. You can then extend this to whatever you want to power.

Tips: You can put a Lever on the side of the block in your Redstone clock, and you can turn the clock on and off with the Lever. You can create clocks with greater delays (much greater, theoretically) by using more Redstone Repeaters in a row.

Screenshot: Minecraft®™ & © 2009–2015 Mojang/Notch.

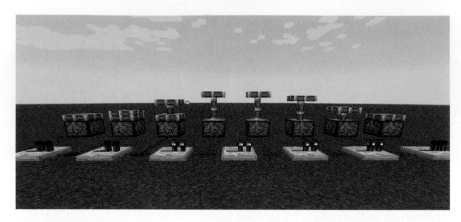

The Piston Wave

What it does: Causes a series of Pistons (or Sticky Pistons) to extend and pull back with each consecutive Piston firing slightly after the last, making a visual wave.

How it works: A clock (see previous First Build section for how to build) powers a series of Redstone Wires in which there is a Redstone Repeater set every other block. The Repeaters are all set to the same delay (does not matter how long), and a signal branches off from the main Redstone Wire directly after each Repeater to a Piston. This makes each Piston fire, and since the signal is delayed by each subsequent Repeater, each Piston fires slightly after the last. The Pistons also immediately retract as the signal from the clock comes in a pulse and is not constant.

You'll Need: 8 Pistons (or Sticky Pistons), 27 Redstone, 8 Redstone Repeaters, 1 Redstone Torch, 1 Random block.

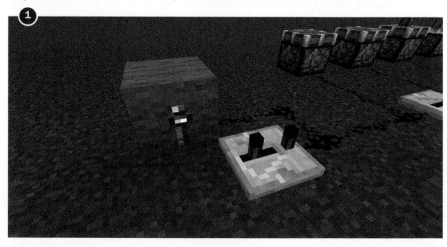

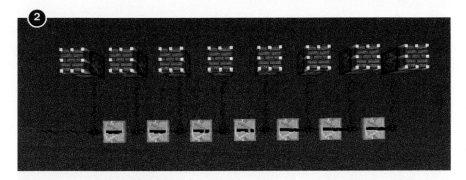

This build really doesn't do much that is practical, but it's fun to see and helps to visualize the effect of Redstone Repeaters on a signal. It combines a few very simple Redstone concepts that have been approached in the previous builds in this section in a fun way that makes a sweet visual Piston wave, and it doesn't take much to build. This construct could be applied to some visual effects you might want to create in complex Redstone maps, but for the most part it is useful simply for the way it demonstrates what a pulsing signal and a signal slowed by Repeaters can both do.

1. Build a clock using the instructions in the previous build. Make sure the out signal from the clock faces where you'd like your line of firing Pistons to be.

2. Attached to the Wire coming out of the clock, put a Redstone Wire, then a Redstone Repeater, and then another Redstone Wire and another Redstone Repeater (make sure that the Repeaters are facing the right way so that the signal continues to the next Wire). Keep doing this until you have placed down the 7 remaining Redstone Repeaters (after using 1 for the clock). It should be a line of alternating Wires and Repeaters attached to the clock, and if the clock is on (as in the Wire has not been broken or it has not been turned off

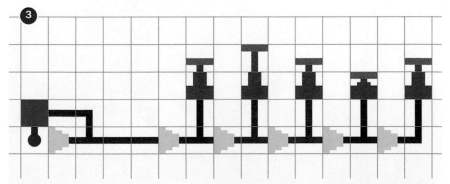

Diagram designed at mordritch.com

with a Lever), you will see the signal pulse through the Redstone Wire and Repeaters one by one. Put each Repeater on the same delay at first (though it doesn't matter which particular tick you set them on, as long as they're all the same), and, if you want, you can go in later and tweak it however you like to test what it does to the wave.

3. Place more Redstone down, this time placing 2 Redstone Wire off each Redstone Wire to the left of every Redstone Repeater you have placed (except, of course, the one in your clock). Also place 2 coming off to the right of the final Repeater. Make sure all wires go in the same direction. Refer to the image to see exactly how to do this.

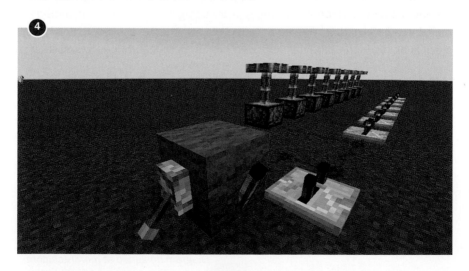

4. Place a Piston facing straight up to the sky at the end of each of these branches of Redstone Wire that you have just created. Note: you may want to turn off the clock while you do this, as when all the Pistons fire it will make a lot of noise until you turn it off. It can get super annoying.

5. When wired up to the clock (and with the clock on), the signal will proliferate through the Wire and each Repeater in turn, taking a few ticks each time before it goes through to the next set of Wires and Repeater. This will cause the signal that goes out to each Piston to come a little behind the signal to the Piston to its left, and the Pistons will fire in a wave. Use this construct to observe how signals can be delayed, and play around with the time that each Repeater is set to in order to get an even better sense of the way time works with Redstone. You can also make this build look a little cooler by doing things like using Sticky Pistons with Glowstone attached instead of regular Pistons.

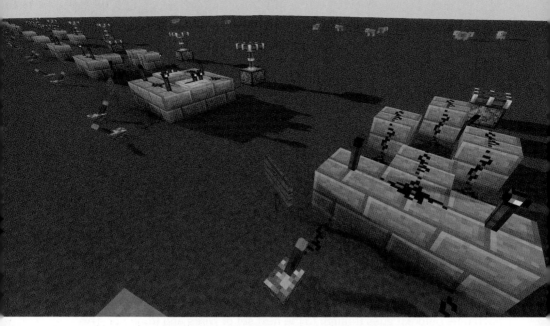

Redstone Gates
What They Are and Why You Need to Know 'Em

Ready to have your brain busted? Well, unless you've already got a good bit of learnin' accomplished in the fields of logic or computer programming/building (and we don't mean installing more memory into your PC, we mean the actual construction of those memory chips), chances are this section of our little guide is going to be a bit of a noggin'-expander. But don't get your head all worried- we mean that in a good way!

What we're tackling in this chapter are the ever-important, all-powerful Redstone gates. These little constructs are simple to build, yet are the hardest part of Redstone to master, and in the end they're what allow most every Redstone build to work. They can be used in everything from a simple mob detection system (which uses a basic NOT gate or so), to the most mind-bogglingly complex Redstone computers that need an engineering degree to understand and build (and which use just about every single version of these gates that there is, and thousands of each).

So what the heck are Redstone gates?

The Deep Explanation

Well, this is actually quite a complex subject, especially for a video game. To start with, know that it's not necessary to grasp the entirety of this concept right now as you read through this chapter. Like much of this book, the important part here is just to read the words over so that you get familiar with the ideas, and then to try and recreate the gates you see in the pictures so that you start using them yourself. Redstone gates are fascinating and are worth learning not only to get better at building in Minecraft, but also because even attempting to understand gates will make you smarter and will help you to learn how actual real-life things like computers and electronics function (which might even help you in a future job!).

But, even some very highly educated people struggle with these concepts, so don't worry about trying to understand the whole thing all at once. Understanding will come with time and practice, and besides, there's always something more to be learned about Redstone gates once you get the hang of all of this you see here.

To get on the right track and to start to understand what Redstone gates are, let's begin with two ideas:

1. Redstone gates are circuits built out of Redstone, very similar to the kind of circuits that make up the wiring in everything electronic in your home, from the somewhat simple wiring that goes through your home to all of its lights, to the incredibly complex wiring that makes up the circuits of the computer or console on which you play Minecraft. Redstone gates, like those circuits, take power signals and combine and manipulate these signals in order to achieve a specific result. For lights, this result means turning on. For Redstone gates, it can mean a variety of things, from causing a Piston to activate to powering the input to yet another Redstone gate.

This works like this: each gate (and each circuit in your electronics) takes these input signals and reads what they are, and then manipulates them based on how the gate (or circuit) is built, and then the gate (or circuit) outputs a new signal based on that manipulation. For real circuits, these outputs have a lot of variety, but for Minecraft's purposes, the output is either ON or OFF. This concept of ON or OFF leads us to our second idea for understanding Redstone gates.

2. Redstone gates are a way to create what are known in the world outside of Minecraft as "logic gates," except you build them in the game. Though Redstone gates are often called circuits, and are very similar to electronic circuitry, it is actually a bit more useful and more apt to compare Redstone gates to the field of logic than to electronics. In logic, various combinations of ON inputs (also sometimes known as 1, A, or HIGH inputs) and OFF inputs (also known as 0, B, or LOW inputs) go into mental constructs known as logic gates that function in much the same way that Redstone gates do, except instead of having "physical" parts like Redstone Torches and Dust and blocks creating the gate (or real physical parts like actual wires, for electronic gates), the gate is all in the mind.

This may make Redstone gates seem more similar to electronic gates than logic gates, since they both require actual construction, but the truth is that electronics feature a lot more special "rules" than Redstone does, which have to do with the physical properties of wires and electricity. Redstone, on the other hand, is created in a virtual world with far fewer rules and restrictions, and which can be referred to as a simulation. Since creating and using logic gates inside your mind by thinking of them can also be thought of as a simulation, you can start to see why logic gates and Redstone gates have a lot in common.

What It Means for Minecraft

In the end, all this fancy talk and high theory doesn't mean much fun for your Minecraft world if you can't actually do anything with Redstone gates. But, since this is a video game, Redstone gates are primarily used to create really fun and/or impressive things in your Minecraft world such as hidden doors, traps, cool lighting rigs and even super complex things like working computers and most of the mini-games you play on Minecraft servers.

In the end, the easiest way to explain Redstone gates in Minecraft terms is to say that they are what allow all of the really complex Redstone builds to work. The end result might be that a pirate ship battle mini-game kicks off in full force, but what you're not seeing when this happens is all of the Redstone gates and logic concepts that are built into the behind-the-scenes that allow the pirate ships to function and do things.

Using Redstone gates is not just important to mastering Redstone, it may be the most important part of the whole field outside of simply knowing how the various Redstone items work. It's not something that almost anyone can understand right off the bat, but if you take the time to try out all of these gates and think about how they work, and how to use them, we promise you that you'll come out the other side as a builder that's 100 times better at Redstone, if not more.

 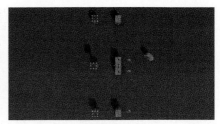

A Couple of Notes Before We Jump In

Before we start unleashing the mighty force of Redstone gate knowledge on your brains, a couple notes on what you're about to read:

The text for each gate explains how and why the gate works, and just gives a bit on how to build them. To actually build each gate yourself, simply copy what you see in the photos and diagrams. Make sure you do it exactly, or else the gates just won't work right. You'll know that you built it right if you get the same results in terms of turning the inputs ON and OFF as you see in the text below the title of each gate.

There are many, many ways to build each of these gates. What we've given you here is 1-3 basic versions of each of the gates that are easy to build and understand, but there are so, so many more ways to build each of them. This is because the rules that make the gates work can be used to construct them in various ways, from ways that are more complex to those that are quicker to those that take more inputs to those that travel in different directions (such as vertically, instead of horizontally). There are hundreds of variations on these builds available online, but for the sake of space, we've stuck to the most common versions for this book. We encourage you to play around with Redstone and see if you can come up with other ways to build these gates, or go online and copy a few layouts from the web to learn even more about them.

This is a very, very basic introduction to logic and electronic circuitry, but there is almost infinitely more information out there on both of these subjects. In fact, each of these would not only take up a whole book on its own, but many hundreds of books could, and have, been written on each. While this book and Minecraft itself are excellent introductions to the concepts behind logic and electronics (we'd say maybe even the best introductions yet), they are not meant to be the whole of knowledge on the subjects, and are really only scratching the surface. Again, if you're interested, seek out info online and even in libraries or schools if you want to know more.

Time to build some gates!

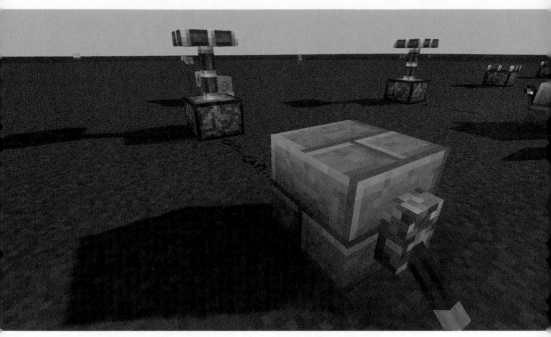

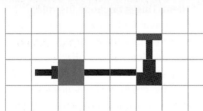

Diagram designed at mordritch.com

INPUT/OUTPUT Gate

ON=ON

OFF=OFF

Short Translation: The signal that is input is the same as the signal that is output.

What it does: The INPUT/OUTPUT gate is really just a regular power source attached to a regular outgoing Redstone wire, but it is still technically a gate. Unlike our other, more complicated examples of logic gates, the signal that is put into the INPUT/OUTPUT circuit is the same as the signal that is output, making it quite simple.

Construction: A Redstone power component powers a block that then has Redstone transmission components carrying that signal away from the block.

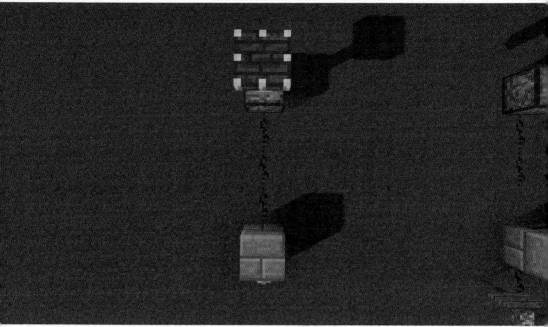

This is the simplest version of a gate, with just an input that outputs the same signal.

If you've learned how Redstone power components can send a power signal through Redstone Dust and other Redstone components when they are turned on, then you also understand the idea behind an INPUT/OUTPUT "gate," because this is pretty much how it works. We include the

INPUT/OUTPUT gate (when it's not really any different from regular Redstone powering) because it gets us thinking in "circuit language," which is different from thinking of regular Redstone concepts.

In the case of the INPUT/OUTPUT gate, think of it as a gate that has an ON (or 1, to use binary terms like a computer does) input and an ON output (1), or an OFF input (or 0) and an OFF (0) output.

Screenshot: Minecraft®™ & © 2009–2015 Mojang/Notch.

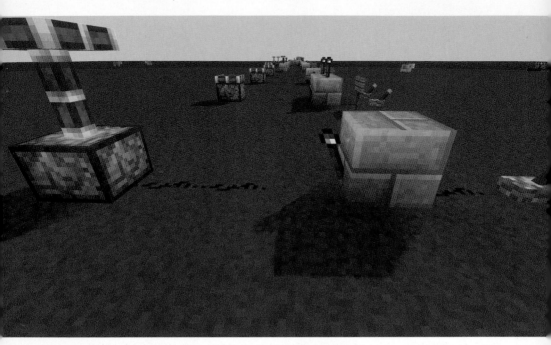

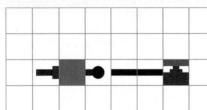

Diagram designed at mordritch.com

NOT Gate

ON=OFF

OFF=ON

Short Translation: The signal that is input is the opposite of the signal that is output.

Also known as: Inverter gate

What it does: The NOT gate reverses whatever signal the input is giving and outputs that reversed signal. So, if the signal going in (input) is ON, the signal going out (output) will be OFF. If, on the other hand, the signal going in is OFF, then the signal going out will be ON.

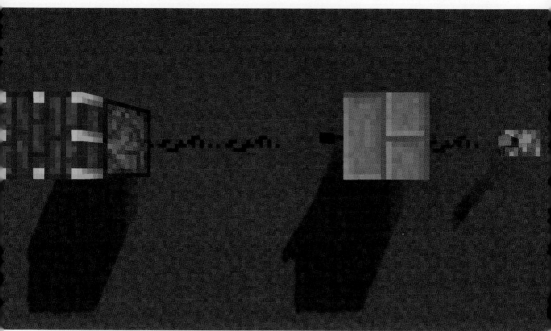

This is a gate that you will find yourself using time and time again, so remembering how it works will be very useful.

Construction: A Redstone power signal powers a block, and that block has a Redstone Torch attached to it, which is turned OFF when the Redstone power component is activated, or vice versa. Redstone transmission components carry that signal from the Torch to elsewhere.

NOT gates are the most important Redstone gate/circuit. They take an input signal and reverse it, meaning if the power going into the NOT gate is ON, then the output coming out of the NOT gate is OFF, and vice versa.

This ability to invert a Redstone signal is used often in builds, especially because other Redstone gates rely on the NOT gate to function. In fact, almost all other types of gates have a NOT gate built into them, or can have in some version.

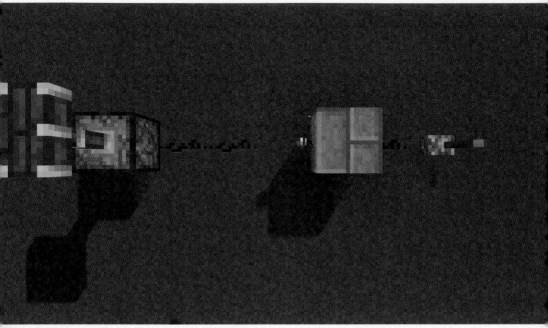

The NOT gate when the input is OFF

There is one very important feature that allows NOT gates to work; in fact, it's why they are used so often, and this feature has to do with Redstone Torches. The feature works thusly: when a Redstone power signal goes into an opaque block, it powers that block. A Redstone Torch attached to that powered block will be turned OFF. If the power signal(s) going into the powered block that caused the block to be powered (ON) is then turned OFF, the Redstone Torch turns ON. This is because it is no longer receiving an ON power signal, and so it has nothing acting on it. So, the Redstone Torch is then in its automatic ON state.

If you look at the images of almost all other gates in this chapter (excluding the INPUT/ OUTPUT gate and some of the simpler gates), you'll see that at some point the gate includes a NOT gate. You can see this when any single power signal goes into a block that has a Redstone Torch attached to it.

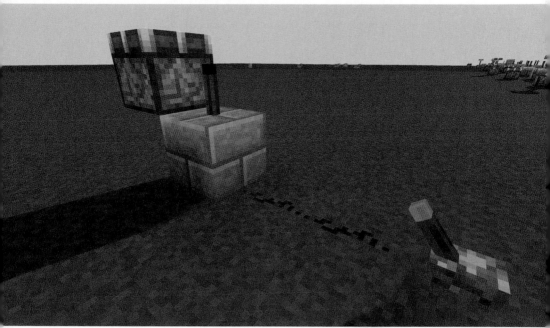

Another version of the NOT gate. There are many, many versions out there.

The end result concerning each gate's output status may vary, but if a signal is reversed at any point in a gate or a build, it uses a NOT gate. This ends up being thoroughly useful not only in circuits, but also on its own. For example, when you want a Redstone Torch to light up when a mob runs over a Pressure Plate. Typically, the Pressure Plate would send a signal to a Redstone Torch and turn it OFF, which seems counter-intuitive. When you build a NOT gate between the Pressure Plate signal and the mob-indicating Redstone Torch, however, you can invert the initial Redstone signal so that the Torch turns ON, and not OFF.

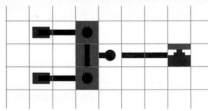

Diagram designed at mordritch.com

AND Gate

ON + ON = ON

ON + OFF = OFF

OFF + ON = OFF

OFF + OFF = OFF

Short Translation: The output signal is ON if both input signals are also ON, otherwise is OFF.

What it does: The AND gate requires that both inputs to it be ON for it to output an ON signal. Think of the output of an AND gate as a special light bulb that requires two switches to be flipped to ON for it to work: if no switches are ON, it won't work, nor will it work with just one switch ON. It must have both inputs ON to output an ON signal (or to light up, in terms of the bulb).

Note the state of the Levers and the Torches in each image, and which combined state causes the Piston to fire.

Construction: Two power signal inputs are each attached to their own NOT gate, and the outputs of those NOT gate are combined with Redstone transmission components and attached to a third NOT gate, which outputs a signal based on its two inputs.

Everything is in the name with the AND gate, and they're quite heavily used both in practical and in advanced logical builds. AND gates compactly combine the signals from two NOT gates to output a signal from a third NOT gate, meaning that the combination of the first two NOT gates outputting an OFF signal creates one ON signal outputting from the third NOT gate. If just one NOT gate in the initial two is outputting ON, or if both initial NOT gates are OFF, it causes the Torch for the third NOT gate to turn OFF, outputting an OFF signal.

Practically speaking, the AND gate can be used to create a situation where just knowing to flip one single Lever to send out an ON signal would not power a creation, forcing a player to know where both input Levers are and to flip them both ON. This is great for secret doors and other sly builds where you might want to hide one or both of the input power components (such as Levers).

Speaking in terms of logic, AND gates can be stacked with themselves and other gates to create complex patterns with varying results. For instance, try this example out: if both inputs to an AND gate are attached to the outputs of two other AND gates (in other words, there are two AND gates whose outputs feed into the two inputs of a third AND gate), you actually need both inputs for the initial two AND gates to be ON for the third AND gate to put out an ON signal. If even just one of the four total input signals across the two initial AND gates is OFF, then the third AND gate will output OFF as well.

OR Gate

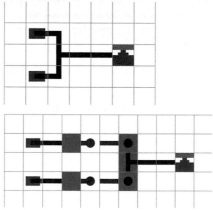

Diagram designed at mordritch.com

ON + ON = ON

ON + OFF = ON

OFF + ON = ON

OFF + OFF = OFF

Short Translation: The output signal is ON if any input signal is ON, including both. Otherwise OFF.

What it does: The OR gate is the opposite of an AND gate in that it always outputs an ON signal unless both inputs are OFF. In terms of real-life systems, think of this as a system that will turn on a light in a room if any of the light switches are turned ON, and will only turn off if all of the light switches are turned OFF.

All three of these are OR gates, and the bottom left is built out of other gates. Can you tell which?

Construction: Like most Redstone circuits, OR gates can be built a variety of ways, including by just attaching multiple power components to a single opaque block with a Redstone signal leading out of it, or by leading a wire of Redstone Dust from two power components so that they combine into one wire. You can also build more complex versions featuring NOT gates.

OR gates are pretty simple to understand: if any ON power signal is going into the OR gate, the OR gate will output an ON signal. This is great for when you want a Redstone build to activate no matter which input is turned ON, and you can stack ON gates in a similar way to AND gates, but with the opposite result.

One thing to note with OR gates is that you might want to isolate the inputs from the gate itself so that you can use them to power other things as well without interfering with the gate. If you just combine Redstone Dust signals like in the above example, it will work, but it can cause problems if you want to use that same Dust signal for anything other than the OR gate (which is likely in complex builds like computers). This is not hugely important to know right now, but it's something to keep in mind.

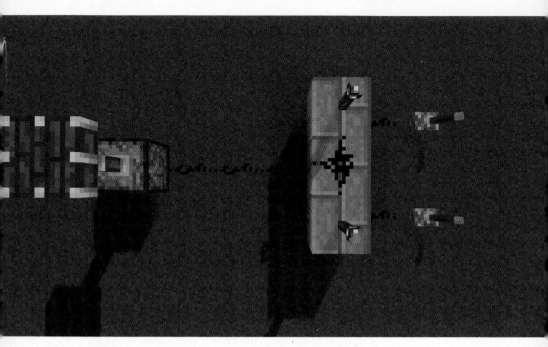

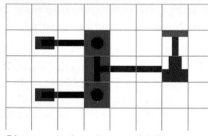

Diagram designed at mordritch.com

NAND Gate

ON + ON = OFF

ON + OFF = ON

OFF + ON = ON

OFF + OFF = ON

Short Translation: The output signal is OFF if both inputs signal are ON. Otherwise ON.

Also known as: Neither-and gate

What it does: The NAND gate will output an ON signal if either of the input signals is turned ON or if both are turned OFF, so it will almost always put out an ON signal unless it is receiving a double ON signal, one from each of its two inputs. A NAND gate is an opposite to an AND gate in this way. All four gates are intimately related to each other, in fact, as you can see by comparing their INPUT + INPUT = OUTPUT charts.

All other gates can be built using a string of NAND gates.

Construction: Easy NAND gates are exactly like the basic AND gate above, except that instead of having a third NOT gate taking the input of the initial two NOT gates, it just has Redstone Dust connecting the two NOT gates. Whereas in an AND gate the signal from either of the two initial NOT gates can cause the third to turn OFF or ON, in a NAND gate the signal from either of the initial NOT gates will cause the output to turn OFF or ON.

NAND gates are the logical extension of the AND gate, except in reverse. It's only when both inputs to a NAND gate are turned ON that it kills the output from the NAND gate. This can be used to deal with conditions when a Redstone build being activated would cause trouble if there was too much input (typically in complex logic circuitry).

For an analogy outside of the game, think of a high-security computer system that requires a signal from two administrators in order to be shut down. If just one administrator sends out their signal, the high-security system remains ON, as it needs both administrators' permission to shut off. This idea can be extended to Redstone circuits and mechanisms that almost always want an ON state.

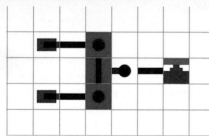

Diagram designed at mordritch.com

NOR Gate

ON + ON = OFF

ON + OFF = OFF

OFF + ON = OFF

OFF + OFF = ON

Short Translation: The output signal is OFF if at least one, or both input signals are ON (either input can be ON). Output signal is ON if both input signals are OFF.

Also known as: Neither-or gate

What it does: The NOR gate will only output an ON signal if there is absolutely no ON signal going into it. This means that it is almost always OFF and is only set to be powered when everything going into it is shut down.

Construction: The NOR gate we use here is actually two NOT gates attached to the two inputs of a single AND gate. In fact, this is actually five NOT gates stuck together,

Note the way that the NOR gate is made of a bunch of NOT gates strung together into one output.

creating a unique output. However, as mentioned before, there are other ways to build NOR gates.

NOR gates are kill-happy, which is a way to say that they will shut down if there is any ON signal going into them at all. They only output an ON signal if there is absolutely no ON signal going into them, making them very useful as kill-switches for your Redstone builds. Think of NOR gates as a build that is useful when you want to absolutely make sure the power is cut to a build unless everything attached to its input is OFF.

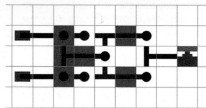

Diagram designed at mordritch.com

XOR Gate

ON + ON = OFF

ON + OFF = ON

OFF + ON = ON

OFF + OFF = OFF

Short Translation: The output signal is ON if only one input signal is ON. Otherwise OFF.

Also known as: Exclusive-or gate

What it does: The XOR gate outputs an ON signal when its inputs are different from each other. Think of it like most normal real-life lighting systems that are controlled by two light switches: you can turn the lights on or off from either light switch by simply flipping one of the two switches. What you're actually doing is either causing that switch to be ON while the other is OFF, in which case the lights are ON, or you're putting both switches in the same state (whether ON or OFF), in which case the lights are OFF.

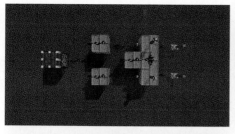

Two versions of the XOR gate, one of which requires Repeaters to function.

Construction: Can be fairly complex. We've given two examples, one of which uses 7 NOT gates attached to each other, and the other of which uses the fact that Redstone Repeaters will only power things in front of them to make the design more compact with only 5 NOT gates. Essentially in both designs the various NOT gates check each other to make sure that only one single power signal is being input to the whole of the XOR gate at a time, or else the signals cancel each other out by the time they reach the final two NOT gates.

This is where we start getting into the somewhat more complex gates in terms of how much they take to build, how they work and what you'd actually use them for. To make it simple, XOR gates are a string of NOT gates that have the result of allowing one of two signals to control the XOR gate's output without having to travel to the other signal and turn it ON or OFF as well. This is useful for situations like the mentioned real-life lighting system that can be controlled from multiple switches.

Say, for instance, that you have a Redstone player trap in the land outside your base. You can hook up a XOR switch to Levers so that the trap can be activated when you look out the Door at the ground level of your base, or from up a Lever in a tower far above the ground. You can also then deactivate the trap from that same location without having to worry about running to the other Lever to deactivate it as well, as flipping just a single Lever for a second time will return the XOR gate to an OFF status.

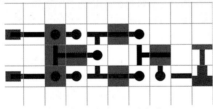

Diagram designed at mordritch.com

XNOR Gate

ON + ON = ON

ON + OFF = OFF

OFF + ON = OFF

OFF + OFF = ON

Short Translation: The output signal is ON if both input signals are the same, and is OFF if they are different.

Also known as: If and only if gate, equivalence gate

What it does: The XNOR gate is the opposite of an XOR gate in that it produces an ON signal when the two inputs are the same.

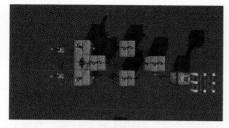

The XNOR latch is a lot more complicated than our other latches, but the rules are still simple for how it works. It's simply some of the other gates attached together!

Construction: The easiest way to think of it is to add a NOT gate to the end of a XOR gate, though It Is slightly more complex than that. See images.

The XNOR gate is a weird one: it's like an AND gate, but instead of having to set both inputs to ON to make the circuit produce an ON signal, you just have to make sure that they're the same. This is both more complex and simpler than an AND gate: it's more complex because it takes more resources to build, and it's simpler because you don't have to worry about making sure that both inputs are set to ON, but only have to flip one of the inputs either to the opposite state to activate a system that is currently turned OFF.

Real-life systems where this could help include a system in which you'd always want there to be a person at each of the input controls, so that it had to be turned on with two people sharing the state of one of the inputs. However, this isn't necessary in the case of very simple systems hooked up to XNOR gates that activate immediately, but only in the case of those whose results are hard to determine immediately through visual means (so the knowledge of the actual state of the inputs is crucial to creating the desired outcome).

Screenshot: Minecraft®™ & © 2009–2015 Mojang/Notch.

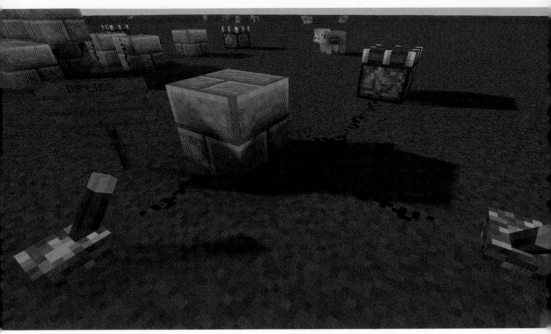

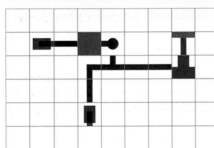

Diagram designed at mordritch.com

IMPLIES Gate

ON (A) + ON (B) = ON

ON (A) + OFF (B) = OFF

OFF (A) + ON (B) = ON

OFF (A) + OFF (B) = ON

Short Translation: The output signal is ON if input A and input B are both ON or both OFF, or if just B is ON. The output is OFF if A is on but not B.

Also known as: If-A-then gate, parent-child gate

A 1-high version of an IMPLIES gate, and one that is more compact horizontally but less compact vertically.

What it does: The IMPLIES gate is different from all other gates in that it has a primary or "parent" input and a secondary or "child" input. The output of an IMPLIES gate will always be ON unless the child input is ON and the parent input is OFF.

Construction: Consists of a NOT gate attached to the child input, which feeds into an INPUT/OUTPUT gate (i.e., just a straight line of Redstone Dust without any kind of inversion or other manipulation of the signal) that goes straight to the output.

The IMPLIES gate Is another weird one, and it's unique among Redstone gates in that it is the only gate where the two inputs are not interchangeable. In the case of the IMPLIES gate, one input can essentially "block" the other input's signal, causing an OFF state even when the other input is ON. We call the "blocking" input the parent input, and the other input the child input.

These are very useful for when you want to have a signal usually propagate on through the IMPLIES gate and to the output, but in some cases would like to be able to shut off the signal without having to manipulate both inputs.

5 Intermediate Builds

You've read about all the items, you've tested out a few builds, and you even know how to build a Redstone gate or two: it's time for some more difficult builds.

The coolest thing about Redstone, perhaps, is that the more difficult the builds get, the more fun and impressive they tend to be. In this chapter, we're going to really start getting some awesome stuff built with our favorite glowy, red material, starting with some sweet new doors for your home, and ending with the terrible might of a couple neat Redstone cannons.

At this point, we're going a bit beyond just making builds, and should be thinking about how they work and how to make them better. We'd suggest that you make each of these by the book (literally) once, and then play around with the ideas and see if you can't come up with more complex or, alternatively, simple ways to do them.

For now though, strap in, fire up your game, and get ready to impress your friends with these five super awesome Redstone builds.

Automatic Double Doors

What it does: Automatically opens both Doors in a set of double Doors at the same time as the player runs across any of four Pressure Plates, two behind and two in front.

How it works: Just two little NOT gates, one hooked up underneath each Iron Door, that are then connected to two more NOT gates. The second pair of NOT gates is hooked up to four Pressure Plates, and it also causes the second set of gates to be OFF until it gets a signal from those Pressure Plates. Pretty easy!

You'll Need: 2 Iron Doors, 4 Pressure Plates, 4 Redstone Torches, 1 Redstone Repeater, 26 Redstone

It's kinda weird, but to get a set of double Doors in Minecraft to open and close at the exact same time is not as simple as just hooking them up to basic Redstone. While you can get them to act as one unit, one Door will usually fire open slightly behind the other. This is due to the amount of time it takes the Redstone signal to propagate from one Door to the next, and while it's not really a big deal, it's not the cleanest or coolest way to get your Doors to open.

Automatic double Doors that work well is a bit of a badge of honor among Redstone creators, and it's used by some as a mark of a person who actually does know a bit about the system. Our first intermediate Redstone build, then, is to get a double Door construct working that will fire both Doors at the same

Screenshot: Minecraft®™ & © 2009–2015 Mojang/Notch.

time when you run over Pressure Plates, and we'll use a few of the lessons we've learned about gates, specifically NOT gates, to get it working.

It's actually a pretty simple system to set up, though it takes a bit of space under your Doors. All it really is, is one pair of NOT gates under the Doors themselves that is hooked up to a second pair of NOT gates. That second pair keeps the first one OFF, and then the signals that the second gate sends are turned OFF themselves when the Pressure Plates the second NOT gates are attached to are activated. This allows the Torches in the first pair of NOT gates to go ON at the exact same time, opening both Doors simultaneously. Nifty!

1. Find a spot where you'd like to have your autodoors. This is a bit tricksy, as you're gonna need to dig out at least 3 blocks of space immediately below your Doors and Pressure Plates. For your first shot at this, as always, we highly recommend trying it in Creative Mode. Barring that, it's best to do this very, very early on when starting a base, as trying to add it in later can be a huge pain.

2. Place your Doors down.

3. Place your two pairs of Pressure Plates down in front of the Doors. Each pair should have 1 block of space between it and the block the Doors are on. Note: this is not 1 block of space including the block the Doors are on. If you don't leave space between the Pressure Plates and the blocks that the Doors open up into and are on the edge of, the build won't work.

4. Dig out space underneath the layer that the Doors and Pressure Plates are on. Leave the layer they're on, but the two layers immediately below should be totally clear in a decent-sized area. You can fill in some of this space later, but we suggest making it rather spacious to begin with (must be at least 7 blocks long in the direction that the Doors are facing, 8 the other way horizontally and 2 deep). This should be one block off-center of where the Doors are, as you see in the image.

5. Place 2 blocks on the floor immediately below the blocks that the Doors are on, leaving a 1 block space of air between these new 2 blocks and the blocks the Doors are on. Do this for the Pressure Plates as well. See picture for reference.

6. Place 2 Redstone Torches on the blocks underneath the Doors (Doors will open for now). Place a Redstone Dust on each of the 4 blocks that are underneath the Pressure Plates.

7. Place a Redstone Torch on the sides of both outside ends (the side 1 block wide) of one of the sets of blocks under the Pressure Plates. Do not do this on both sets, just on one. See image.

8. Connect these Redstone Torches to the blocks underneath the Doors with Redstone Dust. Connect the left Torch on the blocks under the Pressure Plates to the left block under the Doors, and the right Torch to the right block, as you see in the image.

9. Place Redstone wire down coming off one Redstone Dust on the block pair that has Torches on its sides, and place this new wire on the side of the block pair that does not face the blocks under the Doors. What you've just created here, for reference, is two NOT gates under two of your Pressure Plates that lead into two NOT gates under your two Doors. See image.

10. Extend this Redstone wire according to the pattern you see in the image, so that you connect it to the wires on the block pair that has no Redstone Torches without creating a connecting between this new wire and the wires you placed in Step 8. That this strand of wire does not touch the other two is imperative to the build working. This wire is to carry power from the second set of Pressure Plates to the circuit you've built in the previous steps.

11. At some point in the wire you'll need a Redstone Repeater to keep the signal up, so place one down in the wire as you see in the image. Make sure to place this Repeater so that the signal carries to the blocks with the Torches, and away from the blocks without them.

12. Check your build with the images, and test out the Pressure Plates to see if it works. If you've wired it up correctly, stepping on any of the Plates will cause both Doors to open automatically.

13. Bury that build, making sure not to break any of the connections or to put opaque blocks in a place that would break them.

Screenshot: Minecraft®™ & © 2009–2015 Mojang/Notch.

Mob Detection System (or- Day/Night Detector)

What it does: A Redstone Torch in your base turns on when mobs or players run across Pressure Plates in an area you'd like to keep tabs on.

How it works: One or more Pressure Plates is set up outside a base wherever you'd like, and Redstone Dust is run through an underground tunnel a layer below the Plates. This connects the Plates together, and the Dust then goes through the tunnels underground and back to your base or another area where you'd like the mob detection signal to go off. This Dust is hooked up to a NOT gate that leads to a Redstone Torch (a second one, not the one in the NOT gate), which is activated when anything triggers one of the Pressure Plates.

You'll Need: 1 Pressure Plate (any kind), 2 Redstone Torches, Redstone (a decent amount, will vary depending on your build), Daylight Sensor (optional)

One thing any veteran of Minecraftery knows well is that mobs and players can often sneak up on you when you're underground or in a base. It's hard enough to see all around your home even with windows, much less when you're deep underground or in other spots where there's no line of sight to the surrounding area. Usually there's not much you can do except listen (if close enough) and hope you can tell which direction mobs are coming from, but with this Redstone mob detection system, those days of wondering if a Creeper's outside will long be gone.

It's a fairly simple idea: Pressure Plates set up around the area where you want to be alerted to the presence of mobs and players will activate when something runs over them, causing a signal to go to a Redstone Torch in your base. When that Torch (or Torches, if you get fancy with it) lights up, you know that you've got intruders.

The only real tricks to this build are that you'll need to carve out a pretty decent amount of underground space to tunnel the Redstone from your Pressure Plates and into your base, and you'll also need to hook up a NOT gate before the final Redstone Torch so that it goes ON when a mob or player hits the Pressure Plate, and not OFF (you could just leave it without a NOT gate, but having a Torch go OFF when your system detects mobs is a little backwards in our minds).

This is easiest to set up with a small number of Pressure Plates and on the ground floor of your home, but you can add as many as you'd like and send the signal anywhere if you have the patience and resources to dig out all of the tunnels you'd need and wire it up. To send the signal for the detector up or down (say into a tower or cave), you'll need to either build wire staircases or ladders (see the Advanced Wiring chapter).

Another cool feature of the detection system is that it can even be hooked up to other Redstone mechanisms, such as the Pressure Plates that open a Door in your home, a Trapped Chest you want to keep tabs on or even just other Redstone circuits, so that you know when any of these is being used.

Note: Our instructions here are to build the most basic version of this contraption to show you how it works. In this case there will be just a single Pressure Plate and indicator Torch, and the distance between the Pressure Plate and the Torch will be very short. However, using the Redstone knowledge from the rest of this book, you can add more Plates, make the distances greater and even add multiple indicator Torches if you'd like. You can also hide the NOT gate in this build more cleanly than in some of the images here, as well as send the signal vertically if desired.

1. Dig a pit 2 blocks deep into the ground and 5 blocks long (this is just for this example build, it can be any length in your version).

2. Replace the ground-level Dirt block at one end of this pit. At the other end, replace the block at the floor of the pit. See image.

3. Place a Pressure Plate on top of the block that you replaced at ground level.

4. Place a line of Redstone wire across the bottom of the pit, including the space below the Pressure Plate and on top of the block at the other end of the pit.

5. Place a Redstone Torch on the ground outside of the pit at the end of the pit opposite from the Pressure Plate.

6. Put an opaque block in the space above this Redstone Torch, and then place a set of 4 blocks adjacent to the Torch and perpendicular to the pit in the pattern you see in the image.

7. Place Redstone Dust on top of the 2 blocks that are 1 block off the ground, as you see in the image.

8. Place a Redstone Torch on the side of the block that the Redstone Dust leads into. Make sure this is the block that you see in the shot, and not the one above the other Redstone Torch. This second Torch will go OFF immediately, because you have just created two NOT gates, and the first NOT gate (the one directly next to the pit) inverts the signal of the second NOT gate.

9. Test your contraption by stepping on the Pressure Plate. If set up right, the Torch you placed in Step 8 will light up (you'll have to place the Torch on the side of the block that's facing you to see it for now, as you're the one standing on the Plate, but you can move it back later if you want).

10. You can now think about expanding and refining this build. One obvious thing you need to do is to cover up the pit. In our example, you can just place blocks over all of the pit, though you'll have to place a block above the block at end of the pit that's next to the Torch, as you have Redstone Dust on the block below it.

There are many, many variations to this build- for instance, you could build the first NOT gate underground, and have the Torch for the second NOT gate (the indicator that goes on when mobs walk on the Plate) sit on the ground, as in the image. You can also add multiple strands of wire connected to multiple Pressure Plates that all go to the same Redstone Torch indicator, or you could give each Plate its own. Or, you could replace the Pressure Plate and the block it's on with a Daylight Sensor, creating a daylight indicator instead of a mob indicator.

Easy Combination Lock

What it does: A series of Levers acts as a combination lock for an Iron Door, forcing players to turn on the right set of Levers to open the Door.

How it works: An Iron Door sits on the block directly above the Redstone Torch in a NOT gate. If the wrong set of Levers (the wrong "combination") is activated, including none or all Levers, then a signal is going into this NOT gate, causing it to be in an OFF state. Only when the right combination of Levers is flipped will no power be entering the NOT gate, producing an ON signal and causing the Iron Door to open.

You'll Need: 5 Levers, 9 Repeaters, 4 Redstone Torches, 9 Redstone, 1 Iron Door

Keep friends and foes alike from getting into your home with this nice and simple lock build. This is a very cool little build that is quite impressive and which uses a good amount of Redstone theory without taking long to do at all. To explain how it works further, each Lever in the lock is on a block on the ground, and behind each of these blocks is a series of Redstone Repeaters and/or a NOT gate. The Levers that have just Repeaters behind them are the wrong Levers to pull to open the Door, while the ones with Repeaters and NOT gates are the Levers in the correct combination.

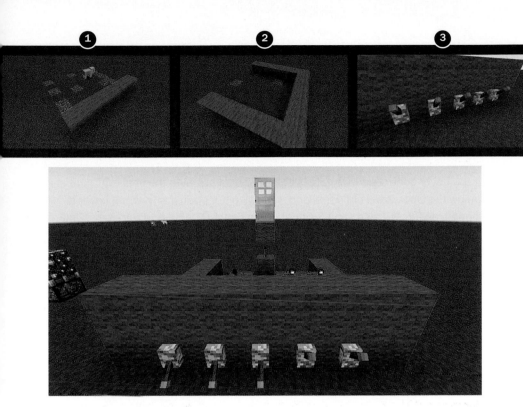

The way this works is that the Repeaters keep the lines of power from each Lever separate from each other (as Repeaters only give power in one direction) and a line of Redstone Dust perpendicularly connects the output to all of the Repeaters and the NOT gates. The signal of this Dust is funneled into just one line of Dust, which then goes into a final NOT gate. Above the Redstone Torch in this final NOT gate is the block on which the Iron Door sits.

When a Lever that is hooked up to just the Repeaters is flipped, it sends power all the way down to the final NOT gate, meaning any time any of the wrong Levers are flipped, the NOT gate is OFF and the Door stays closed. The other NOT gates in the build, the three that are behind the Levers in the combination, are automatically set to send an ON signal to the final NOT gate when their Levers are not activated, which in turn shuts the final NOT gate's output OFF. Each of the signals from the Lever-controlled NOT gates must be turned OFF by flipping its corresponding Lever in order for all NOT gates to stop sending out a signal.

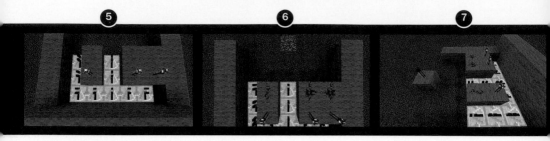

If any Lever-controlled NOT gate is still sending a signal to the final NOT gate below the Door, it will not open, and it will also not open if any wrong Lever is flipped, as this will also send a signal to the final NOT gate and turn it off. Only when all incorrect Levers are off and all correct Levers are on will there be no signal going to the final NOT gate, and the Door will open.

We've built this lock here using Wool blocks for ease of build, but the best idea for this construct is to use blocks that are quite difficult to break open, as you want to hide the Repeaters and NOT gates behind the Levers so that people can't see the combination. When done right (especially on servers where you can designate some blocks as unbreakable), it's a very effective deterrent to those who don't know the combination and are unwilling to sit and figure it out.

We also suggest, again, that you build this lock in Creative Mode or in a new base first, as opposed to adding it to an existing base, as it takes up a lot of space.

1. Build a line of blocks 7 long.

2. Place 5 more blocks coming off of each end of the line of 7, as in the picture. We also went ahead and added a second layer of blocks to the original 7 at this point, but this is not necessary to do until the end of the build.

3. Place Levers on the front side (opposite from the direction of the lines of 5 blocks) of the middle 5 blocks on the edge of your build that is 7 blocks long. See image.

4. Decide which 3 Levers you want to use for your combination. In our example, we picked Levers 2, 4 and 5 going left to right.

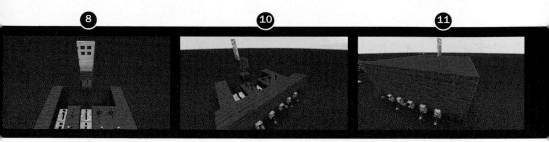

5. Go to the other side of the blocks from the Levers, and place down a row of Repeaters on the ground, all facing away from the Levers (so they're powered when the Levers are activated).

6. Create another two rows of Repeaters after this initial row of Repeaters, but only for the Levers that are not your chosen three for the combination. Instead of Repeaters for these three, you want to place 2 opaque blocks down, with a Torch at the end closest to the Levers on each set of 2 blocks. These are NOT gates, and they're what set your combination. See image.

7. Place Redstone Dust down on the second block in the pairs of 2 blocks that make up your combination columns, and then place Redstone across the ground behind the third row of Repeaters and the blocks you just put Dust on. See picture.

8. Place one Redstone Dust coming off the middle of the row of Redstone you placed in Step 7, and then place a block directly after that, and put a Redstone Torch on that block. This is another NOT gate.

9. Place a block directly above the Redstone Torch you just placed, and put your Iron Door on top of this block.

10. You can now go flip your Levers, and if it was built correctly, the Door will only open if the 3 Levers in the combination are ON, and all others are OFF.

11. You can then fill in the rest of the space around the door with blocks, hiding the contraption from sight! We suggest heavy-duty blocks like Obsidian, so that no one can break into your lock and find out the code, or destroy it.

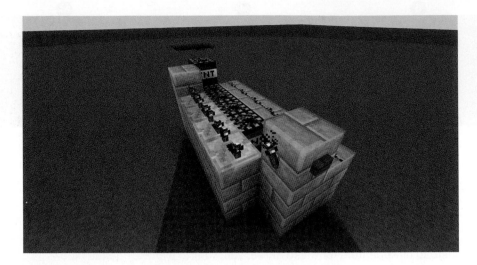

TNT Cannon #1- Easy Standard TNT Cannon
(thanks to minegab for the design)

What it does: Fires a single shot of TNT a decent distance away from the cannon.

How it works: Uses the property of Water that says that activated TNT will float in Water and not blow up anything around it, but will blow up still and launch other activated TNT that is on a block around it. In this version, a single Redstone power component sends a signal down two paths- a first path that is that is straight Redstone, and a second path that starts with a NOT gate in an ON state and then goes through 4 Repeaters, and which is thus on a delay. The first signal instantly activates 4 TNT (called the "charge") that are laid in a channel with a Water source behind it, which then flows forward, catching the TNT and pushing it to the end of the cannon. The second signal turns off the NOT gate, goes through the 4 Repeaters and turns them off in turn, and this allows a second NOT gate at the end of the Repeater line (and which was therefore OFF before) to invert and give a power signal to a final block of TNT set above the others. This activates a few ticks after the rest, so when the 4 TNT explode, their force launches the final block of TNT out and forward, after which it shortly blows up itself.

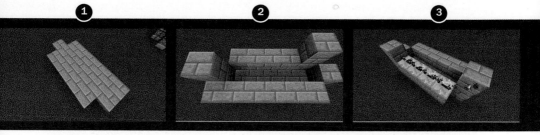

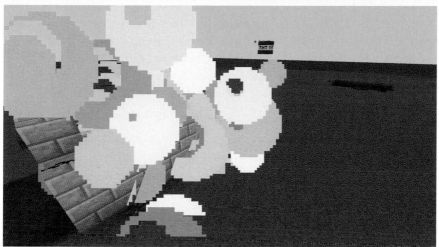

You'll Need: 30 of any high resistance block (Obsidian is great, but at least use Stone), 5 TNT (more to reload), 4 Redstone Repeaters, 2 Redstone Torches, 6 Redstone, 1 Button, 1 Bucket of Water

TNT cannons are beast. Just about every Minecrafter loves these guys, and we'll bet that this cannon (or our second, even more beastly one) will be one of the very first Redstone builds you show off to your friends when you get it figured out.

This particular model is one of the very most basic cannons, though it kicks things up a notch from the most simple TNT cannons by using just one split signal instead of two separate ones. Easier cannons don't use Repeaters, but instead use Redstone wire where the Repeaters in this build are, and they hook that up to its own Button. In that type of build, the Button that activates the "charge" (again, the TNT used to launch the final block of TNT, which is itself called the "shot") is pressed, the player waits for a few ticks, and then the second Button that activates the shot is pressed.

In our build, things are a bit more elegant. It does the job quite nicely, though the shot distance is not all that far, and the damage is fairly minimal. This cannon still has to be reloaded by hand to shoot again, but it makes for an excellent and quick lesson on splitting Redstone signals, using Repeaters and NOT gates, and manipulating TNT with Redstone. Plus, stuff blows up! Yay, stuff blowin' up!

A note: if for some reason your shot explodes before the charge, or if your charge goes off and it's not in Water, your TNT cannon will probably just blow itself up instead of your target. This is why we recommend you build the cannon out of sturdy stuff. If you build it right and it fires correctly, however, it doesn't matter much what you build it out of as long as it is opaque.

1. **Build a pattern** of blocks that copies what you see in the image here.

2. **Build more blocks** on top of this pattern of blocks the exact same way you see in this second image. This is the housing for your cannon.

3. **On the end of the cannon** with a block sticking out of the middle of the cannon, place a Redstone Torch on its left side. Add Repeaters facing away from this Torch to the left wall of the cannon, stopping when you hit the other of the two tall blocks on the cannon. See image.

4. **Go back to the tall block** in the middle of the cannon, on which you put the Redstone Torch. On the back side of this block (opposite the length of the cannon), place a Button. Then run Redstone wire up the side of the cannon that's opposite to the Repeaters. Place this all the way down the side to the end.

5. Drop a Bucket of Water into the channel in your cannon on the side that has the block with the Button. Then add a final Redstone Torch to the far side of the tall block on the opposite side of the cannon (the one without the Button). Use the image for reference, and note that you need the Water to be flowing away from the Button.

6. Add one block of TNT on the single block sticking out of the far end of the cannon. It should be adjacent to the Redstone Torch at this end. Then place 4 blocks of TNT into the channel in the cannon, placing them starting from the end that holds the other TNT block and going back towards the Water source. Make sure not to place a block that covers the Water source, however, as this will likely result in the cannon exploding when you fire it.

7. Now, when you press the Button, the cannon will first ignite the blocks of TNT in the channel (the charge), dropping them into the Water, and it will then ignite the block at the end of the cannon (the shot). When the charge TNT blocks explode, they will launch the shot TNT block, if done correctly.

8. Reload, blow more junk up!

TNT Cannon #2- Rapid-Fire Scattershot Cannon

What it does: Fires a huge number of TNT shots 3 at a time a very large distance and covering an enormous area.

How it works: If you've read how the first cannon works, this one is much the same in basic principle, but kicks things up a notch or 500. Instead of hand-placing TNT blocks into a channel and activating them, this version uses Dispensers to repeatedly throw the "charge" TNT blocks into a Water channel set up directly above another series of Dispensers, which throw the "shot" TNT blocks above, slightly ahead and, in terms of time, slightly after the charge TNT blocks explode. This is done by building a fast pulser behind the cannon itself and then manually connecting it to Redstone already hooked up to the bottom row of Dispensers. You then wait a second or two before manually (and quickly!) adding another row of 3 Redstone that connects the pulser to the top row of Dispensers as well.

You'll Need: 8 Dispensers, a ton of TNT (whole heaps of it), 3 Slabs, 1 Lever, 2 Redstone Repeaters, about 17 Redstone Dust, 2 Buckets of Water, a few random blocks

If you thought the first cannon was fun, wait til you get one of these bad boys firing. It's not exactly the prettiest build, as it's fired not by activating a power component, but instead by manually laying down extra Redstone and connecting it to a pulse circuit (aka a "pulser"), but in terms of glorious destruction and lookin' cool, it's pretty unbeatable.

It's also pretty simple to build, and it adds a bit more to the concepts we've been playing around with so far. It throws in the new idea of pulsers (more in the Advanced Wiring chapter) and adds Dispensers to the mix in a new way, this time using TNT. We also deal with the fact that we can't put the shot-firing Dispensers on top of the charge-firing Dispensers, as we need the shot to be activated at a different tick than the charge. This is also why we have to manually lay down the 3 Redstone Dust on top of the Dispensers slightly after the charge Dispensers are hooked up to the pulser. Speaking of, we also do a little bit of shift-click Redstone placement on our Dispensers here, another concept that is good to get familiar with.

If done right (and it can easily go wrong the first few times), this cannon will spew out a wave of destruction and chaos that is almost unrivaled in Minecraft. So, don't point this thing at anything you like! It goes farther than you'd think, and it will outright decimate an area larger than a Village in mere seconds. In fact, we highly suggest pointing one of these at a Village at some point, just for the lulz.

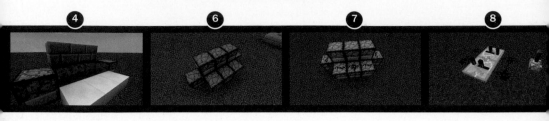

1. Place 2 Dispensers facing each other with 3 blocks of space in between them.

2. Place a line of 3 Slabs one block forward and between these 2 Dispensers, as you see in the photo.

3. Place a line of 3 Dispensers facing the slabs, but 1 block back from and between the original 2 Dispensers, leaving a gap 1 block tall and 3 wide between the original 2 Dispensers, the 3 Dispensers in the back and the 3 Slabs in the front.

4. Drop 1 Water Bucket on the ground at one end of this gap, and then the second at the other end. You need to drop 2 total in order for this to work. Then put blocks of any kind on top of the 3 Dispensers that are facing toward the Slabs.

5. Place 3 more Dispensers on the side of the blocks you just placed, still facing the Slabs.

6. Destroy the 3 blocks you placed in Step 4, so that the back of the cannon looks like this image.

7. Place Redstone Dust on top of all of the Dispensers on the bottom layer of the cannon by holding the Shift key and clicking to place Redstone Dust like you normally would. Also add one Redstone Dust on the ground block at the two back corners of the cannon, and one on the ground leading away from the cannon. All of the Dust should connect, as you see in the shot.

8. Build a pulser a few blocks behind the cannon on the back side of it. To build a pulser, place 2 Redstone Repeaters and 4 Redstone Dust in the pattern you see in the image, and then send a signal into it. To send a signal into a pulser, you need to place a Lever adjacent to the Dust in the pulser, and then flip the Lever ON and OFF as fast as you can. If you did it right, the pulser will show a signal turning OFF and ON very quickly. If you did it wrong,

it will show no signal or a steady signal, and you'll have to break the pulser's connection, re-connect it and try again with the Lever.

9. Fill all of the Dispensers with as much TNT as you'd like. Note that you need quite a bit in each for this to work, and only the TNT in the top 3 will be fired away from the cannon. The bottom layer of Dispensers is what fires the "charges," while the top is what fires the "shots."

10. To fire this crazy cannon (and it is quite crazy indeed), you need to perform a tricky maneuver. First, connect the Redstone Dust attached to the bottom layer of Dispensers to your pulser. Then very, very quickly jump on top of the bottom layer of Dispensers, wait about 1 second, then place a line of Redstone Dust on top of the top layer of Dispensers as well. You'll need to use the Shift key again to do this, and it will connect the top layer of Dispensers to the Redstone Dust on the bottom layer, in turn connecting the top layer to the pulser.

11. If done right, you'll almost immediately start seeing wave after awesome wave of TNT firing out in a wide spread from the cannon, going very far and outright wrecking all in its path. Again, we can't recommend enough that you try this on a village. It's really, really funny.

Redstone Challenge

Try to come up with ways to make this build's activation more elegant. Is there some other way you can come up with to get the bottom and then the top Dispensers to fire, instead of having to place Redstone manually? Would the top level have to be attached to its own pulser, or could it still use the same pulser as the bottom level, but still get the signal on a slight delay? And how could you go about sending a signal from the pulser to either set of Dispensers by using a power component to activate the whole contraption, instead of manually creating a Redstone Dust connection?

We've got a some ideas of our own, but try out a few things and see what you can come up with!

Advanced Wiring Concepts and Terms

Before we jump into our final advanced build, let's talk a bit about some of the more advanced Redstone subjects. That's right kiddos; we're on to the crazy parts of Redstone now! Nice work making it this far.

In this chapter, we're going to give you an overview of some of the topics that Redstone engineers like yourself should start to tackle once they've got a firm foundation in the basics of Redstone. This is for when you'd like to kick things up a notch and learn more about the absolutely insane things people have been able to get Redstone to do when they really know their stuff.

We're just going to touch briefly on these advanced topics and give you a little info on each to get you familiar with them, as these topics could fill entire an entire book on their own and we just don't have the space. That being said, this brief overview will give you plenty of info to work with and should get you thinking about how to incorporate these advanced Redstone tactics into your own builds. If you're looking for more info, give each of these terms a search online, and you'll find more details by the truckload.

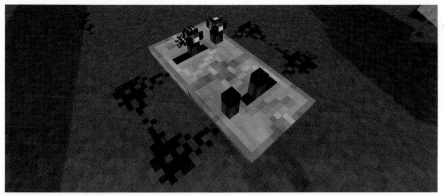

This is a basic pulser. You can't tell with the static picture, but this is blinking in a pattern.

Transmission Circuits

On top of the basic transmission items like Redstone Repeaters and Dust and the circuits we've discussed in previous chapters like our chapter on logic gates, there are a few other constructs that are commonly used to transmit a Redstone signal.

Bridge: Bridges are when one Redstone wire crosses over another without interacting with it. These can be created in a variety of ways, but the basic idea is simply that they are constructs that keep the two wires or circuits from interacting while still passing very close to each other.

Pulsers: As the name would suggest, pulsers or pulse circuits are parts of Redstone systems that send a signal that turns ON, then OFF, then ON again. These can be created in a large variety of ways, with the difference being the frequency of the pulse, the way the pulse is able to be turned ON and OFF (or not) and whether the pulse sends a signal in an ON>OFF>ON pattern, or in an OFF>ON>OFF pattern.

Detectors: Detectors are a variant of pulsers that create a specific type of pulse when certain situations are detected. "Edge detectors," for instance, create a pulse output at the moment of either detecting the beginning, or the end of another Redstone signal. "Pulse length detectors" output a signal pulse when detecting another pulse that is of a specific length, and "Comparator update detectors" pulse when they detect a Comparator that is updated by a change in a storage item's inventory. A fourth kind of detector is the "block update detector," or BUD, which is a very special and useful kind of detector that we'll talk about in its own section in just a few pages.

Memory Circuits

Where Redstone gates are constructs that take certain input signals into them and then output a new signal, meaning that their state is always a result of what is currently being input into them, memory circuits are able to take certain combinations of inputs and store a state based on which inputs have been recently put in. Essentially, memory circuits remember what inputs have been put into them, and they will keep remembering until other inputs occur. This is very similar to very (very, very) basic computer memory, as memory circuits typically stores 1 bit of information (either 0/OFF or 1/ON), though they can also store more. While there are a huge number of types of memory circuits that can be made, there are a few basic versions that people tend to use most often in Minecraft.

Latches: There are two basic types of memory circuits called latches- the RS latch and the JK latch. The RS latch is a circuit that takes two inputs, one which sets the RS latch to have an ON output, and the other which sets the latch to have an OFF output. One of the most well-known and widely used Minecraft circuits outside of gates is called an RS NOR latch, which, as you might have guessed, uses a NOR gate. JK latches are very similar to RS latches, except that when both inputs are ON at the same time, it will toggle the output from ON to OFF.

A basic T flip-flop. Knowing how to make these and what makes it work is something that really does separate a novice from a master Redstoner.

Flip-Flops: Like latches, there are two basic circuits known as "flip-flops"- the T flip-flop and the D flip-flop. A T flip-flop is another type of circuit that is used very often in builds, and it is also known as a "toggle," because inputting a pulse of power into a T flip-flop will cause it to toggle between an output state of ON and OFF. This means that when a pulse of ON power goes into a T flip-flop that is already outputting an ON signal, the T flip-flop will start outputting an OFF signal and will keep doing so until another pulse of power goes through it. D flip-flops, on the other hand, have two inputs: a clock (or C) that pulses power and a "data" input (or D) that holds a current state. When the C input pulses through a D flip-flop, it causes the output of the D flip-flop to be equal to whatever state that the D input is in while between pulses.

Counters: Counters are memory circuits that can store not just two states, but many states.

Using Torch towers is essential to powering most builds with multiple vertical layers.

Ladders, Torch Towers and Staircases

Redstone Dust is great for transmitting a Redstone signal horizontally, but when you need the signal to move vertically up or downwards, things get a bit tricky. Redstone Dust will typically only move a signal up in a staggered "staircase"-esque build, but creative players have managed to come up with a couple of other methods for vertically moving a signal, called Torch towers and ladders, respectively.

Staircase: The most basic method for moving a signal up or down, staircases look like their namesake, as they involve a block being one block above or below another and one block to the side. Redstone Dust can be placed on top of both blocks, connecting them, and a power signal can be sent through them.

Torch Tower: Torch Towers use the property of Redstone Torches that says that they will power an opaque block placed above them. By placing a block on top of a Redstone Torch, and then another Redstone Torch on top of that, and then repeating this a third time on top of this second Torch, we are able to move a Redstone signal straight upwards. This is actually creating multiple NOT gates stacked on top of each other, and is a very efficient way to transmit a signal vertically, though it does not work downwards.

Ladder: Ladders involve placing transparent blocks like Glowstone or Slabs in a vertical "checkerboard" pattern, placing Redstone Dust on each block as the ladder goes up. A signal can be hooked up to the bottom of a ladder, and because the blocks are transparent, it will propagate up the rest of the ladder. Also only works vertically.

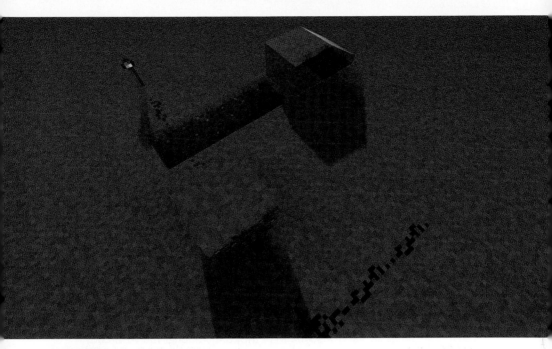

Block Update Detectors

We talked about detectors a few pages ago, but to refresh, they are pulsers that create a signal pulse only when they detect certain conditions. Of the various detectors, block update detectors or BUDs are probably the most common and useful. These take advantage of a "bug" in Minecraft that causes Redstone circuits or mechanisms not to recognize that they should be receiving a signal until the game sends a "block update" to the area. Block updates are basically the game checking the state of each block and seeing if it should change, and they are triggered by actions or events in the game, including placing blocks nearby, Grass growing, a natural block of Redstone being punched or stepped on, and many other ways.

Though there are many types of BUDs, in all BUDs there is one block that is the "sensor" block, which is the block that does not realize it should be receiving an update. Players then force an update by causing one of the previously mentioned or other events to occur, the sensor block gets an update, and the circuit it is attached to receives a short pulse of power. The circuit then goes back to "sleep," and the power goes off.

Redstone Building Terms

As practitioners of very complex subject, Redstone engineers have come up with many special terms to describe what they are creating. You've already heard many of them, but here are a few more terms to use that will help you to communicate info about your builds, not to mention impress your friends and other engineers.

1-High (Flat)/1-Wide- **Refer to the shape and dimensions of a build. 1-high or flat builds are only 1 block tall, while 1-wide are only 1 block across in one direction.**

Analog/Binary/Unary: Refer to the transmission of power through certain circuits where the state of the power and the type of circuit are used to represent numbers. "Analog" transmission means that the power level of the input of the transmission is the same as the output, and it can have 16 states (0-15 power). "Binary" transmission refers to transmission where multiple lines of transmitted power each have their own state, and where each state makes up one digit in a single binary number (binary numbers look like this- 1101100, 001, 0100 etc.). "Unary" refers to multiple lines of transmission where the number represented is selected by which of the lines of transmission is powered. So, if the 9th line of transmission is powered, the number represented is 9.

Cannon names: This is maybe the most complex subject in this chapter, oddly enough, and we don't have space to fully explain the complexities of naming cannons, but suffice it to say that there is a very specific system that players have created to name cannons which quickly tells other players information about that cannon. The formula for naming cannons is, to give the simple explanation, as follows:

[DV].[EV].[TA].[MR] [Cannon nickname]

Each value is a number, except the last.

DV= damage value (accuracy, power and speed combined)

EV= ergonomic value, meaning difficulty of build (average of construction, Redstone and TNT values)

TA= amount of TNT used

MR= maximum block range can fire

Cannon nickname= what the player calls the cannon

To learn more about this, check out the extensive article on the Minecraft wiki.

Flush: Flush means that the build doesn't extend beyond a flat floor, wall or ceiling and which provides power to the other side of the floor, wall or ceiling.

Hipster: Doesn't mean what you think, but instead means that you don't see any Redstone components before or after a Redstone construct performs its operation. A build is still "hipster" if you can see them during operation.

Instant: The output of a build activates right away after the input activates, with 0 ticks of delay.

Seamless: Seamless means that the build is totally hidden behind a flat floor, ceiling or wall when not activated, but which when activated interacts with the other side of the wall.

Silent: As you'd expect, these are builds that don't make noise. So, Piston builds usually aren't silent.

Stackable/Tileable: Terms that are opposites of each other, where stackable means that you can place multiple exact copies of a build directly next to each other, and the builds can all be controlled together as one, and tileable means that copies of the build can be placed directly next to each other and still controlled separately.

Final Lesson:
An Advanced Build

Now, it's time to put all of the knowledge you've (hopefully!) picked up from the rest of this book to work in a build that's more than a little complicated, and also more than a little awesome.

You know about Redstone gates, you've had a little bit of info on some advanced wiring concepts, and you've whetted your appetite for builds with a few beginner and intermediate options. But this, girls and boys, is the big one: the 3x3 Piston door.

Of course, the truth is that this build would actually be considered quite simple by many Redstone masters, but that's the beauty of Redstone: like all truly rich subjects of learning, each time you get to a point where you feel like you've understood something about Redstone, you realize that there's just so much more out there still to learn.

So, we aren't saying this is advanced by, say, Sethbling or pg5's standards (both could probably build this one handed and asleep), but for those who have just recently begun their journey toward Redstone engineering dominance, it most certainly earns the term advanced. Firstly because this build exemplifies many of the most important qualities about Redstoning, including elegance, efficiency, circuits working separately and together, gates and more. And secondly, because when you build this Piston door, you can truly say you've done something awesome with Redstone.

Think of this as at once your final Redstone exam, and your final lesson. It's fairly simple to follow the instructions to build this guy, but the important part here is to think about why each part does what it does. We'll give you a little bit of the info, but we'd like to encourage you to do some of the discovery on your own, as nothing will solidify a lesson better than that eureka moment when you realize through your own thought processes what it is that makes a complex Redstone build truly tick.

All the info you need to understand this build is in the pages of this book, and there's ever more out there online and in the heads of the Redstone engineers building on Minecraft servers across the world. Build it, think about it, and don't be afraid to go back through these pages or to seek out an expert to get more explanation.

Once you truly understand what's going on in this build, well, we'll just say this: Welcome to the Redstone engineering corps, miner.

Mumbo Jumbo's Tiny 3x3 Piston Door

What it does: Uses just one Lever to open and close a door made out of a 3x3 section of blocks that, when open, hide away into the structure of the build

How it Works: Essentially, it's a series of Sticky Pistons that extend and retract blocks from the side and the top of the door frame so that all blocks in the door are removed (to open) and then replaced when closed. It does this using three circuits, all controlled by one Lever. The power signal from the Lever goes to each circuit in turn. Different parts of the build is receiving power at different speeds due to the Repeaters in the build and because of various broken and unbroken circuits, which all causes the various Pistons in the build to fire at different times, pushing and pulling the blocks involved in the door at just the right time.

It's a rather elegant and easy(ish) to build contraption, yet is also fairly advanced in its composition, involving NOT gates, a mini Torch ladder, delayed signals, breaking and creating circuits, a monostable circuit involving a Comparator, a Hopper and a Dropper (more on that in the instructions) and a double extender Piston array.

You'll Need: 12 Sticky Pistons, 1 Lever, 1 Comparator, 1 Dropper, 1 Hopper, 1 Detector Rail, 3 Repeaters, 18 Redstone, 3 Redstone Torches, many opaque blocks

The 3x3 Piston door is a bit of a legendary step in the process of becoming a master Redstone engineer. This is because it doesn't just involve solving a simple problem (i.e. "I need a door here"); it also contains a problem within itself. This is that a 3x3 door made of blocks has one block in the center that must be pushed and pulled along with the rest of the build to be truly well-done, but if we were just to build this door using Pistons surrounding a 3x3 space, no Piston would normally be able to reach that middle block. The other blocks in the door and the other Pistons would be in the way, meaning it would be left floating alone, looking terrible.

This means that we have to figure out a way to manipulate that block with Pistons as well as the others. This, oh miners, is the kind of problem that Redstone engineers love to solve. Being able to successfully create a build that solves problems like this is what separates a Redstone dabbler from a true member of the Redstone engineering corps, and it's a heck of a lot of fun along the way.

So how are we going to solve this problem? Well, as we said, we aren't going to give you the answers to how every single detail of how this build works, as we think it's important to leave some things for you to discover on your own, but the gist of it is this: we are going to set up some normal(ish) Sticky Piston arrays for the rest of the blocks around the middle block and the block below it, and we're going to build a special Piston design to take care of extending and retracting those two pesky middle blocks.

The basic idea of the build is that we're going to use a double Piston extender (aka a DPE) that will push first the middle, and then the bottom middle block up into the door one at a time. When it retracts, it will pull the bottom middle one out first, and then go back and grab the top middle one.

A third Piston will feed the second block (the bottom middle one) to the DPE after the DPE has pushed the first middle block in (when closing the door), and that same third Piston is used to pull the bottom middle block off the DPE after the DPE has snatched the block when the door is opening. This third Piston helping out allows the DPE to be clear to grab the middle block. It also, however, means that the DPE has to fire twice: first it fires so that just the top Piston in the DPE activates, grabs the bottom middle block, then retracts, and then the third Piston grabs the block from the retracted top Piston in the DPE and moves it out of the way. Second, the DPE fires again, and this time the bottom Piston in the DPE fires first, pushing the top Piston up, and then that top Piston fires too, grabbing the middle block. The top Piston in the DPE then retracts, and then the bottom one retracts too. This works in the opposite way when closing the door.

We know, it's a bit confusing, but once you see it in action it will make a lot more sense.

To get this to even happen, however, we have to build an array of circuits at the bottom of the door construct that cause power to reach the three Pistons involved in the pulling and pushing of the two middle blocks at specific times, and that power signal also has to be activated, be cut off, and be activated again multiple times with just one flick of a Lever, and it has to go to different pistons in the DPE trio at different times. To get this effect, we have to create some somewhat complicated circuits, including one on the left side of the build that uses a power signal that is delayed through Repeaters, which causes it to fire a Piston that pushes a block, which cuts itself off and then reactivates itself. We also have to build a circuit on the right side of the build that uses what is called a monostable circuit.

The rest of the Pistons in the build also have to fire in order to extend and retract the rest of the blocks that make up the door, and all of this has to be wired together to be activated by flipping just one single Lever. This means the build must carry a power signal vertically as well as downwards at points, and since the point of all of this is do the build in a very small area that can fit into most bases (7x2 blocks horizontally and 9 vertically), we have to be very, very efficient with how we get that current to travel up and down to the other Pistons.

Now you can see why this build is your final lesson in this book: it's not too hard to build when you have the instructions, but understanding it is something else entirely.

Redstone Challenge

While you're building this, don't just try to understand how it works, also try to think about how someone came up with this idea. There are many, many 3x3 Piston door designs out there, but this is one of the best and most famous because it is so incredibly efficient and compact. See if you can come up with another way to do it without worrying about how big it is. Then, see if you can take your version of the build and make it more compact. We guarantee you that if you weren't already amazed at the elegance and cheap item cost of this build before, you will be after you try your own.

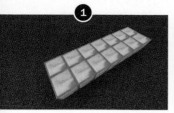

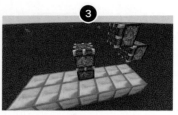

1. Build or mark off a 7x2 block area of horizontal space which will be the bottom of the build. We're going to be referring to the "front" and "back" of the build as well as the two sides, so pick one of the long sides and start thinking of it as the front of the build now. The portal for the door itself will have its bottom block at 5 blocks off the ground, so if you're building this in a base, make sure to keep that in mind. As always, we can't suggest enough that you try this out in Creative Mode before trying to fit it into a base.

2. Place a Sticky Piston facing up on the back middle block of the 7x2 area, and then another Sticky Piston facing up on top of that first Sticky Piston.

3. Place two more Sticky Pistons to the right of the first two Pistons as you see in the image here, still on the back row, but one should be in the right corner one block off the bottom of the build, and the other should be one block to the left and one block up from this first Piston. Make sure these two new Pistons are facing in toward the middle of the build.

4. Build an L shape out of opaque blocks on the right side, front row of the 7x2 area, leaving one empty block on the far right, as seen in the image. Put a dot of Redstone Dust on the leftmost block in the L, and put a Redstone Torch on the right side of the top block of the L. This is a NOT gate. Note that in our build we're using different colored blocks for each one of the three main parts of the circuits that make up this build, and we suggest doing the same so that you can keep better track of what's happening.

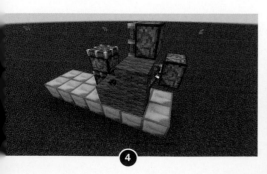
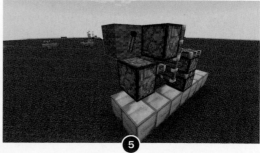

5. Go to the back side of the build and place a block immediately above the last Redstone Torch you placed, and place another Redstone Torch on this new block, but facing the back of the build. This is another NOT gate and is a small Redstone ladder.

6. Place a block in front of the head of the Piston that extended when you set the first Redstone Torch down (the only extended Piston, which is the one facing toward the middle on the bottom on the back of the build).

7. Move back to the front right side of the build, and remove the block at the bottom right corner of the L of opaque blocks. Replace that block with a Detector Rail. Set the Rail to face the way it is in the image, which is going left to right (you may have to put a second one down temporarily to do so). Put a line of Redstone Dust on the block to the right of the Detector Rail, as in the image. The Detector Rail doesn't actually function in the build except to make sure that the Redstone Dust faces it, and not any other part of the build (which is crucial).

8. Remove the back right corner block of the 7x2 base of your build and replace it with a Dropper facing up. Put one item of any kind in this Dropper.

9. Shift click and place a Hopper so that it is right above the Dropper and attached to it.

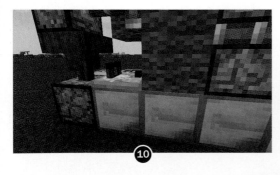

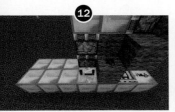

10. Place a Comparator on the empty block to the right of the Hopper (when facing the build from the back) so that it is facing away from the Hopper and toward the Piston two blocks to the right. Then put a block between the Comparator and that Piston. What we've built here with the Hopper and the Dropper and the Comparator is what is called a "falling edge monostable circuit." A "monostable circuit" is a circuit whose output will remain in the same state (ON or OFF) until a power signal is input into it again, and "falling edge" is a term that refers to a power signal being output only at the moment that an input power signal is turned OFF. This is a rather complex topic, but the gist of what happens is that when we flip the Lever that controls the build to ON, it causes the Comparator to read the inventory of the Hopper, which is just pushing the single item back into the Dropper, and this Comparator pulses a single signal with a power level of 1. This happens at the end of the power pulse going through the build. This is important for our DPE because we need the top piston in the DPE to pulse (quickly activate and then deactivate) when we are trying to retract the middle blocks. This is the most complex part of this build in terms of theory, and there is a lot more info on these kinds of circuits online.

11. Return to the front of the build and place two opaque blocks, one on top of the DPE and one on the block to the right of this block you just placed. These blocks are what will make up the middle two blocks of your door, aka the blocks that cause all the trouble with 3x3 doors.

12. Place a Repeater facing left and set to 4 ticks in front of the bottom Piston of the DPE.

13. Place a block to the left of this Repeater (we are using a different color now because this is a separate part of the circuit), and place a Sticky Piston on top of this block facing left.

14. Place a block in front of the head of this Piston, and place a Repeater under this new block. The Repeater should also face left and should be set to 2 ticks. Place one Redstone on the block in front of this Repeater. This is the last block on the far left front edge of the build.

15. Place a block on the far left back corner of the build, and then place a block that is one block up and one block to the right of this new block (see image). Place Redstone on both of these blocks (it will connect to the Redstone you just placed in the last step).

16. Go to the back of the build and put a Repeater set to 4 ticks facing left (so it faces toward the direction of the Pistons in the middle of the build) under the block you just placed last (the one that is one above the base of the build). Place a block directly to the left of this Repeater, and place Redstone Dust on top of this last block.

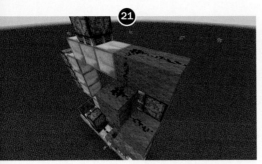

17. Place a block directly above the Redstone you just placed in Step 16 (see image, block should go 3 blocks from the base of the build). This block is important, as it cuts off the signal from the Redstone beneath it to areas of the build that should not receive it. You can now go back to the front of the build and place a Lever on the block to the right of the Redstone Repeater in the middle of the build and flip it to see the DPE in action. If set up right, it will push two blocks up into the middle of the build when flipped ON, and will retract them when flipped OFF. This is the hardest part of the build, so pat yourself on your back, because it's done!

18. Facing the front of the build, copy the row of 3 blocks and 3 Sticky Pistons seen in the image on the right side of the build. The Pistons should face inward to the blocks you are placing. Then add the top row of 3 blocks, with one Sticky Piston facing down directly into the top middle block. All blocks that you're placing that have a Piston facing into them are part of your door proper.

19. Complete the "circle" of the door by adding 3 more blocks and 3 more inward facing Sticky Pistons on the left side of the build, as seen in the image.

Screenshot: Minecraft®™ & © 2009–2015 Mojang/Notch.

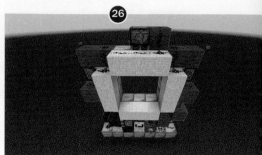

20. Move to the highest block in the front row on the right side of your build (in the image for Step 19 it is the magenta block on the far right of the image, and it also has a Redstone Torch on it facing to the back of the build). Put a Redstone Torch on the very top of this block (it now has two Torches, one on the back and one on the top). Place a block directly above this new Torch (we used a new color block for a new part of the circuit), and put Redstone Dust on top of this block. Don't worry about the Piston that fires here, it's supposed to.

21. Place another block one up and one to the left of the block you just placed, then another block that's one up and one to the back of the build from that new block, and then a third one that is one block to the right of that block as well (see image). Place Redstone Dust on all of these blocks.

22. Place a block to the right of the Piston that is on the top of the build and facing down, and put Redstone on this block (it will connect with what you have just placed).

23. Place 3 blocks, one in front of each of the 3 blocks that make up the top part of the door (the Piston is facing down into the middle block of these 3 top door blocks). Then place one block a block down and to the left of these 3. For the 4 blocks you are placing, you want to use a type of block that you like the look of, because this will be the frame around your door from this side. Place Redstone on all 4 door frame blocks you just placed.

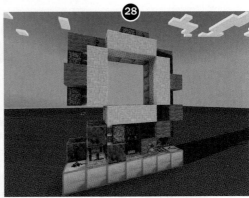

24. Place 2 blocks on the back row of the build as you see in the image (one block up and back from the last block you placed, the one that was one block below the other door frame blocks). These 2 new blocks will be on the same level as the top of the door frame. Place Redstone on both of these blocks (it will connect to the single door frame block below these 2 new blocks).

25. Place one block on the far left front edge of the build and 2 blocks down from the blocks you just placed (see image). Place Redstone on this block. It should connect to the single door frame block that is slightly below the other 3 door frame blocks. Your door is now fully powered!

26. Complete your frame with blocks of the same type, as seen in the image. You'll have to replace the top block on the right side of the frame with a frame block (instead of a circuit-colored block), and you'll need to replace the Redstone Dust on this block when you do so.

27. Go back down to your Lever, and flip it! If you did everything right, the Pistons will fire and the door will open and close as you flip the Lever. Make sure not to flip it too fast, however, as it takes a second to completely open and shut.

28. Congratulate yourself for being a Redstone genius-in-training!

Chapter 4

Mods & More!

Skins, Resource Packs And Shaders:

Making Your Minecraft Pretty

Minecraft is rather unique among games- this is something all players know. One way that it is unique that can sometimes go overlooked, however, is that Minecraft's structure of being mostly blocks with textures on them allows the look of Minecraft to be customized to a degree that few other games have ever seen. Because players and creative folk out in the world can basically take that blocky structure and create their own textures to lay over it, the exact same world and characters can be changed in nearly infinite ways to look differently, making for perhaps the most customizable visuals in any game ever created.

There are three basic components to Minecraft's visuals that can be customized: skins, texture or "resource" packs, and the trickier, but oh so awesome shaders. If you're looking to pretty up your Minecraft game and create an entirely unique look that can sometimes change even a standard Minecraft landscape into something worthy of a million screenshots, here's how you do that.

Skins:

Changing Your Character's Look

By far the easiest facet of your Minecraft visuals to give a facelift to is literally the face (and body) of your Minecraft character. Ole Steve, your standard Minecraft character model, is great and all, but at some point when playing online it gets pretty boring to look like every other schmoe out there. That's when it's time to change your Minecraft skin, and doing so is very, very easy.

How to Change

PC/Mac- Changing your skin on the PC or Mac versions of the games is actually done online through the official Minecraft website. Just head over to minecraft.net and click on the "Profile" button at the top of the screen. Sign into your profile, and the very next page will ask you if you want to change your skin. All you do then is to select one of the two character models (the only difference is that one has slightly skinnier arms), and then you click "Browse" and find the skin file on your computer. After that it's just a matter of uploading the file! Super simple, all around.

Console: Skins on console versions are changed in the game menu when you're in a game. Skins are located under the Help & Options menu, and though you can't upload custom or self-made skins like you can for PC or Mac, there are many, many skinpacks available on console to purchase, most of which have a free trial with a few free skins in them.

Where to Get Skins

Kind of a creepy sentence, no? Well, in this case, we're talkin' the non-fleshy kind of skins, so don't worry. Skins for the PC and Mac version are readily available online in the thousands, and finding them is as simple as heading to a skin database (another creepy phrase!) and just picking one out and downloading it.

A few of the biggest skin databases include Planet Minecraft, The Skindex, MinecraftSkins.net and the SkinCache.

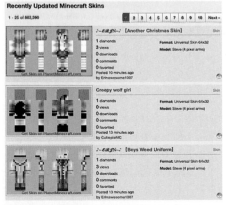

Top: The page on minecraft.net where skins can be changed for PC/Mac/ Linux. Middle: A few minutes on any big Minecraft server will show you the wild variety of skins that are out there. Bottom: A typical selection of fan-made skins on PlanetMinecraft.

Making Your Own Skin

The creepy sentences keep coming! Making your own skin is a pretty simple process, as all skins are actually just a flat image that is wrapped around the character model. A wide variety of programs exists out there to help you create and test skins yourself, and it does not take much time to become a master skinner. Some of the best include NovaSkin, Miners Need Cool Shoes and MCSkinner, the first two of which are actually used completely online in a browser. The Minecraft Wiki has a great list of skinning programs to check out if creating your own look interests you, so just Google "Minecraft skin program," and you'll see the list.

Resource/Texture Packs

Where skins change the look of your character, resource packs, also called texture packs, change the look of the actual blocks in your game. They can also change things like the way Water looks and the way the sky and even the sun and moon appear, making them very powerful tools to create a new experience in your game.

How to Change

PC/Mac- Mojang has included a nice little shortcut in Minecraft to make adding a new resource pack quite easy. Simply start up the game, and then go to Options in the menus. Click on Resource Packs, and then hit the Open Resource Pack Folder button. You'll then need to either quit the game or turn Fullscreen to OFF in the Video settings, and you will see a window open that is the folder named Resource Packs. Then, simply copy-paste the .zip resource pack files that you want to add into the folder!

Console: Like skins, resource packs on the console are limited to the ones that are officially available, but there are quite a few of these out there. On the console, resource packs are officially known as "texture packs," and they

must be loaded before you load the actual game world. It's actually one of the options when you select a world, right there on the screen as you confirm your selection, and you simply pick the one you want. Like skins, you can also purchase extra texture packs if you wish for pretty cheap ($1).

Where to Get Resource/Texture Packs

Resource/texture packs for the PC and Mac can also be found online, again at sites like Planet Minecraft, resourcepack.net, MinecraftTexturePacks.net and Curse's Minecraft Texture Packs page. The Minecraft Forum is perhaps the best place to get packs, as you'll see players upload them and update very frequently, and it provides a great place for other players to post pictures of their worlds with the packs turned on and discuss them.

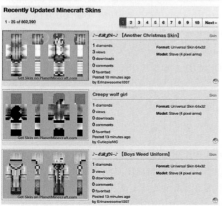

Top: The page on minecraft.net where skins can be changed for PC/Mac/ Linux. Middle: A few minutes on any big Minecraft server will show you the wild variety of skins that are out there. Bottom: A typical selection of fan-made skins on PlanetMinecraft.

Making Your Own Resource Packs

This is also totally possible, though it is much, much more intensive than creating a Minecraft skin. Again, there are a wide variety of

Screenshot: Minecraft®™ & © 2009–2015 Mojang/Notch.

The same scene in a variety of shaders. Particularly note the differences in the Water, the shadows and the way the focus works.

programs out there to help you out with this, and using Google to find the Minecraft Wiki's Resource Pack Creators page is your best bet. Successfully creating a resource pack is a pretty big undertaking however, as you'll need to think carefully about how every texture you create will look in your world and together with the textures of other blocks. We'd suggest using YouTube to get some tutorials on the specific program you choose, which should help tremendously.

Shaders

Shaders are by far the most powerful visuals-changing feature of the game, as they actually change the way that light and pixels are displayed. When you've seen those really gorgeous photos of Minecraft with lots of realistic shadows and lighting effects, they are always created in a Minecraft world that has shaders enabled. It's by far one of the most dramatic ways to change your game, with some players saying that they simply can't go back to playing without shaders on. However, shaders are PC/Mac/Linux only, they're somewhat difficult to install, and they require a pretty powerful computer to be able to run and actually play the game (and not just take a quick screenshot).

How to Change

There are a few built-in shaders for Minecraft on the computer, which can be found by clicking the "Super Secret Settings" button in the menus in-game. However, these are mostly just pixel shaders and not very good to play with. The shaders that people use to actually play the game require that you install the Forge modloader (files and instructions at files.minecraftforge. net), and you then need to install the Shaders Mod (found at http://bit.ly/ ShadersModLink with instructions).

Once this is installed, you'll need to make a shaderpacks folder in your main Minecraft folder (the same place where you find the folders for your screenshots, saves and mods), and then download and place shaderpacks into the shaderpacks folder. Once you've got it all set up like the instructions at the Shaders Mod page tell you, you'll be able to load your Forge mod profile through the Minecraft launcher, open a world, and then hit the ESC key to go to your options. In your Video settings you will now have a Shaders option, where you can select which shader you want to use.

Where to Get Shaders

There aren't nearly as many shaders out there to download as skins and resource packs, but some of our favorites, and the ones used in this book, include Sonic Ether's Unbelievable Shaders, Sildur's Vibrant Shaders, MrMeep_x3's Shaders and DocteurDread's Shaders. Most of these have their own page on the Forums, so just Google the name and you'll find them easily.

Spotlight Corner: Servers And Mods

Nothing gives Minecraft more life, extended playability and new thrills like the servers and mods that users have built around this game. What started as a simple mining game has gone places Notch likely never dreamed of through the work of the intrepid creators on the modding and server designing fronts. In fact, when most players first discover either of these communities, they tend to feel like they're playing an entirely different game, though the blocky graphics tell them that it's still Minecraft.

It might look like Minecraft, but these servers and mods take Minecraft's unbeatable adaptability and turn the game into just about anything that creators can think of. Want to play an MMO version of Minecraft, complete with skill trees, classes, a giant world and quests? That's out there. Feel like a silly Smash Bros. style brawl of quickness and chaos? Definitely exists. Want to turn into a hamster, fly to the moon and create a colony of Pokemon? Those are all mods, and there are servers that host each and every one of them.

This is our list of the mods and servers we think are absolutely killing it right now, and if you or anyone you know have ever expressed boredom with vanilla Minecraft, we'd bet that just a single one of these will get you right back into the blocky fray. These are just a handful of the many, many servers and mods that exist as well, so if you like anything here, chances are there are at least a dozen more out there that you'll dig just as much.

So without further ado, here's our newest edition of the hot mods and servers list to get your little Diamond-loving selves into.

Servers: Worlds Waiting for You Online

As varied as one person's Minecraft world is from another, servers are even crazier. There are plain Survival and Creative servers, role playing servers, competition servers, Factions servers and infinite more variations, and servers can hold as few as 0 other people or as many as 10,000+! It's one of the best parts of Minecraft, and each of the servers in our list here is absolutely worth at least a little peeking around.

2b2t

Server Address: 2b2t.org

So...2b2t is crazy. It is a world where the idea is that anything goes, at all, and it is not supposed to be reset ever. Unfortunately, it was reset once recently, due to the need for an update, but this is actually kind of good because as 2b2t goes along, it gets outright wild. This server is really like no other, and in fact, it's like no other thing in gaming. Because people cheat wildly, grief relentlessly and absolutely wreck the area for thousands of blocks around the spawn, 2b2t's landscape turns into a nightmare wasteland which you will probably not survive. Be warned: 2b2t is not for the faint of heart or the sensitive. You will die, people will attack you and wreck/steal whatever you have, and you will very likely run into some offensive language and behavior here. That being said, it's an experience like no other and completely fun, if you're ready for what awaits you.

Arkham Network

Server Address: mc.arkhamnetwork.org

The Arkham Network consistently comes up in best-of lists for Minecraft servers because it is one of the most well-oiled and fun competitive servers that exist today. You'll almost always find thousands of other players on the Arkham Network no matter when you log in, and it features a semi-rotating crop of the most popular styles of play and mini-games, adding more as they are invented. As Minecraft communities go, this is one of the strongest, and they take entertaining you with mini-games very seriously.

Empire

Server Address: play.emc.gs

It may surprise some of you to learn that the server in these images, Empire Minecraft, is actually a Survival server. Yes, it looks like a Creative Mode server, but that's because Empire employs a very interesting system wherein players live in a Survival world, but are given plots of protected land within a giant town on the server. So, though players can die and explore the world like a normal survival server outside of town, they end up building enormous, oft-amazing creations within the huge city that has built up in Empire. Additionally, there are other add-ons to vanilla Minecraft to be found here, including new mobs and bosses and an economy system.

Typically images like these would come from Creative servers, but Empire is a special place! Their unique rules and world structure allows for awesome town plots like these in a Survival Mode server.

One of the best parts of big servers like Arkham network is that everything from the hub to the mini-game maps is professionally designed and looks amazing.

Extronus

Server Address: pvp.extronus.net

Most servers choose either vanilla Minecraft, Creative Mode or do many mini-games, but not Extronus. No, here the players are about one thing and one thing only: Factions. A part of the Arkham Network that has grown into its own thing, Extronus takes this mini-game to the extreme by creating an entire, thriving server dedicated to it, and the culture there is pretty intensely into the game.

Extronus' Factions zones are very nicely designed with interesting aesthetics like this ice world look, as opposed to the typical vanilla world that many Factions servers contain.

There are actually a few Factions servers rolled into one server hub here, each of which has an awesome aesthetic theme that has been handcrafted, such as the ice world you see in the photo. As they say in Extronus "Choose YOUR path and build your Empire."

Hypixel

Server Address: mc hyplxel net

The great Hypixel's personally hosted server, hypixel.net is another quality competition/PvP server and one of the more frequented servers period online. Since it is run by one of the bigger personalities in the game, you'll often find "celeb" players here as well as a very well-updated list of mini-games and competitions. Plus, because of the quality of folks involved, everything in it runs very smoothly and looks incredible! In fact, many mini-games were actually created specifically for this server, like the Blitz game we profile in our Mini-Games chapter of this book. Hypixel's home is a benchmark server for other servers, in that it's where trends are born and server methods are perfected, so why not spend a little time at one of the web's best locations?

Few servers can boast either hubs as gorgeous as Hypixel's or mini-games as fun and creative.

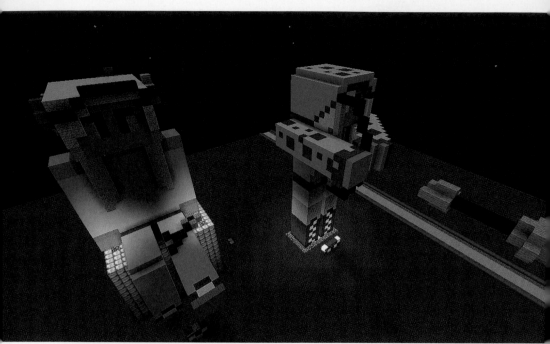

A personal favorite of this author, Lichcraft is a server that has just about every major mode and does all of it well.

Lichcraft

Server Address: us.lichcraft.com

Consistently ranked among the top(if not at the top) servers online, Lichcraft is similar to Hypixel and the Arkham Network but with a few different games to play, including Survival, Skygrid, kit PVP, Duels, Prison, MineZ and an excellent couple of Factions servers that are well populated and nicely run. It's just a solid server all around, and that's why it continues to be one of the best-known and most frequented servers in the game.

MindCrack

Server Address: us.playmindcrack.com

There are actually two MindCrack servers (at least): the private one played on by Guude and the other members of the famous MindCrack Network, which is the subject of many incredibly popular YouTube video series', and then the public MindCrack server, which is this one. While it's pretty hard to get an invitation to the private MindCrack server, the public server is an example of the highest quality server that a regular Minecrafter can get on. Not only can you tour the maps from old seasons of the MindCrack video series', literally stepping virtual foot where some of the best Crafters in the world once built, you can also play the mini-games created by this untouchably talented crew of builders and YouTubers. Many of the great Redstone engineer SethBling's mini-game creations are tested first on this server, such as the wild and explosive Missile Wars game he created with Cubehamster, and indeed most of the mini-games found here are not seen elsewhere. Along with 2b2t, Hypixel and WesterosCraft, the MindCrack server sits among online royalty when it comes to public servers.

Here you see the team select for the awesome Mineplex Arcade, and the image above is of one of the games featured in said Arcade. In this game every player looks like a Villager and is in a sea of real Villagers. You have to try and figure out who is real and kill them, and every so often everyone changes into their normal form for a few seconds. Super fun!

Mineplex

Server Address: us.mineplex.com

A top mini-game server, Mineplex typically is one of the very busiest servers, often with over 10,000 players online at a time. In fact, at the time of this writing it has a whopping 13,354 Minecrafters on it enjoying the entertainments it has to offer. Mineplex is professionally run, with server hosts that really pay attention to the desires of their virtual denizens and who are constantly adding new features, tweaking things to be better and throwing special events just to make things that much more fun. Maybe one of the best features on any server is Mineplex's Arcade, where they mix up a ton of fun mini-games that play one after the other, so you only have to load into a lobby once.

Treasure Island

Server Address: ticreative org

Treasure Island is actually a collection of servers, like many of the others on this list, and it hosts many of the popular styles from PvP to Skyblock, but for here we're focusing on the subserver that focuses on Creative Mode. This is because the Treasure Island Creative server is incredible when it comes to the amount and quality of builds that can be found there. In

Treasure Island takes Creative Mode quite seriously, as is readily apparent when you spend a little time around the 0,0 coordinates, where most of the oldest and best plots are located.

fact, Treasure Island goes so far as to have a whole series of islands to build on and a system where players can judge other players' creations and give them points that earn ranks. The higher rank you are, the more islands you have access to build on, meaning that some islands are exclusively built on by those players that the community deems to be most skilled.

WesterosCraft

Server Address: mc.westeroscraft.com,
but has its own special launcher that should be used

Now, there are probably other servers out there with builders as skilled and dedicated as those at WesterosCraft, but frankly, we've never seen one that beats it. If you want an example of what a truly talented and committed group of people can do with their time, this is the server that you want to check out. The idea is that they are building a detail-oriented replica of the world from the A Song of Ice and Fire books and the Game of Thrones TV show, including both the giant continent of Westeros and the bigger continent of Essos. This project has been going along for years, and they've built an area that is, as they say, about the size of Los Angeles in real life. While the locations they've painstakingly crafted are all stunning, perhaps even more impressive are the incredible server testing grounds located around the 3D map of the world, where the master builders that put this server together try out their creations before doing them for real. If you want to learn how to be a better builder in any way, from the creation of buildings all the way down to trees (they have a whole forest of tester trees, each in its own labeled square, and it's quite beautiful), you could not do better than to spend some time just flying over the WesterosCraft testing grounds. Good people of WesterosCraft, the writers of this book salute your efforts as truly awesome in the original sense of the word.

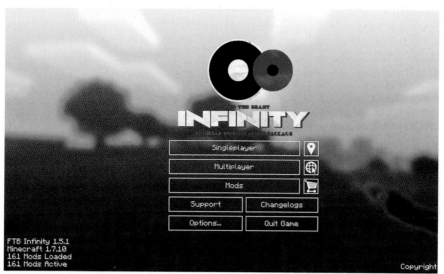

If you've done your work right, you should be seeing custom modded versions of Minecraft just like this one in no time flat!

How To Install Your Mods

Right, so here's the one tricky bit when it comes to mods: Installing mods can be a bit of a pain.

Mods are just plain fun, once you get them installed, that is. We think that the experiences in modded Minecraft are as good as any others in gaming, bar none, and a lot of people out there agree with us.

That being said, getting a mod installed can (but won't always) take a bit of work.

Typically it's not hard at all. Most Minecraft mods are loaded the same way, and you just have to learn it once to get it forever. Those kinds of mods go through the Forge program, where you only have to worry about making sure all mods are for the same version of Minecraft and that you put the mod into the correct folder.

It's only a matter of time before you start seeing Minecraft's world in a whole new way.

Sometimes, though, it takes a little doing. Each computer is different, and each situation is unique when getting a mod working, both for the computer and for the mod. This book and this chapter can guide you to a point, but it's so different from one mod to the next that you always want to read the mod's instructions on its page and follow them to the letter. Luckily almost all mod creators include detailed instructions at the mod's link, and we've included the links to every mod in this book, so you should be able to easily find each mod's specific installation instructions.

Sometimes even that isn't enough, though, and there's always the chance that you might have to ask for help in the Minecraft Forums or on the mod's page. Don't hesitate to do that, though remember to remain polite. This is also part of the mod culture; mods are made by fans, so they're rarely an exact science, and getting mods to run is a traditional part of the experience for all games, and all gamers seeking to mod them. Each mod has an online presence somewhere, and if you have the time to invest in it, you will be able to get almost every mod running on your own rig.

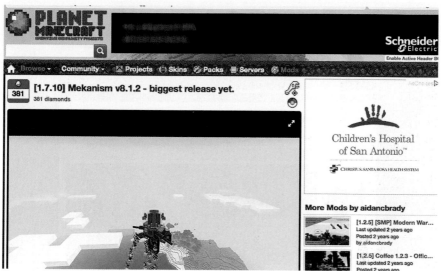

You'll become very familiar with pages like this one when you start getting into modding.

The hope is that you'll be able to avoid doing too much work for a mod, though. A little instruction in basic mod installation will be all you need 80% of the time, and that's what we've got for you here.

Where to Get Mods

We've included a link to every mod in this book (except for the ones that go through a modloader, which don't require a link), but in general when looking for a mod, there are four locations at which you'll find most mods:

Planet Minecraft: The prime directory of all Minecraft creations, including maps, texture packs and, as is most pertinent to this book, mods. The vast majority of mods have a Planet Minecraft page that has a link to download them, info about the mod, photos, and/or video of the mod and a comment section. Not all PMC profiles are kept totally up-to-date, however, though many are.

The Minecraft Forums are an indispensible resource for anyone interested in mods, as you can not only get mods there, you can also learn how to install them and speak to the creators and community, which is especially great if you're having any trouble getting a mod to run.

The Minecraft Forum: The Minecraft Forum is the other primary website where mods keep a major presence, along with Planet Minecraft. Though they are a bit less formal of a project-holding site, in that the entries for the mods are just forum posts (though often well-structured and heavily informed ones). At the current time it is more common for a mod to have an up-to-date, well-crafted Minecraft Forum post than a good Planet Minecraft post. Often, though, the big mods have both. In this book you'll find more Minecraft Forum links than any other, and you won't go wrong from following one, when it comes to getting mods working.

The Curse Page: The Curse company is extensively involved in online gaming, and they have a major presence within the Minecraft community. Not only does the Minecraft Wiki, the prime repository for Minecraft knowledge online, fall under the Curse banner, Curse also hosts downloads for many Minecraft mods. A lot of the big mods have a Curse page in addition to a PMC and/ or Minecraft Forum page. Though these don't have the comment section interaction or the pure Minecraft focus that the other mod links have, Curse pages are very reliable and consistently updated, and some mod creators consider their Curse page to be the best one to share with potential users.

This is an example of an individual mod creator page for the lovely food mod Still Hungry! Using these pages is one great way to help mod creators out a bit.

Individual Mod Creator Pages: Mod creators don't make a lot of money doing what they do. They work on a game that already makes its money separately, and the only way they get compensated is from user donations or from getting hits on their mod links. By far the best way to support mod creators is to use their own website to download a mod, as it will directly reflect on hits on their site and will direct you to the download link that pays them the most , both of which earn them money. Not only that, but creators' websites always have the up-to-the-minute download info, updates and guides to mods, so they are always preferable when it comes to getting a new mod.

The rule is this: Google it, and try to find the personal page for the mod creator. If you can't, go with PMC, the Minecraft Forum, or Curse. Avoid most other sites at all costs, as few good mods have no presence at the main sites, and there are definitely sites out there with some dubious downloads on offer.

The links you need for forge are down at the bottom of this page. There are a few different ones, but the Install link typically is the best one.

Forge really is quite simple to install, especially since it tells you if you did it right at the end!

Forge: The Program That Makes Most Mods Work

http://files.minecraftforge.net/

The first step to getting Minecraft mods going on your computer is to install the Forge mod loading program.

To do this, you'll have to download the Forge installer from the link above and then run it. At the link above, simply scroll down to the "Downloads" section, and then pick the version of Minecraft you would like to run mods in. Note: this is most likely going to be Minecraft 1.8, 1.7.10, or 1.6.4. If you decide you want to run mods for a different version of Minecraft later, you'll just come back to this link and download and install that one.

To actually download the file, make sure you've clicked on the version you want, and then look below where it says "Download Recommended" (if it only says "Download Latest," look there instead). Click the "Installer" button (Windows users can also just use the Installer-win" button, but either will work), and then save the file to your computer.

Before you open that file and install it, you need to make sure that you have opened Minecraft at least once. Most likely you already have, but if you're jumping right into modding, make sure you open the game first and then close out again. This must be done because certain files and folders Forge needs aren't created until Minecraft runs for the first time.

When that's done, run the file you downloaded from Forge. It will pop up a window asking if you want to "Install Client," "Install Server," or "Extract." Select "Install Client," and ignore the file location at the bottom and just hit OK. It should then show that it's downloading and installing Forge, and if you did it right, you'll see it tell you that it was successful.

On a Mac, this is the menu you want to drop down while pressing the "alt" key in order to find the Library. On a PC, use the Run program and type in "%AppData%/.minecraft" to find the Minecraft folder.

Finding and Installing Mods for Forge

To actually get mods loaded into Forge, you will need to do a few things.

1. Get some mods! This is the easy part- just go to one of the links in this book, or head to Planet Minecraft, the Minecraft Forums, or the Curse webpage and search around for mods. There are tons on each of these, and a good idea for which to pick is to go with those that have a lot of downloads (each site lists these differently, though for the Forums you'll just have to look at how many comments the mod's page has instead of download numbers). Make sure that you are getting the correct mod for the version of Forge you have installed (and remember that you can always download and install other versions of Forge).

Note: When installing mods for the first time, you should always add just one mod at a time. This way if a mod causes Minecraft to crash, you know which one did it. In fact, we highly recommend that you only install one mod period for your first go at modded Minecraft, and wait until you get the hang of how to install mods before adding any more to a single game.

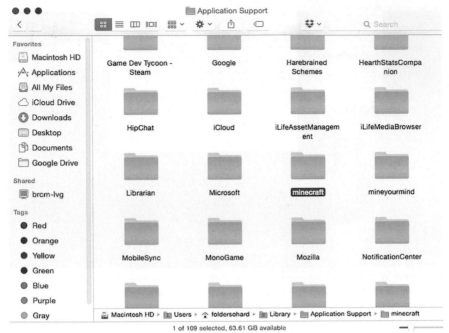

Macintosh HD ▸ ▒ Users ▸ ⌂ foldersohard ▸ ▒ Library ▸ ▒ Application Support ▸ ▒ minecraft

1 of 109 selected, 63.61 GB available

There's that pesky Minecraft folder! You'll be coming back to this a lot if you get into modding, so remember how to find it quickly to save time.

2. Find the mods folder. To run a Forge mod, you have to put it in a folder called "mods" inside the "minecraft" folder on your computer. There are two ways to find this folder:

A. Locate it manually by finding the folder at the following location, depending on your operating system:
- **Windows:** C:\Users\You\AppData\Roaming\.minecraft or %AppData%\.minecraft
- **Linux:** ~/.minecraft
- **Mac:** ~/Library/Application Support/minecraf

For Windows, you can open "Run" and simply type "%AppData%\.minecraft" into it, and it will bring it up.

Clicking that "Open resource pack folder" button can help you find the Minecraft folder if you're having a little trouble.

For Mac, open a Finder window, and navigate to the Library folder by holding the "alt" key and clicking "Go" up in the top menu bar. This will show the Library folder as an option; click on that, and then "Application Support," and then "minecraft."

B. Run Minecraft, and go to "Options." Click "Resource Packs," and then "Open resource pack folder." This is easiest done when in "Windowed" mode and not Fullscreen, but either way it will open up the "resource packs" folder in a new window in your operating system. All you have to do then is to go up one folder to the folder "resource packs" is in, and you're in the "minecraft" folder.

3. Move mods into the "mods" folder. In the "minecraft" folder, there should be an empty folder called "mods." If you don't see this, go ahead and create it now. Once you've found it or created it, all you have to do is move the .jar file that you downloaded for each mod into the "mods" folder. Don't open or extract these files, just move them as they are. If the mod file is not a .jar, and is a .zip, you may need to extract the .zip and get the .jar out of it, and then move that over to the "mods" folder.

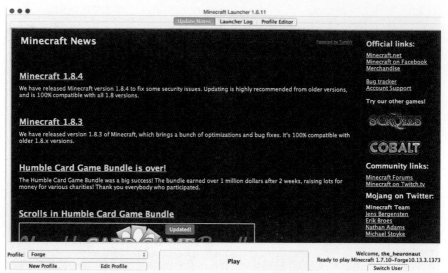

Note the "Forge" profile loaded in the left corner, and the mention of Forge in the right-hand corner as well. This is a Minecraft game that's ready to play some mods!

4. Open the Minecraft launcher and select the Forge profile. When you open the Minecraft launcher, you'll see on the bottom left that there is an option to change which "Profile" you are running. To run mods, you'll need to select and run the Forge profile, which should automatically show up there after you've installed Forge. Note: If you need to, you can click "New Profile" and create a Forge profile yourself. To do this, you'll need to click the "Use version:" dropdown menu and then select the version of Forge you want to run. This can be useful to do if you want to have multiple Forge versions on your computer at once, creating a different profile for each.

5. Check the corner of the launcher. If it says "Ready to play Minecraft" and then something that includes the word "Forge" after it, you're ready to go!

6. Click "Play," and launch Minecraft! If it worked, you will see the regular Minecraft menu (or a new one, depending on the mod), but there will be information in the bottom left hand corner that says Forge is loaded and gives a count of the mods you have running.

7. Start a game! You can usually tell if mods are working by checking the Inventory screen.

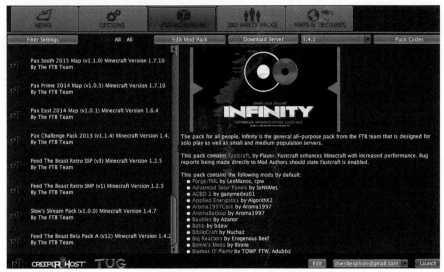

This is what the Feed the Beast mod loader looks like. A little different from regular Minecraft, and it makes loading up complex modpacks a breeze.

Other Ways to Install Mods

Forge is by far the most commonly used program to run mods, but there are two other ways, the first of which is also pretty well-used by mod players.

1. The Technic and Feed the Beast Launchers: These are two programs that you can use instead of the regular Minecraft launcher, and each makes it very easy to load mods or modpacks. All you have to do is download the file for each launcher, and then open it (only run one at a time, of course) and log into your Minecraft account (the same login you use normally).

There will be a list of mods that you can choose from, and all you have to do to play one is to select it and tell the launcher to "Play" or "Launch." It will then do all of the downloading, installing and launching for you, and should kick you right into the modded game. If something goes wrong, try launching again, and if that doesn't work, head to the Technic or FTB sites to get assistance (they have a lot of people there to help).

This is the Technic loader, another major mod loader with a set of stellar mods and packs to play.

2. Manual installation: Mods can be installed manually without Forge or a launcher, and in fact that's how people used to have to do it before all of these convenient launchers and loaders existed. The instructions to do this are pretty complicated though, and it's easy to mess up your game doing so. If you're interested in doing things the hard way, this is easy to Google, but we highly recommend using one of the more standard ways of installing mods.

Mixing Mods- A Few Tips

Some mods are big enough that people often play them on their own, but for the most part, people run more than one mod at the same time. We've touched on this a little bit throughout this chapter, but here are some tips to get the best experience when it comes to mixing mods:

- Always make sure all mods are for the same version of Minecraft.

- Always make sure you are running the correct version of Forge for your mods.

When you get mods going and actually get in the game, you can tell which ones loaded in correctly by checking the "Mods" button on the menu, which will get you a big list like this one.

- Install one mod at a time, and run Minecraft between each installation to make sure it works. This will show you which mod is breaking your game if it won't load, something that is very frustrating and tedious to figure out if you have loaded a ton of mods at once.

- Don't overload your computer. Very powerful computers can run a lot of mods at once, but anything less than top-of-the-line models will have trouble the more mods you load in. Keep it at a reasonable level for the kind of machine you have in order to make sure your game runs smoothly.

- Check online for lists of mods that work well together. Many mod creators actually list a few that work well with their mod on their mod's page, and other players have created lists online that go even further.

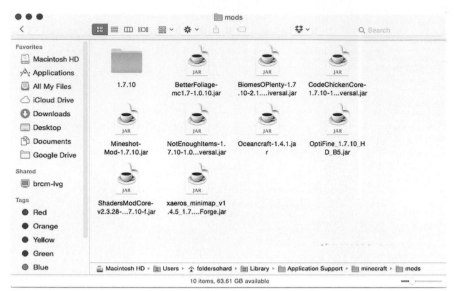

What the mods folder can look like when you get a bunch of mods loaded into it correctly.

Troubleshooting Mods in General

Sometimes a mod just won't work, and there doesn't seem to be a reason why. You can do everything right in installing it, and it can still cause issues in your game or even cause it not to load at all.

This happens, and while each situation will be different, we can give you a few tips for if it happens to you:

* Make sure you know which mod is causing the crash. Remove all other mods and test it alone. If it works alone, it may be conflicting with another mod. If it still doesn't, you know which mod is the culprit.

* Save any information that Minecraft gives you when it crashes. It will usually give a crash report, and may even give an error in the game.

Sometimes mods will crash; that's ok! It happens to everyone, and it usually just means that one or more of your mods are in conflict with another, so you just have to figure out which mods aren't playing well together.

- Check the mod page. Someone else has probably had the same problem you are having, and there is always a lot of discussion on fixes in the comments on Planet Minecraft and the Minecraft Forums. Check there before asking for help.

- Google the problem as well. Sometimes the best troubleshooting discussions are on other pages away from the mod page.

- If you still have trouble, try posting your own request in the Forums. Don't direct message the mod creator though, they tend to hate this and are less likely to get back to you. When you post, make sure to include all information you can about the mod, what version you're trying to run, what computer you are on, what the game said when it crashed and anything else you can think of that might be relevant. Oh, and be nice and patient! People are there to help you, but they won't want to if you are a pest.

Utility Mods
Tweaking the Interface and More

Utility Mods are those mods that don't actually add any blocks, biomes, items, mobs, systems, or any other physical changes to the game of Minecraft, but which instead add something to the user interface or otherwise just make the game easier to use and play.

For instance, one of the most popular Utility Mod types is the minimap, which (as you might suspect) adds a little map to the corner of your game, making it much easier to navigate the wild world of Minecraft. Other mods might make finding out information about items easier, or help you find something in the world (like the Horse Locator mod we'll talk about in this chapter).

Most of these mods are very lightweight, meaning they're easy to install, don't change a lot about the game and don't take a lot of computer power to run, and they're all thoroughly useful in their own respective ways. Because of this, Utility Mods are among the most commonly used mods by Minecraft players, and you'll often hear about people using them or find them stuck into modpacks.

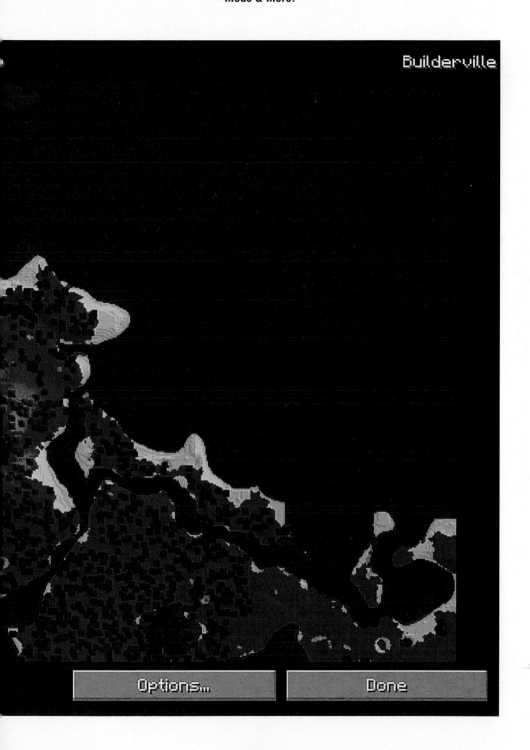

Builderville

Options...

Done

X-Ray Mod

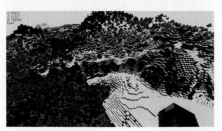

In one sentence: Lets you toggle the ability to see through blocks (whichever ones you want!).

Creator: AmbientOcclusion

Version: 1.6.4-1.8.1

Installed Through: Manually- Forge, LiteLoader, Technic

Where you can find it:

http://bit.ly/XRayModMinecraft

Complexity Level: 1.5 Diamonds

One of the very hardest parts of Minecraft is finding what you need in the wide, confusing worlds you create. Whether it's a special kind of resource, a structure like a cave or a fortress, a mob or another player that's sneaking around, or even your own base (if you got a little lost, as we all can do at times), the X-Ray Mod can help you look right through all the blocks around you to find it.

This mod is toggled on and off with a single key and works very quickly without a lot of drag on your system, and it also can be configured to see through only the blocks you want it to. In other words, if you care about Redstone but don't need Iron right now, you can set this mod to just look for Redstone and to look right through Iron. This can be done to most kinds of blocks, making the X-Ray Mod one of the most powerful tools to save time and energy that's out there. However, using this mod is not okay on all servers, as some consider it cheating. Make sure you use this only on your own worlds or on servers that specifically allow it. No one wants to get the banhammer dropped on their head!

Horse Locator

In one sentence: Finds your horse for you!

Version: 1.7.10

Installed Through: Forge (manually)

Where you can find it:

http://bit.ly/HorseLocator

Complexity Level: 1 Diamond

: Horse Tamed? [false]   × You can hide/unhide this GUI by pressing F9. ×
Owner: none
Baby Horse? [false]
Coords: X: -19 | Y: 70 | Z: -744
^Away: 9 | Y^Away: 0 | Z^Away: -2
Jmp: 3.45 | Speed: 12.85 | HP:

This mod is for everyone who loves horses in Minecraft, or really just anyone who wants to find one easily. This is a super-lightweight mod that simply adds a little bit of text to the corner of your window to tell you when horses are near. It gives a description of the horse, tells you if it belongs to someone and who, and shows you how far away it is. Once you've actually claimed a horse, you can then use it to find it again no matter where it is. Never lose your horsey pal again!

Horse Locator

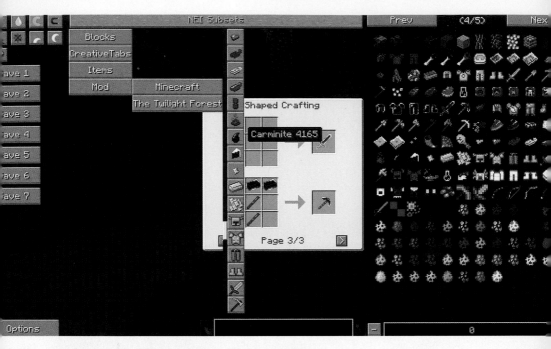

Not Enough Items

In one sentence: A very powerful utility mod that is mostly for gaining information on items (including those from other mods) such as recipes and the like, but which can also do things like save and load inventories, change the weather and time and more.

Version: Pretty much all from 1.8 and back

Installed Through: Forge (manually) NOTE: You need both the NEI download and the CodeChickenCore file installed in your mods folder for this mod to work

Where you can find it:

http://bit.ly/NotEnoughItemsForum, http://bit.ly/NotEnoughItemsDownloadsPage

Complexity Level: 3 Diamonds

Mods & More!

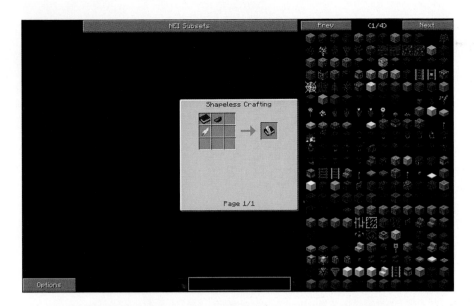

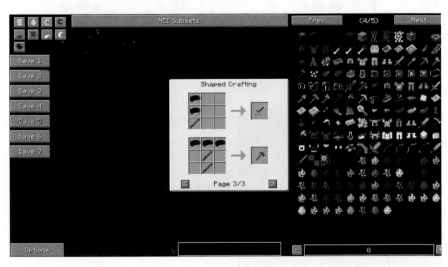

Zan's Minimap/VoxelMap

In one sentence: A highly customizable, very powerful but lightweight mini-map that can show you just about anything you want including mobs and user-set waypoints.

Version: 1.6.4/1.7.10/1.8

Installed Through: Forge (manually)

Where you can find it:

http://bit.ly/VoxelMapLink

Complexity Level: 1.5 Diamonds

When it comes to minimaps, the VoxelMap (also sometimes known as Zan's minimap) is not only among the most popular, but also the most powerful and customizable. The basic use is that it adds a minimap to the corner of your

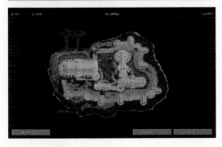

screen, but it doesn't stop there. You can go into the options for VoxelMap, which also reveals a much larger version of the map (another great feature) and change a huge number of things, including whether it shows mobs (and which kinds, even down to specific mobs) or biomes, has a chunk grid or shows other players, among many other options. You can also change the size and shape, and you can even add named and colored waypoints that will show up both on the big and small map, making it very easy to find things again. This is a beast of a map mod, and it's no surprise that it is very commonly used by Minecraft players.

Item Mods
More Things, More Fun!

Minecraft is a game built around a few key things: mobs, blocks, and items. In that last category, many different types of items can be found, ranging from those that help the player interact with the world (such as tools and weapons) to those that manipulate other blocks and items in crafting systems, to food, to those that are mostly there for fun and looks.

This chapter deals mostly with those last two categories and the mods that specifically add more food and fun items to the game. This is because most of the mods that add things like new tools and weapons or crafting systems fit better into the categories of Combat mods and Magic, Tech and Crafting Systems, as the mods they come in are more specifically geared toward those subjects.

There are, however, many other mods whose sole purpose is to bring a swarm of new items into the game that aren't predominantly about laying waste to foes or adding in a new, complex crafting system. These mods are more about the items they bring themselves, which serve to add a little flavor, color and aesthetically pleasing attributes to Minecraft builds. Or in the case of the TNT Mod, to give you new ways to blow up all that cute stuff you or someone else built, which is some fun all in itself. Here are seven of the best mods that will give you dozens upon dozens of new items to play around with and use to make your creations more perfectly realized.

Mr. Crayfish Furniture Mod

Creator: Mr. Crayfish

In one sentence: A mod that's all about decking your home out in furniture, and with an aesthetic that's made to look like it fits right in with regular vanilla Minecraft.

Version: 1.6.4, 1.7.2, 1.7.10
Installed Through: Forge (manually)

Where you can find it:
http://bit.ly/MrCrayfishFurnitureMod

Complexity Level: 2 Diamonds

Adds Items?: Yes

Mr. Crayfish's Furniture Mod consistently ranks in the Top 5 Minecraft mods on the Planet Minecraft page, because it does what it does well, efficiently and in a way that makes it seems like it fits right into regular Minecraft. Many mods add a whole new thing into Minecraft that look out of place in the regular game, which can also be fun, but Mr. Crayfish has done a very good job to make his furniture items have the same look and feel of regular Minecraft items, while greatly expanding what you can add to your home.

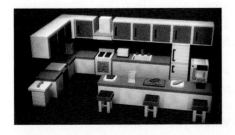

Speaking of what you can add, it's basically everything you'd expect from a regular real-world house, like a fridge, chairs of different types, sinks, blinds, tables, lighting, radios, computers, TVs, and even some weirder stuff like bushes and fire detectors. This is one of those mods that you'll find on a lot of servers, and it's very lightweight, so it's an excellent addition for those wanting to kick their regular home up a notch without changing the game too much.

DecoCraft

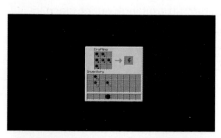

Creator: ProfMobius, RazzleberryFox, Noppes and the DecoCraft team

In one sentence: Brings a set of items called "Deco Clay" into the game, with which you can craft many different decorative items.

Version: 1.6.4, 1.7.2, 1.7.10
Installed Through: Forge (manually) or through the Technic Pack
Where you can find it:
bit.ly/DecoCraftModLink

Complexity Level: 2.5 Diamonds
Adds Items?: Yes

Quirky and cute is the name of the game with the DecoCraft mod which is chock full of items that fit that description, most of which are meant to lend your home a little fun and personality. There are objects for both indoors (beds, toys, lighting, plumbing, decorations etc.) and outdoors (signs, things to make a park, outdoor decorations), and all of them are crafted using various combinations of different colors of Deco Clay.

The Deco folks take decoration in the game to new heights, and are also quite good at utilizing their own creations on their server, where they have built some great spaces nicely filled with the Deco items.

Still Hungry!

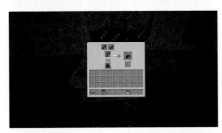

Creator: 17CupsofCoffee, DizzyAlyx, and BethW08

In one sentence: A culinary experience inside of Minecraft, adding a new cooking station, cider and beer making and 60+ new food items.

Version: 1.7.2, 1.7.4, 1.7.10
Installed Through: Forge (manually)
Where you can find it
http://bit.ly/StillHungryMod

Complexity Level: 2.5 Diamonds
Adds Items?: Yes

Edibles is another place where vanilla Minecraft chooses simplicity and few options over a more complex system. Still Hungry makes the days of choosing between a few meats, bread, and soup history, adding in not just a

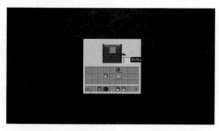

grocery store worth of food, but also the options to get complex with your cooking.

Much of the new gastronomic wonder of this mod comes from a new crafting system for food done through the Stove item added by Still Hungry. It's got a couple slots for combinations of food, which are cooked in Frying Pans or Mugs. Cider and beer can also be concocted with Barrels, which we don't hate one bit. When you're done and ready to head out for the day, you can also take your meal with you in a Lunchbox that stores up to 6 different food items, saving the rest of your valuable inventory space for other cool junk.

Nomnomnom indeed.

Land & Biome Design Mods
A Better View

Minecraft's many biomes are lovely, excitin' places to get your dig-and-build on, but after a little while exploring the swamps, mesas, forests, deserts, and more that vanilla 'Craft has to offer, you do start to wonder what the world of Minecraft would be like if it was just a little more varied.

Enter the land and biome design mods, whose sole purpose is to take that vanilla landscape and turn it into something more complex, varied and simply awesome. These mods run the gamut from those that add new biomes into Minecraft that generate the same way the regular ones do, but contain a different, new set of plants and an all-new look, to those that change the land in more specific ways, such as adding new features to existing biomes. There's even one that plants a dang new dimension right into your vanilla world, which essentially acts like a separate, magical biome replete with its own flora and fauna that's accessed by a secret portal! It's, quite literally, a whole new world out there with land and biome design mods, and it's just waiting for you to load it up and step into it.

Biomes o' Plenty

Creator: Glitchfiend

In one sentence: New biomes, and plenty of 'em, even in the Nether!

Version: 1.6.4-1.8

Installed Through: Forge (manually)

Where you can find it:
http://bit.ly/BiomesOPlentyMod

Complexity Level: 2 Diamonds

Adds Items?: Yes

Adds Mobs?: No

75 new biomes. Yep, that is not a typo, this mod adds 75 entire new biomes to your vanilla Minecraft world. That's 75 new biomes to play in, dig up, and build giant bases in, and many of 'em have a whole new set of plants and materials to turn into cool new stuff. It's a veritable smorgasbord of plants and pretty landscapes. It's especially spectacular with shader mods, and for those of you who are all about the exploration, the Next Horizon style Crafters, this is the one you want. It even goes so far as to add a bunch of neat stuff to the Nether which, let's face it, could use a facelift.

The Twilight Forest

Creator: Benimatic

In one sentence: A new, fantastical dimension of glimmering dusk adventures through a magical forest, complete with fascinating creatures, an adventure to follow and all manner of new plants and blocks to discover.

Version: 1.7.10 and way back
Installed Through: Forge (manually) or through the FTB Launcher
Where you can find it:
http://bit.ly/TwilightForestPage

Complexity Level: 3.5 Diamonds
Adds Items?: Yes
Adds Mobs?: Yes

The Twilight Forest mod is one of our very favorites, as it is just so darn enchanting. As opposed to other biome mods, this one is not just randomly created in the world; you actually have to build a portal to it and jump in. Once you do that, you'll find yourself surrounded by what might be the most aesthetically wonderful realm in all of modded Minecraft, with its own set of biomes and areas, not to mention unique mobs and things to experience. It truly is the premier fantasy environment in Minecraft, and it feels like you just stepped into the pages of a 1970s fantasy adventure novel, or the land of the movie Legend.

Once you do step into this perpetual twilight land, you'll notice immediately that everything is different. Deer and Fireflies and Bighorns roam the land, and the towering trees are not even a bit like the ones from regular Minecraft. There is also much to fear in this new world, which will throw over a dozen new hostile mobs at you, such as the Kobold and Swarm Spider or bosses like the Naga, Hydra, and Lich.

There is a bit of an RPG element to the story of this land, as well as to its aesthetic, as it is set up to have a progression from boss to boss, and the land itself is designed to draw you through these progressions. Along the way you'll find well over a hundred new blocks and items to mine, manipulate, craft and master, all with a fantasy bent and totally fun to discover. It is a beautiful place and a beautiful mod, and it's one every Crafter who has ever been interested in fantasy should check out.

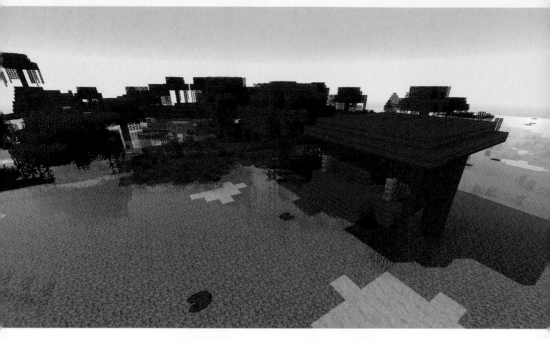

OceanCraft

Creator: thomassu

In one sentence: Utterly transforms the ocean biome into a much more dynamic place, full of life and with many new craft-ready blocks, plus an overhauled generation system.

Version: 1.5.2, 1.6.4, 1.7.2, 1.7.10
Installed Through: Forge (manually)
Where you can find it:
http://bit.ly/OceanCraftModLink
Complexity Level: 2.5 Diamonds
Adds Items?: Yes
Adds Mobs?: Yes

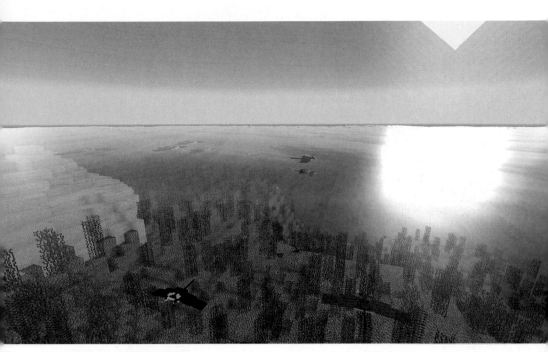

The Oceancraft mod could easily fit into the Mobs or Adventure Enhancer chapters, because it adds so many creatures and general things to experience to your game, but because it is so biome-centric, and it also heavily manipulates the spawning of that biome, it fits best here in this book. Oceancraft is the beach-lover's dream come true in Minecraft, taking the regular, pretty boring seascape of the game and making it much more like the real beach.

The life of the ocean is a major part of this mod, with Crabs, Orcas, Sea Turtles and all manner of ocean-faring mobs added, and it doesn't shirk the plantlife either, adding a wide variety of water fauna. Coral is also a big part of this mod, being a new craftable material in the vein of ores, allowing for armor and tools to be made of its pink porous self. Speaking of items, Oceancraft has many, all sticking to its oceanic theme.

Oceancraft even adds new generated structures and land, from the way the floor of the sea looks itself to new ground structures near it, such as the huts of the Beachvillager. While this mod is by no means the most extensive or comprehensive mod, it does manage to massively enhance one very particular biome in a way few other mods do, and it makes it heaps more fun to live by the sea in Minecraft.

Combat Mods

Turning the Fights Up a Notch

Minecraft is a rare game in that combat is more a side thing and not the main focus of the game, but that is really only true in vanilla Minecraft. Even in plain ole 'Craft, people do get up to quite a lot of bashin' and smashin', and if you go to just about any online server, the amount of battling you do goes up quite a large amount. Even though Minecraft isn't really built around combat, people have come up with some really awesome ways to do PvP in this game, and have gotten really good at it, and in no part of the game is that more true than when it comes to mod-aided Minecraft combat.

Combat mods come in a lot of shapes and sizes, from those that just add a few little weapons, to those that deal more with helping you get more information about combat, to those that totally overhaul the whole weapons and fighting systems. Here, you'll find all of these types, as we've collected a group of mods that represent the best of the combat mods available today.

Better PvP

Creator: xaero96

In one sentence: Gives you stats and other information on combat and combat-related things through the user interface, plus Xaero's minimap and some handy tweaks to make things like running and eating food much easier.

Version: 1.7.10, 1.8
Installed Through: Forge (manually)
Where you can find it:
http://bit.ly/BetterPVP
Complexity Level: 1.5 Diamonds

Adds Items?: No
Adds Mobs?: No

This might be considered a utility mod, if it weren't so specifically for use in combat. Better PvP is designed to give you much, much more information on combat situations than you would normally have. Better PvP adds info like weapon and armor status, potion effects, Arrow counts, and enchantment statuses, as well as giving indicators of quick combat events, such as when you're being shot by arrows, when you gain or lose XP, or when something is about to explode near you. Additionally, this thing will cut down on your need to jump in and out of inventory or use inefficient button combinations in combat by giving you options like binding food eating to a certain key or making sprinting much easier.

And to sweeten the deal, Xaero includes his very good little minimap (which you can find on its own in our Utility Mods chapter) with Better PvP, which is highly useful in combat both for its ability to show the enemies and land around and for its feature that shows you where your last death occurred. All in all, an immensely useful combat mod which doesn't actually change the way combat works in vanilla Minecraft by adding items or new systems.

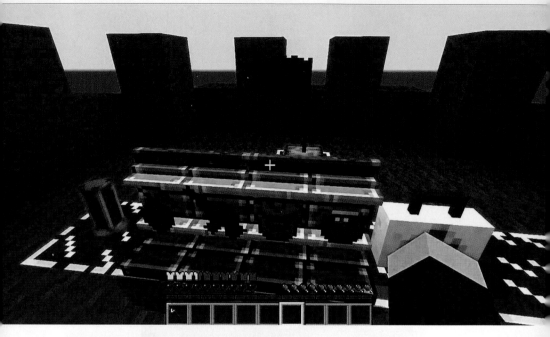

Paintball Mod

Creator: IKinx

In one sentence: Play paintball in Minecraft with a variety of weapons and equipment like flags and base creators that create a minigame similar to real-life paintball.

Version: 1.6.2 through 1.8
Installed Through: Forge (manually)
Where you can find it:
http://bit.ly/PaintballMod

Complexity Level: 2 Diamonds

Adds Items?: Yes
Adds Mobs?: No

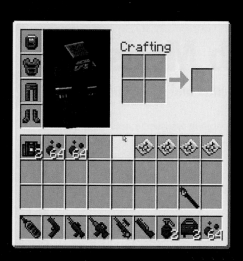

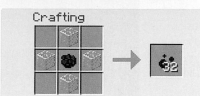

If you've ever played real-life paintball with a good crew of friends at the right paintball place (and a bit of pain doesn't phase you), you know that the excitement and camaraderie and chaos can be just a huge amount of fun. Mod creator IKinx (who is looking to make a career of this, so make sure to support them if you can!) has brought this very thrill to our favorite building game with the awesome Paintball Mod, which features everything you need to get a game going. This includes a huge number of weapon types (pistols, sniper rifles, machine guns, shotguns, grenades and more), as well as ammo and items to set up your gameplay area, like automatic base creators and flags. All of this is craftable, and IKinx has conveniently provided downloads for server-side mod stuff on his site as well, if you have your own server goin'.

Mob Mods
More Friends and More Foes

Every time Mojang releases a new mod with a Minecraft update, it's a big ole deal, and everyone goes crazy about the new creature roaming the lands of Minecraft. What modded Minecraft players know that those who just play vanilla might not, however, is that you can have that feeling times thirty or so all at once, right now!

Mob mods (it's fun to say, isn't it?) are some of the most requested things that Minecraft players getting into the modding scene ask for, and that makes a lot of sense, as adding even one new creature into the game really does liven it up a big amount. Luckily, mod creators have gone out there and added just about every imaginable creature to Minecraft and jammed them all into mods that are among the easiest to install and the least likely to mess up your existing worlds. If you're lookin' for a few new friends to hang out with (or enemies to slay!), one or two of the mods in this chapter will set you right.

Screenshot: Minecraft®™ & © 2009–2015 Mojang/Notch.

More Mobs Mod

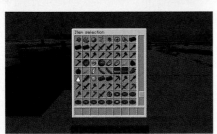

Creator: SimJoo

In one sentence: All the mobs you could ever want, including new human mobs, and some neat items like Wings.

Version: 1.7.2, 1.7.10

Installed Through: Forge (manually)
Where you can find it:
http://bit.ly/MoreMobsmod

Complexity Level: 2 Diamonds

Adds Items?: Yes
Adds Mobs?: Oh yes

This is the big one when it comes to adding new types of mobs to your Minecraft world, as it features well over 30 new mobs of all different shapes, sizes, and types. It also adds a few neat new craftable items like Fire tools and Wings, which make it a double whammy of a mod. Primarily though, this is mostly a big-time mob mod, and the list of the mobs this mod adds reads like a zoo directory. Check it out:

ANIMALS	NETHER MOBS	HUMANS
Dog (different from trained Wolf)	Evil Steve	Priest
Zebra	Reaper	Knight
Rabbit (different from vanilla)	Lava	Lumberjack
Hedgehog	Lava Snake	Merchant
Lion		New Villager
Penguin	END MOBS	
Swamp Crawler	Sprender	MONSTERS
Goat	Crender	Ghosts (Orange/Purple)
Bee	EnderPig	Dark Zombie
	Endead	Ent
	EnderCube	Creep
	EndPC	Burning Obsidian
	Skelender	

Mythical Creatures

Creator: HurricaneSHLBHP

In one sentence: A creature mod that adds all manner of fun, fantastical creatures like dragons, crocodiles and some ponies you might recognize, as well as some item additions like extra-long swords and enchanted armor.

Version: 1.6.4
Installed Through: Forge (manually)
Where you can find it:
http://bit.ly/MythicalCreaturesMod

Complexity Level: 2 Diamonds
Adds Items?: Yes
Adds Mobs?: Yes

This mod doesn't mess around with systems or anything fancy, but in terms of the kinds of mods it adds, it's the most imaginative on this list. It's all fantasy stuff here, turning your Minecraft world into a land of mythical (thus the name!) and quite dangerous beasts. Plus, you get the fun addition of some cool items to play around with, including, as they say on their forum page "stuff that can cause ridiculously huge explosions." This is another good one for when you don't want to add in anything too complex, you just want to make your existing world a little more flavorful.

Mythical Creatures

Millénaire

Creator: Kinniken

In one sentence: Adds five new types of Villages to Minecraft, each of which has its own culture and an extensive amount of new items and Villager types, and which can grow, trade and interact with the player in a large number of ways.

Version: 1.7.2, 1.7.10
Installed Through: Forge (manually) or through the Millénaire mod installer
Where you can find it:
http://millenaire.org/
Complexity Level: 3.5 Diamonds
Adds Items?: Yes
Adds Mobs?: Yes

The basic idea of Millénaire is simple, but in actuality this is one of the more complex and comprehensive mods out there, so much so that it would almost be a total conversion mod if it weren't otherwise set in vanilla Minecraft. The core concept is that there are various cultures of Villagers around the Minecraft world in randomly generated Villages, and these Villagers all have jobs like mining or chopping Wood (instead of just milling about). There is a leader, a trading hall and there are many ways to interact with the Villages, including helping them get items they need to build their Village and taking quests from them.

On top of this, you can also gain a reputation with these Villages and even become a leader, which in turn allows you the option to build your own Village that you can control (in terms of what they do and build). The Creation Quest you can get from the Villages is also a pretty big change to the game, as it adds in a little backstory for the Minecraft world and sends the player on an epic quest to gather items and information. All-in-all, Millénaire is a way to really spice up and populate the regular Minecraft world, turning it into more of an RPG builder game with a plot and characters, as opposed to being just about what the player wants to do. It's very cool, and one of the best ways to bring excitement back into the game if you're a little bored with regular Crafting.

Building Mods

Quick Buildings & More

Building is awesome, but sometimes it's not really what you want to spend time on in Minecraft. Say you want to get into some combat, or do some exploring of a new mod-having to sit and build a whole home, or using a very basic, crappy home really aren't great options.

That's why there are convenient quick-building mods out there, like the two we're showing off in this chapter. They essentially do the same thing in two different ways for two different reasons, that being that they allow you to very, very quickly spawn pre-built structures of different types right into your world without having to do any of the work.

Note: Technically, many of the mods in the rest of our book deal with building, such as those that add new block types, but we consider those to be more crafting and general mods. The mods here are more about making building faster and easier, as opposed to giving you more objects to build with. For those types of mods, check out the Items and the Adventure Enhancer chapters, along with a few other mods scattered throughout our book.

Instant Structures Mod

Creator: MaggiCraft

In one sentence: Spawn all sorts of different structures into your Minecraft world with just one click, or spawn different sized chunks of blocks.

Version: 1.7.10, 1.8
Installed Through: Forge (manually)
Where you can find it:
http://bit.ly/InstantStructuresForum

Complexity Level: 2.5 Diamonds
Adds Items?: No
Adds Mobs?: No

Over 170 different structures of various sizes and types are packed into this mod, whose goal is to help players speed up creation in their own worlds. Whether you just want a quick medieval windmill in your city and don't want to have to design one yourself, or you have found the perfect spot for a house and need one quick, the Instant Structures Mod has you covered. The selection of available structures is staggering, including everything from entire cities, to boats of all shapes and styles, to a ton of houses and generic buildings, to even statues, pixel art, a huge number of vehicles and so much more.

Perhaps even more awesome, this mod also includes a feature that allows you to spawn custom-sized shapes of different kinds, like pyramids and spheres, or remove blocks in an area. And the icing on the cake is that this feature also lets you scan your own structures into its system, allowing you to replicate them wherever you wish! It is a triumph of quick building, and a great mod for those who are looking to cut a few corners.

Instant Massive Structures Mod

Creator: SimJoo

In one sentence: Add a variety of simple structures into your Minecraft world with a single click, as opposed to the highly complex builds of MaggiCraft's mod.

Version: 1.6.4, 1.7.2, 1.7.10
Installed Through: Forge (manually)
Where you can find it:
bit.ly/InstantMassiveStructures

Complexity Level: 2 Diamonds
Adds Items?: No
Adds Mobs?: No

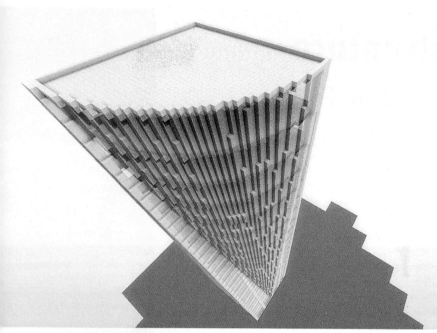

While the Instant Structures Mod is great, its builds are pretty much the kind of thing you'd see as complete builds on a server or as a downloadable map. That's great, but it doesn't allow for much customization, as they're already pretty much done. If you're looking more for something that will add simple structures that you can then tweak and build on, turning them into your own creation, this is the building mod you want.

Now, that isn't to say that the builds in this mod are all just utterly simple. There are some quite nicely designed buildings and vehicles in here as well, such as a very well-done tower. However, the idea here is to keep things more simple and leave space for the user to create their own thing out of them, and that makes it one of the most useful mods there is when it comes to speeding up building.

Adventure Enhancers

Mods That Give You More To Do On Your Journey

Outside of building things, adventure and fantastical experiences are what Minecraft is all about. Though some players choose to spend all their time crafting, mining and perfecting their home, which is also great fun, there are those of us who feel the itch to gear up and head out into the wilderness each time we see the sun rise over those virtual mountains in the distance.

You never know what will be over that next rise, what creatures or land features await, and one of Minecraft's best qualities is its ability to make you say "Whoa, come check this out!"

That's what this chapter is all about: mods that add more of those "Whoa" adventuring moments to your game. Many of these mods could fit in other chapters in this book, as they often add mobs, items, biomes, systems and just about everything else we've talked about, but we've given them a special category because these mods almost all add more than one of those things, and some even add all of them.

Additionally, the focus of these mods is more about directing your overall Minecraft experience in a certain direction, such as injecting an ancient Egyptian adventure into your game (Atum), making survival more realistic and difficult (TerrafirmaCraft) or turning dungeons into huge, mightily challenging structures (Chocolate Quest, Roguelike Dungeons). They are, each one, an adventure in themselves, and they will enhance the fun, magic, and wonder of the overall journey in your Minecraft world tremendously.

Screenshot: Minecraft®™ & © 2009–2015 Mojang/Notch.

The Aether 2

Creators: Brandon "Kingbdogz" Pearce and Emile van Krieke

In one sentence: Adds a sky dimension that's basically the counterpart to the Nether, with a light, happy and airy aesthetic instead of a hellish one.

Version: Automatic
Installed Through: Aether Launcher or Forge (also requires Guilded Games Utility)
Where you can find it:
http://bit.ly/Aether2Link

Complexity Level: 3 Diamonds
Adds Items?: Yes
Adds Mobs?: Yes

The Aether mod adds a new dimension to your world that is the polar opposite of the Nether. The Aether is a sky dimension, and it keeps with that theme by including flying animals (Pigs with wings!), lots of cloud- based items and a very fluffy and light look and feel. It's also a huge challenge, however, as it adds in three neat little Aether dungeons that have dangerous mobs and bosses in them, and each of which has a reward.

It's a quite enduringly popular Minecraft mod, both for its look and for the fact that it's just very well done. As opposed to many mods, The Aether feels at once complete, complex, and perfectly at home in the world of Minecraft, and though it does add a very big number of new items, block types and mobs, all of that stuff can only be picked up or seen in The Aether itself, meaning that the rest of your Minecraft world will stay the same. This makes it feel like just a really big update to the regular game, as opposed to mods that make Minecraft feel like a totally different game (though that's fun too!).

Galacticraft

Creator: micdoodle8

In one sentence: Craft through all new systems to build, launch and fly a rocket, going all the way to the moon and Mars!

Version: 1.7.10 and back to 1.4.7

Installed through: Forge (manually), and is also in many modpacks

Where you can find it:
http://bit.ly/GalacticraftMod

Complexity Level: 4.5 Diamonds
Adds Items?: Yes
Adds Mobs?: Yes

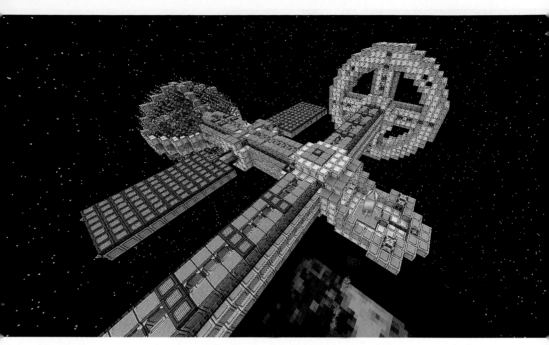

Included in many modpacks (such as A Era do Futuro), Galacticraft deserves its own section because what it does is just so darn cool: it lets you build a rocketship and go to space! SPACE! In actuality, Galacticraft is a lot more than that, adding entire new systems and hundreds of new items and block-types to the game, all of which have a high-tech, sci-fi kind of theme to them.

The "space" you go to in Galacticraft is pretty awesome too, being basically three new dimensions that you can travel to and build in. These include the Moon (no longer just a bunch of pixels hanging in the sky, but an actual place you can fly to and stand on!), the space around the earth (meant to be as if you're in orbit, and you can build space stations there) and Mars. If you fire this mod up and are lookin' to take a rocket up to see what you can find, however, make sure you bring a spacesuit, as even virtual space doesn't have a whole lot of air for your character to breathe!

(Though excellent on its own, we'd suggest grabbing Galacticraft in Technic's Tekkit modpack, which is made to make Galacticraft even better by adding other cool mods.

Camping Mod

Creator: Rikmuld

In one sentence: Make every night out in the wilderness a classic adventure with camping gear and a new campfire cooking system!

Version: 1.4.7, 1.5.1, 1.5.2, 1.6.2, 1.6.4, 1.7.10
Installed Through: Forge (manually)
Where you can find it:
http://bit.ly/CampingModLink

Complexity Level: 1.5 Diamonds
Adds Items?: Yes
Adds Mobs?: Yes

Some of the mods in this chapter add an entire new world to adventure in, while others, like this Camping Mod, are there to make your adventures feel more complete and rich. This mod is one of our favorites for just that reason, as it adds in the fun and comfort of camping and campfires to vanilla Minecraft.

This mod is very well-realized, as it contains not just new items like a Pan, Tents, Sleeping Bags and logs to sit on, it also adds a cooking system through a special Cooking Campfire, and even a couple new wild mobs (Bear and

Arctic Fox)! You can even roast marshmallows, which is just a great touch.

Your nights out in the world on your exploration trips will never be dark and dreary again, with this adorable and fun little mod.

Shape Shifter

Creator: zacuke

In one sentence: Become every mob in the game, complete with special powers for each mob.

Version: 1.6.4
Installed Through: Forge (manually)
Where you can find it:
http://bit.ly/ShapeShifterMod

Complexity Level: 2 Diamonds
Adds Items?: No
Adds Mobs?: No, but tweaks them

This mod doesn't change the look of the game really at all, and it could be considered on the smaller and less complex end of the spectrums, but it is a bit of a game changer. That's because the shape shifting ability it gives you, which lets you become any mob in the game, really changes the way you move about and interact with the world of Minecraft.

That's not hard to imagine, when you think about what you'd do in vanilla Minecraft if you could suddenly become an Ender Dragon and fly around. Each mob has an ability or two like this, and it makes for a very different experience without changing what the rest of the game is like. It's even more pronounced on multiplayer, and we highly suggest getting a bunch of your friends around and Squid-ing about the ocean just for fun.

Most popular mobs to turn into, data gathered by zacuke:

1. Dragon
2. Ocelot
3. Bat
4. Creeper
5. Enderman
6. Spider
7. Villager
8. Zombie
9. Ghast
10. Wither
11. Wolf
12. Silverfish
13. Sheep
14. Chicken
15. Slime
16. Pig
17. Golem
18. Skeleton
19. Blaze
20. Squid
21. Magmacube
22. Witch
23. Snowman
24. Cow
25. Mooshroom
??. Horse

FloorBallCraft

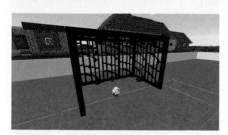

Creator: TheLarsinator

In one sentence: Adds everything you need to play a game similar to hockey or lacrosse in Minecraft.

Version: 1.6.4, 1.7.2, 1.7.10

Installed Through: Forge (manually)

Where you can find it:
http://bit.ly/FloorBallCraft
Complexity Level: 2 Diamonds
Adds Items?: Yes
Adds Mobs?: No

Salming Quest 2

We're using the term "adventure" a bit loosely here, but hey, stopping to play a highly competitive game in the middle of nowhere against your rivals can totally be a part of an adventure, right? We think it just adds another layer of fun and more memories to the game, and that's why we've put the fun and lightweight FloorBallCraft in this chapter.

FloorBallCraft has two options: you can either use the items that come with it to build your own court on which to play, including even painting the lines down and crafting a Goal piece-by-piece, or you can just download a pre-made rink and get to playin'! The game itself is, as mentioned, much the same as hockey or lacrosse where you're just trying to use a stick to get a ball in a net, and it works pretty well for a game built inside of another game. Well worth a try, and hey, maybe you could even get a league going if you get enough friends!

LotsOMobs

Creator: TheLarsinator

In one sentence: Primarily a large-scale mob adder, but this mod goes in the adventure chapter because it also adds dimensions, items, crops systems, and blocks.

Version: 1.6.2, 1.6.4, 1.7.2, 1.7.10, 1.8

Installed Through: Forge (manually)

Where you can find it:
http://bit.ly/LotsOMobsMod
Complexity Level: 3.5 Diamonds
Adds Items?: Yes
Adds Mobs?: Yes

Made by the same guy that did FloorBallCraft, LotsOMobs is a more traditional Minecraft adventure enhancing mod. You might think from the name and the fact that it includes more than 45 new mobs that it would go in our mobs chapter, but this mod goes far beyond its namesake and adds in many other features to kick your adventure into another gear.

Maybe the most awesome additions are the new dimensions LotsOMobs adds in, which include an Ice Age and a Dinosaur Dimension. Guess what you'll find in that last one? Yep, a whole lot of dinos, all ready to stomp you flat and eat your little Crafter body.

There are also new tools, crops, weapons, blocks, and more in this mod, as well as new tanning and DNA systems that allow you to create some of the items and even mobs added by LotsOMobs. TheLarsinator is a very good modder with a lot of interesting stuff to offer the community, and LotsOMobs may be his best work. It's certainly worth a go for the Dino Dimension alone.

The Technic Mod Launcher

Of the mod loaders out there, the Technic Launcher is among the two most popular that do all the work for you (along with Feed the Beast's loader), and for good reason. Not only is it simple, cool-looking, and very stable, it also includes some of the best mods and modpacks that have yet been called into the Minecraft world. In fact, many of the most beloved mods in existence, like Galacticraft and Thaumcraft, are contained in the major Technic modpacks alongside some lesser known mods (turn yourself into a hamster!), and the result is an experience that we think might possibly be the best way to play Minecraft.

To get Technic mods going on your own system is a thoroughly simple process. Simply head to this link and get the loader: www.technicpack.net/

Once you've done that, you can browse through various mods on the loader itself if you're looking for their big-time mods, or you can use the Technic website to find some of the more obscure mods. Installing is as easy as pressing the install button on the loader or, for those smaller mods from the site, you can snag a mod's link and copy-paste it into the "Add Pack or Search" of the Technic loader's "Modpacks" tab. When it comes to loading in a large number of mods, especially when trying to get mods to work together, it doesn't come easier than the Technic loader.

Pixelmon

In one sentence: Turns Minecraft into a 3D first-person Pokémon game, with just about everything you'd hope for from such a mod.

Approximate Mod Count: 1, except in versions where it is bundled with other mods

Complexity Level: 3 Diamonds

Adds Items?: Yes

Adds Mobs?: Yes

It's no secret that Pokémon is one of the most popular and long-lasting game series of all time, so the fact that the hardcore modding community for Minecraft has gone out and recreated Pokémon inside of their own game or that it's the most popular Technic mod should be no big shock to anyone. Pixelmon is just that mod, and to answer your questions: Yes, there are Pokémon wandering around; yes, you can catch them; yes, you can fight them with trainers and other players; and yes, it all works.

Though you can just load this one up through the Technic launcher and play in your own world, we'd also suggest jumping on one of the official servers (just go to multiplayer instead of single player, and they're listed) where people have actually gone so far as to build functioning Pokémon Centers, gyms, and even the Elite Four! Plus, you can show off your sick Mewtwo and find hundreds of other players to battle with. This one's a treat, whether you're a longtime Pokémon fan or just like the idea of a bunch of adorable battle creatures wandering around your Minecraft home.

Note: there are quite a few versions of Pixelmon out there, as well as a lot of knock-offs, so make sure you're downloading the one you want when you go looking for it.

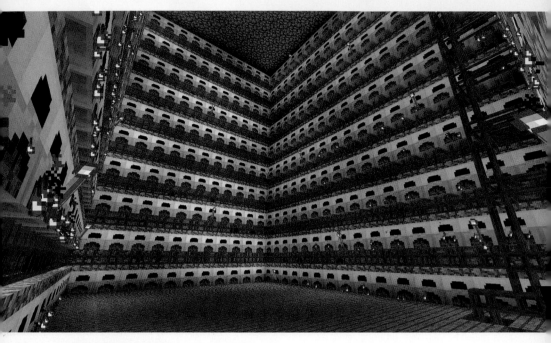

Tekkit

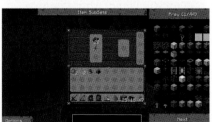

In one sentence: The be-all, end-all granddaddy of technology and system modpacks.

Approximate Mod Count: 60+

Complexity Level: 5 Diamonds

Adds Items?: Yes

Adds Mobs?: Yes

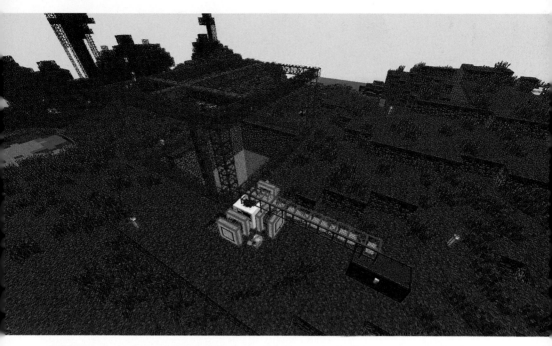

Tekkit is one of the big boys of the modding scene, having been around for quite some time as the answer to your question: why can't I have more systems than Redstone in Minecraft? In terms of what Tekkit contains, it has about sixty mods all packed together, with the idea that you are adding an immense amount of building items and technology (hence "Tekkit") like factory mechanisms, rocketships, and powersuits to your Minecraft.

For those who are into making Minecraft's blocky world automated and complex, taking each thing you can find and utilizing it to make more amazing things happen, you won't find one better or more loved than Tekkit. There's a reason this thing has been popular for so long, and that's because it's a tech-lover's dream.

A Era do Futuro

In one sentence: A major collection of popular mods with a wide scope that adds a little of everything.

Approximate Mod Count: 40+

Complexity Level: 5 Diamonds

Adds Items?: Yes

Adds Mobs?: Yes

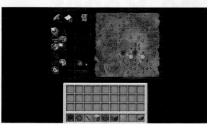

A Era do Futuro is a highly popular modpack on the Technic system, and that's not surprising one bit: A Era contains over 40 of the Minecraft world's most beloved mods. In a nutshell, it overhauls pretty much every facet of the game, including the biomes (with mod Extra Biomes XL), the mobs (Mo'Zombies, Mutant Creatures, Primitive Mobs, and more), the weapons (Asgard Shield, Legend Gear, More Bows, and more), and just about everything else. With A Era do Futuro, you'll be able to build amazing machines, fly to space, travel through a fantasy forest dimension, and ever so much more, making it one of the best modpacks to wet your whistle with when starting out. Even the trees are amazing in this one!

The Feed The Beast Mod Launcher

Alongside the Technic Launcher, the Feed the Beast Launcher is one of the two big names in the modding community. FTB has been around for a long time in the Minecraft world, and in fact it started out way back when modpacks weren't that easy to find. The group that became Feed the Beast had a challenge map they had put together that required a lot of tech mods, and when they made it public, they realized that trying to get all of the mods, maps, and other files to players in a way that would actually allow them to play it would be very difficult.

So, they came up with the idea to package everything together in a modpack, and to also go the extra step to make a launcher that would make everything start up smoothly and easily. Over the years, this original FTB pack was updated, added to, and made into various versions, and now the FTB launcher is home to a series of modpacks that are some of the most comprehensive and technical on the internet.

Opposite and above: You can tell from just these two images the wide variety of mod types you'll find in FTB modpacks. Here you've got a mix of tech mods on the left, and some dark magic mods going on the right, both from FTB.

For this chapter we're going to do things a little different, because there's just too much to show for FTB and too many great packs to talk about. Instead of profiling each pack in our regular way, we're going to give a list of some of the best FTB packs and a bit about them alongside a scattering of FTB screens meant to give you an idea of the huge variety of mods and experiences available in FTB.

Find almost all of these packs and the launcher at:
http://www.feed-the-beast.com

Highlights from the Feed the Beast mods and packs:
FTB Infinity- This is the mother of all modpacks, the big daddy of packs that have a ton of mods, and the Feed the Beast flagship pack. This is the latest version of that original pack that has since been passed around for years simply for the quality of experiences it adds to a vanilla game. It has far over 100 mods, and its well-rounded inclusions feature everything from mods that turn you into a wizard to those that will allow you to add crazy new tech functions that were previously impossible.

FTB modpacks add in an enormous number of new blocks to play with, something you can see in this image by Drullkus.

A serious builder's dream, Infinity contains all the mods you could ever need to make just about any kind of structure, system, machine, or other creation, plus some fun stuff like the ultra-cool Mystcraft (based on the game Myst, lets you create custom dimensions to travel to!). Yep: FTB Infinity is super, super complicated, but that's half the fun! Using its systems, you can automate just about every part of Minecraft, if you know how. If you're looking for a way to spice up your game, and you're up for the challenge of building complex structures, FTB Infinity is the be-all-end-all of tech and builder packs.

Direwolf20: Named after the YouTuber and Minecraft player Direwolf20, this is a less intense FTB pack that still packs a lot of punch. It's kind of a "best of" tech pack with some biome and adventure mods thrown in, and it's a very good one without being as overwhelming as Infinity.

Trident: Take the tech and mechanics of FTB's other packs, especially Infinity, but instead of playing in regular Survival or Creative mode, this pack sets up a PvP experience between three teams in a desert wasteland.

Heavy tech is a big part of FTB packs like Infinity or Tech World.

The idea is that an apocalypse of some sort has happened, and three factions have found what seems to be the only place with Water in this part of the world. Using a large number of tech and other mods, players in each faction have to build their infrastructure up, arm themselves and compete for resources while attempting to achieve preset victory conditions. The whole thing can take about a month, and is one of the biggest challenges in the Minecraft universe.

Mage Quest: Only perhaps the most comprehensive pack of magic-based mods ever to be created for Minecraft. This one eschews the tech and makes every major magic mod in Minecraft work perfectly together, also adding a bunch of smaller, lesser-known packs. This is a true fantasy adventure of epic proportions, and after a few months playing, you'll be able to command the forces of nature to perform your every whim.

FTB Lite: Whether because it just has so many mods that it's overwhelming mentally, or because those mods are overwhelming your computer (which is very possible), Feed the Beast has put out a Lite version of its main modpack, FTB Infinity. FTB Lite is a very good pack to start out with, either for those new to FTB, or those new to modded Minecraft period.

Definitely get online and explore the massive number of packs that are out there besides the big FTB packs, like Jovian here!

Jovian: This is an example of a user-created pack, which launchers like FTB make possible. Jovian was created by player Biochao and can be found at: http://bit.ly/JovianModpack. It features a heavy number of mods, but is not just a regular Survival world otherwise. Instead, the idea is that you have crash landed a spaceship on Callisto, one of Jupiter's moons, and you have to try to not only survive, but to thrive and to eventually leave this moon. Callisto is, as Jovian's site says, "the most heavily cratered object in the solar system," and you will find yourself not alone on this alien rock. These kind of unofficial modpacks that can be loaded through FTB are one of the launcher's strengths, allowing for creators to give players a very easy, workable way to get into complex modpacks.

Other Great FTB Packs:
- Resurrection
- Monster
- Horizons
- Tech World 2/Magic World 2
- Test Pack Please Ignore

Mini-Games Galore!

Ah, mini-games! Those saviors of Minecraft that take our vanilla-jaded minds and turn them onto something new and awesome that makes Minecraft feel like a whole new game.

Of course, we do love vanilla Minecraft, but after countless dozens of hours, even the world's best game can get a little old hat. Lucky for us Crafters, Minecraft is set up so that it is ideal for intrepid creators around the world to modify and turn into all sorts of other games.

Servers like mc.hypixel.net are where mini-games not only get played, but created and tested by thousands upon thousands of players each day.

We call these mini-games, and they're essentially just alternative ways to play Minecraft. Some of them are just slight tweaks to the Survival Mode that manage to make it feel entirely new and unique, while others barely resemble anything you'd see or do in a regular game of vanilla Crafting.

As we've done with the last few editions of our book, here are a few of our favorite current mini-games in the Minecraft world today, as well as a bit more info on some of the modes we've talked about in the past.

Factions

Factions has a very active chat with auctions and a multitude of chat commands that are important to your game.

Type: Long-Term Complex Survival Variant

Factions is among the most popular Minecraft mini-games, and it's also one of the most in-depth when it comes to what you can do. The basic idea is that you are in a regular Survival world with many other players (typically there's no limit to the amount), but you have the added ability to join a faction.

Factions are essentially teams of players that can claim a "chunk" of land for their faction. Only players that are members of the faction can open chests or build or destroy anything by hand on a faction's land. Non-members will find themselves unable to affect another faction's land, except by using TNT, Lava

Playing Factions is best done with friends, whether those you know in the real world or those met online, because a one person faction can't get much done. Find a faction to join, or get some buddies together to make one of your own!

or Water dropped onto it. Typically, you can't be hurt on your faction's claimed land, as well.

Land chunks extend from the bedrock to sky and can claimed by using Power, which each player has in a certain amount, and some of which is lost when the player dies. Usually a player starts with 10 Power, claims land using 1 Power and loses 3 Power on death, but this can be different between servers. When a player joins a faction, their Power is added to the faction total, allowing the faction to claim more land. Be warned though: when you lose Power from dying, that Power will be subtracted from your faction's total. If your faction ever has less power than it has claimed chunks of land, you can start to lose that land. Over time, your Power can grow back, thankfully, but this happens very, very slowly.

The goal of Factions is to grow your faction, get more money (used to buy items and/or land), recruit new faction members and declare war against or ally up with other factions. So basically, it turns (almost) vanilla Minecraft into an all out tribal war. It's a never-ending brutal war for domination and land, and it's one heck of a cool way to compete in Minecraft over an extended period of time.

Paintball

Type: One-Shot-Kill Deathmatch

If UHC and Factions seem a little too much commitment and effort for your Minecrafting session, Paintball is on the opposite side of the spectrum of mini-games in that it's quick, easy and doesn't require much knowledge of the ins and outs of Minecraft.

Paintball is pretty easy to pick up: all you do is run around a map trying to hit players with "paintballs," which are actually just Snowballs under a different name. If you hit a player once, they are immediately warped back to spawn and you and your team get points. The first team to get a certain amount of points or the team with the most points after a set amount of time wins. On some servers getting "kills" earns you coins that you can use to purchase powerups for either you or your team, like a triple-shot or reducing the amount of deaths your team has.

Screenshot: Minecraft®™ & © 2009-2015 Mojang/Notch.

Top and Middle: Flying Snowballs are a common sight in Paintball; in fact you'll probably never see so many in the air at once anywhere else in Minecraft! Bottom: Each match of Paintball has players select a team by picking a colored Wool block in a little pre-game room.

And that's it! Pretty simple, no? Don't be fooled though; while picking up a game of Paintball is easy and you're probably going to get at least a few kills in every match you play, there are some players that have taken this little mini-game rather seriously indeed and can hit other players with ease from far across the map. With practice, though, you can become one of these skillshot aficionados and start to get your name in the Top 3 of the scoresheet with regularity.

TNT Run

Type: No Weapon Spleef Variant

A game that seems easy, and is another simple one to understand, but which will put your jumping and navigational skills to the test like few others. TNT Run has been around for a long time, and it involves running around in an arena on a flat surface which will fall out underneath you as you go. That means that if you step on a block, you better move quick because soon that block will drop and you'll fall to the next layer below.

The idea is to keep moving around and create holes in the ground as you move that other players fall into. Since these players are creating more holes themselves, you'll need to keep on your toes and plan out where you run, deftly jumping any holes that you can't run around.

When you fall to the next layer, you'll do the same thing there, and the player that is able to keep from falling through the final layer of the arena and into the darkness below is the winner.

Some players get a little confused about TNT Run's name, as there are no explosions in this mini-game. The reason the game is named after the 'splodiest block in Minecraft is that there is a block of TNT under each block that makes up the layers of the arena. The game has been specially designed so that walking on the Sand or Gravel blocks that make up the floor of each layer causes the TNT to activate beneath the Sand or Gravel, causing the Sand or Gravel to fall, though without causing an explosion. Essentially it's just a trick to get the game to work, so no need to worry about getting blown up in this mini-game. Just worry about where you're going to put your feet next!

TNT Wiza
Red
Blue
Kills
Point Alph
Point Bet
Point Gam

Wizards

Type: Magic Kit Command Point PVP

Who doesn't want to be a wizard? We know we're into the idea of wrathfully slingin' the powers of magic at our foes, and that's why we love the Wizards mini-game. This one is a simple PVP "capture the command point" mode that has each player pick a team and a kit, and each kit is a different type of wizard with a variety of unique powers.

The powers and wizard-types run the gamut from fireball throwers to ice wizards and more, and each class typically has an exploding spell attack that has a special feature to it, like a fireball that burns enemies (a Fire Charge

Top and Middle: As you can see from these images, the maps in Wizards get absolutely wrecked by the end of a match, which is a major part of the fun. Bottom: Select your Wizard class before each match, or you can let it assign you one automatically.

shot when a staff is used), and a special defensive power, like an instant teleport. Most powers take "mana," which in this case is the icons in your hunger bar, which are used up quickly but also regenerate very quickly. Once you've selected your wizard-type, it's locked in for the rest of the match, so make sure to try a few out and find one you're good with.

The red pad with the beam of light coming out of it is one of the command points in a Wizards match, which you need to go stand on in order to secure it for your team.

The matches themselves are set in an arena that is decently sized and typically contains all destructible blocks, which makes Wizards somewhat unique to PVP matches, which often feature indestructible arenas. Wizards arenas are like this because the powers at the disposal of each wizard in the match are mighty forces of nature that tend to explode and cause area damage, and part of the fun of Wizards matches is that the explosions wreck the environment as the match goes along. And, since the gravity is much lower in Wizards matches, you can jump just about anywhere, making every block in the arena part of the battleground. By the time a winner is announced, the whole arena will be in glorious ruins.

The combat in Wizards is a little different from many such fast-paced PVP mini-games, as although your spells have spectacular effects and do damage in an area, each wizard is actually pretty tough to kill and will not go down without more than a couple direct hits. Additionally, you aren't just trying to kill your enemies, you're also trying to walk on two different command points so that you capture them for your team. If enemy players are on the command point, they will start capturing it for their team instead, and the more players from one team on the command point, the more likely it is to go to that team. Once it's been captured, the other team has to keep enemy players off of it to capture it back, otherwise it will keep going fully back to the team that last captured it.

Points rack up for a team based on the amount of time a command point has been owned by that team, and when one team reaches 2000 points, they win this mighty struggle of magic users.

Wizards is as chaotic as it gets, but its balance of excellent unique classes, destructible terrain, low gravity, heavily armored players and the PVP + command points structure makes for one of the best PVP experiences in the world of Minecraft.

Here's the list of Wizards classes and their powers:

Fire Wizard
Attack Power: Launches a fireball
Defense Power: Instant teleportation

Kinetic Wizard
Attack Power: High damage, short-range railgun
Defense Power: Gravity gun

Ice Wizard
Attack Power: Freeze shot to slow enemies
Defense Power: Puts up a wall of Ice

Wither Wizard
Attack Power: Exploding extra-poisonous Wither skull shot
Defense Power: An extra row of "absorption hearts"

Blood Wizard
Attack Power: Normal attack costs 2 hearts instead of mana
Defense Power: Has a Splash Potion that instantly regenerates health

Blitz

Type: Fast Survival Games Variant

Survival Games is one of the most popular mini-games, and it has been for a long time, but Blitz is our favorite version of Survival Games. It takes the basic concept of an arena with Chests with items scattered around it and kit selection and makes the competition much fiercer and quicker by having smaller arenas, crazier kits and a special Blitz Star that spawns every so often and gives the finder extra powers.

There are a ton of kits in Blitz (far too many to list here), each of which has very specific traits and powers, and

After the initial countdown, players rush from their starting points to the Chests in the center (middle image), after which it's an all-out fight for survival across a decently large map, though one that's smaller and faster than that of most Survival Games matches.

each of which can be upgraded from level I to level X. Some of the kits are free, while others require winning and purchasing to access, and the level of the kit determines the amount and quality of items you get from it and your appearance.

Games of Blitz start out like other Survival Games matches, with players spread out evenly in a circle around a group of Chests. When the countdown finishes, players are able to move and can either risk running to the Chests to try and get items before other players, or they can just run off into the map. PVP is immediately enabled in Blitz, but the items from your kit will not appear in your inventory until 60 seconds into the match. The arenas are decently sized with many hiding spots, and they also contain quite a few hidden Chests, which contain random items like those in the center of the spawn point.

Strategy in Blitz is fairly complex and requires quick changes and thinking. You'll have to decide whether to risk going for Chests or simply to hide and wait for your kit, and you'll be playing against all sorts of other kits, including those that are far above your level. Being higher level does not necessarily guarantee a kill in Blitz, however, as it is still pretty easy to kill someone with a good kit if you catch them at the right time with the right items, especially before they get their kit. You also have a player tracker in the form of a compass, which will show you the direction of the closest player, which can help both offensively and defensively. Because of these reasons, good kits are highly useful, but not a game-breaker.

The Blitz Star, while also not a breaker, certainly is a game changer, as it spawns randomly on the map every 5 minutes and allows the finder to select from a variety of special one-time boosts. There are 18 of these, and they can do everything from teleporting to the closest player and dealing 10 damage, making all arrows one-shot-kill players for a 30 second period, steal hit points from players in a radius around the player or give extra regeneration and much more. All Blitz Stars also give Regeneration II for 30 seconds, which is useful all on its own.

Combine all of this together, and you get a very complex game that moves much quicker than regular Survival Games, which can sometimes go on for a very long time. Typically many players are killed before they even get their kits in the first 60 seconds of each match, but that being said, the last few players in a game of Blitz can often still take a decent amount of time to pick each other off.

While Survival Games is still going strong as one of the top mini-games for Minecraft, we think Blitz gives it a little kick-in-the-pants both in terms of pacing and complexity (with the addition of the Blitz Star and better kits) that makes us favor it over the original. Of course, that's not too surprising considering that this mini-game is one of the always-great Hypixel server creations.

A Guide To Winning Ultra Hardcore

Minecraft's Best Mini Game

If horse racing is the sport of kings, Ultra HardCore or UHC is the mini-game of Minecraft monarchs. By that we mean it's the game for the very best of the best when it comes to Minecraft, and only those players who truly know what they're doing in survival mode can ever hope to last for more than 20 minutes or so, much less win a game of UHC. Go peep the YouTube channels of any member of the Mindcrack Network, which regularly engages in riveting UHC brawls, to see the kind of skills it takes to get good at this mini-game.

What makes UHC so gosh darned hard? Well, that'd be in the name: it's not just Hardcore Mode, which means one death and you're out, it's Ultra HardCore mode, which means it's hard to impossible to even heal. Otherwise it's a fight

NOTE:

Hiding your achievements is an excellent UHC strategy, because knowing what another player is doing is extremely helpful to defeating them in this mode. You can do this by having just one player on a team craft all of your Crafting Tables, handing them out to the other players. You get the "Benchmarking" achievement only when you pick up a Crafting Table from the output slot of either your inventory crafting menu or from a Crafting Table output. Since you have to get achievements in a specific order in order to get the next one, skipping the Benchmarking achievement will mean that your achievements stop showing, even if you complete the necessary action. This will help spread confusion and disinformation, giving you a distinct advantage. Does not work in single player UHC, however, unless you steal someone else's Crafting Table.

to the death in Survival Mode, typically on a small (and sometimes shrinking!) map, but the fact that you have to be very careful not to even lose one heart carelessly is what makes UHC so hard, and so thrilling.

While learning to be the best of the best at UHC requires mastery of just about all things Survival, meaning you'll want to simply learn all you can about the game, this is a mini-guide to the mode that will give you a leg up on your opponents and make you much more likely to survive. Remember though: these are just tips! UHC is all about general Minecraft knowledge and adaptability, so make sure to learn about the basics of the game as well, and never be afraid to try a bold new strategy if it makes sense in the situation.

1. Don't waste time, especially at the beginning. You simply can't mess around when playing UHC, especially right at the beginning. While later stages of the match are harder to do with perfect efficiency, like Diamond/Gold hunting or Arrow creating, everything you need to do at the beginning can be done either rightly or wrongly. That is to say, you can be quick about it, or you can do it badly. When you start a

match of UHC, you need to acquire food, Wood, Crafting Tables and basic gear as quickly as you can, or else another team or competitor will be ahead of you and thus much more likely to win.

2. Know the specific rules of the server and the match. Not all UHC matches are the same. Some spawn you with a gear kit, some have shrinking borders, some allow healing with potions while others only allow it with Golden Apples or not at all. Know the rules of the specific server you're on and the match

you're in, or else you may spend a lot of time trying to do something that just won't work.

3. Be entirely, overly careful. Do not take damage from anything except a player or a mob, and avoid that at all costs. Falling damage or damage from Lava, drowning or hitting a teammate is really something that should not happen in a UHC match, and if it does, it means you are less likely to win. Paranoia based security is the name of the game: if it seems even a little dangerous, get away from it ASAP. Do not make risky jumps if possible, stay out of dark places when possible (even dark forests) and run away from all hostile mobs (especially Skeletons), don't even get near Lava in most situations. It's just not worth it unless you have awesome armor, which you won't for a while.

4. Get the right resources, ignore the others. Not everything is useful in UHC. Here's a list of things you want, everything else can be ignored or dropped for the most part:

- **Raw resources:** Wood, Coal, Iron, Gold, Diamond, Emerald (Emerald only in case you see a Village— Lapis Lazuli (for enchanting in v1.8 or above)
- **Food, especially Apples but do not eat Apples** (they are for making Golden Apples)

- **Feathers and Flint** (for Arrows)
- **Sugar Cane and Leather** (to make Books for enchanting)
- **Obsidian** (for Enchanting Table, best made instead of hunted)
- **String** (for Bows)

Specialty items for specific strategies:

- **Bones** (to tame Wolves who will fight for you)
- **Brewing items** (Sand/Glass, Blaze Rods and Nether Wart etc., to make Potions. Very, very dangerous but can work if done carefully.)

5. Go underground quickly. Once you've gathered whatever food you can on the surface and have plenty of Wood, Crafting Tables and basic tools, you need to get underground and start hunting ores and Spiders ASAP. The best option is to find caves and follow them, or safely go down a ravine, but if you can't find any of these quickly, go ahead and just start digging down in a staircase. You need ore, because as our next step says...

6. Gear is essential. Gear is what will make you win or lose UHC. Outside of ambushes and accidents, the people with the best gear almost always win the match, so it is your number one priority. Gear is important in the following order, with the most important at the the top, and you would do well to focus on acquiring each in this order:

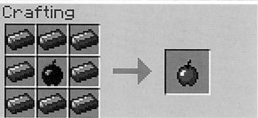

- Stone Sword and tools
- Armor (the best kind you can make)
- Food
- Better Sword, and Bow and Arrows (equally important)
- Golden Apples
- Potions

7. Consider the Nether. This is very risky, but there are also massive benefits if you survive. The Nether will put you away from most other players, who will be scared to venture there, and it will give you the opportunity to collect Blaze Rods and Nether Wart to make potions. However, do not go to the Nether if you are not very, very good at surviving in it, and never go without at least Iron Armor, a Bow and an Iron Sword, if not better gear.

8. Be sneaky and vigilant at all times. Many players in UHC get killed simply because they were focusing too much on resource hunting and gear crafting and they didn't notice that someone was sneaking up on them. Make sure you're scanning your surroundings for other players at all times, and try to stay out of sight or underground whenever possible. Also, use the darkness trick to see other players' nametags: dig a hole or place blocks on all sides of you so that you are in total darkness, then look in every direction. If there is any player near you, you'll see their nametag. Beware though; other players use this trick, so if you think someone might be looking for you, go into sneak

Screenshot: Minecraft®™ & © 2009–2015 Mojang/Notch.

mode with the crouch key. This hides your nametag, allowing you to remain safely hidden.

9. Pay attention to coordinates. It's a good idea to keep your coordinates up and watch them at all times. This is because you want to know where you've been in order not to go over the same area repeatedly, and so you know where you are in relation to the center of the map. The center is where players will most often have to pass through, making it the most dangerous area as well as the best hunting grounds. This strategy is especially important for matches with shrinking maps.

10. Bring the fight to the enemy. When you're all geared up, don't just wait around for other players to ambush them. Do this some, but do it on the move. A player that's moving is much harder to target and is much more likely to get the drop on other players and defeat them. If you're geared up, be bold and take the fight to your enemies, but of course do this stealthily and carefully.

There is little in Minecraft as rewarding as outsmarting, out-surviving and simply outcrafting everyone else in a UHC match. It's thrilling, nail-biting fun that we can't recommend enough, and with this little guide, you are much more likely to come out on top.

NOTE: This is not as common a game on servers as some of the other mini-games, primarily because it's challenging, but also because it takes a bit of time and quite a few people to play. A match can last anywhere from 30 minutes to three or four hours, and it's best played with at least 8 people or 4 teams. That being said, it's the pinnacle of Minecraft competition, and it should be played by all Crafters1.

Chapter 5

Minecraft, YouTube and a New Kind of Star

An Interview with TheDiamondMinecart

Daniel "TheDiamondMinecart" Middleton • YouTube Creator

Here we see TDM in his custom skin along with his popular video characters Dr. Trayaurus and his skeleton dog Grim.

YouTube is the future of entertainment.

More than movies, more than TV, more than music, the world of YouTube channels and the hugely popular personalities that run them is one of the fastest growing entertainment forms in the world, especially with kids. In fact, according to a poll taken by Variety magazine, teenagers are now far more likely to recognize YouTube stars than they are the most famous actors in the world (the most-recognized non-YouTuber, Paul Walker, came in at a distant 6th place in the poll).

To put it even more into perspective, the videos YouTube stars make on their channels often out-do huge music videos and movie trailers to become the most watched things on YouTube, and the medium racks up many billions of views every month. That's right: billions, and it's not all just for fun either. Through the ads program which shows advertisements before or alongside

videos, YouTube channel-runners are able to make actual money from their videos. When those videos start to earn thousands, then millions of views, they earn more money with every view, making YouTube channels not only quite popular, but quite lucrative as well.

Much of what these suddenly super-famous YouTube stars focus on in their videos is that other titan of the "new" entertainment, video gaming. Particularly, stars upload sessions of themselves playing and reacting to their favorite games in a genre of video know as the Let's Play, a phenomenon in its own right that sits within the overall YouTube phenomenon.

Daniel Middleton is one such YouTuber who has combined this idea of Let's Play YouTube videos with the world's most popular video game, *Minecraft*. His channel is called TheDiamondMinecart (https://www.youtube.com/user/TheDiamondMinecart), and on it he uploads Let's Plays of Minecraft just about every day. TheDiamondMinecart, or TDM as it's known, has a very large

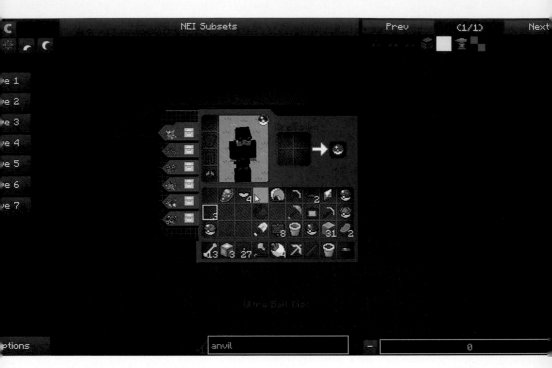

following, with 15+ videos with over 5 million views, 200+ with over 1 million, and as of the writing of this book, 3,349,246 subscribers to his channel on YouTube.

That last number is more people than live in the city of Chicago by about 500k. To call it impressive is to understate massively, but how does this all work? What exactly do YouTubers like Dan do, and how does it get so popular?

We asked Dan to describe the YouTube channel-runner's job, and this is how he put it: "My job consists of using my imagination for cool new video ideas, recording those ideas within Minecraft (and sometimes other games too!), taking those recordings and editing them together to create the final piece and then creating the artwork to go with the video when it goes live on YouTube." Though to the casual viewer it may look similar to regular gaming, Dan says

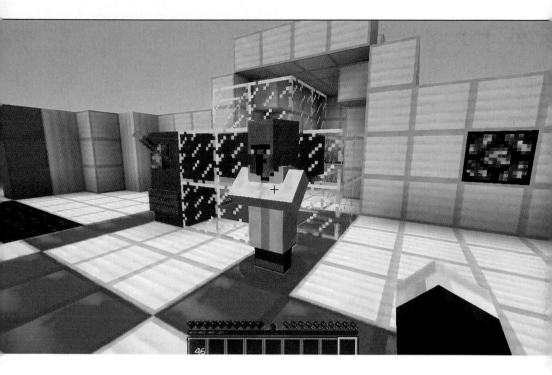

that there's a lot more to it than that, adding "I do get to play and record video games every day, but there's also a lot of behind-the-scenes too."

Anyone can start a YouTube channel with just a few clicks, but it takes gaming know-how, special recording equipment (such as high fidelity microphones and powerful video capture software), passion, dedication and not just a little charisma to gain a following like that of Dan and his fellow YouTube stars. As he says, it doesn't happen overnight, but took months of work and practice before he really hit a chord with viewers and his channel took off. "I would say my first big break was over the summer of 2013. I had been making Minecraft videos everyday for a few months, but when the summer hit and I started showcasing Mods for the game and bringing my own stories into those videos, people seemed to really connect with them and it has got me to where I am today."

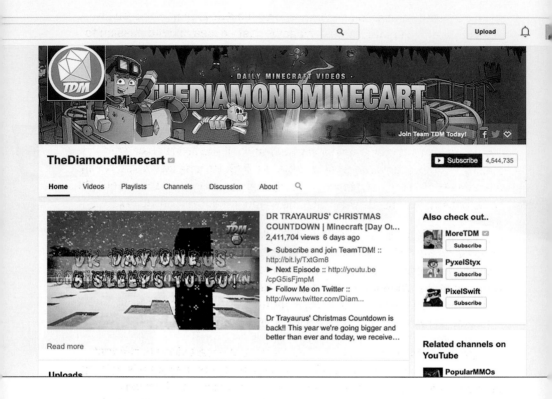

The 22 year-old says that his channel's growth from a small following to his millions of subscribers happened "Very quick!", adding "I literally just finished my university degree and education as a whole and over the summer, the YouTube channel exploded." But in one way it's no surprise that he'd fit so well into the Let's Play world. Dan is and always has been a passionate gamer, telling us, "I have always been a huge fan of video games, playing since I was very young, all the way up until now. They have always been a big part of my life; I have dabbled in video game design, digital art, animation and simply just playing games while going through education, and the website YouTube gives me the perfect platform to show my video creations to the world."

With gaming being bigger than it ever has been, it's the ideal time for game-based YouTubers to make their mark, and Dan believes things are only going to get bigger for video games. "I think the gaming industry is really at a peak right now," he said, "with the internet being so powerful in the creation and growth of video games. You don't have to be a big developer with a huge team any more to create a smash hit game, just an idea and the passion to put it together, just like with Minecraft. I'd say the industry will continue to grow with the importance of the internet and I also think eSports are another huge way of getting gaming out to the masses."

For those who think YouTube Creator sounds like a fun job, Dan has a lot of encouraging advice, telling kids who are looking to start their own channel, "Make sure you're having fun doing what you do. If you aren't having fun making a video, your viewers will be able to tell. So as long as you are having fun doing YouTube then keep at it! Getting popular doesn't happen overnight so be patient, and maybe you'll find one of your great creations go far!"

And don't worry if you don't know what you're doing right away; Dan learned his skills on the job! "The whole process of starting a YouTube channel with limited knowledge of how it works and the programs/games you are working with is really fascinating, so starting from knowing everything really wouldn't be the same. The best part of being a YouTuber is that you can create whatever you want, while learning new skills all the time."

Though it only takes one look at a TheDiamondMinecart video to see that Dan is a young man with heaps of both talent and personality, he is nothing but humble and appreciative about his success, telling us, "I am very privileged to be able to have [TheDiamondMinecart] as my full time job."

Whether you're a gamer, have another interest or simply want to talk to the world, YouTube is a place where you can start sharing your thoughts with almost no set up and at no cost, making it one of the most accessible entertainment industries in history. All you need is a free channel, a way to record, a little software, an idea, and some time. And who knows? You might just be the next YouTube star that all the kids are talking about.

Screenshot: Minecraft®™ & © 2009–2015 Mojang/Notch.